A HANDSEL

LIZ LOCHHEAD

A HANDSEL

NEW & COLLECTED POEMS

First published in 2023 in Great Britain in Hardback
by Polygon, an imprint of Birlinn Ltd

Birlinn Ltd
West Newington House
10 Newington Road
Edinburgh
EH9 1QS

9 8 7 6 5 4 3 2 1

www.polygonbooks.co.uk

ISBN 978 1 84697 651 3
eBook ISBN 978 1 78885 635 5

British Library Cataloguing-in-Publication Data
A catalogue record for this book is available on
request from the British Library.

Typeset in Verdigris MVB Pro by The Foundry, Edinburgh
Printed and bound in Great Britain by Bell & Bain, Glasgow

In memory of my father and mother, John and Margaret Lochhead,
and my husband Tom Logan

CONTENTS

NEW &
UNCOLLECTED
POEMS

(2023)

COMING TO POETRY
An Ode

Reading you, John Keats, at seventy I hurt
pierced again by your beauty that is truth,
was truth to me and my fourteen-year-old heart.
Knowing nothing of nightingales, my melting youth –
still blind to the perfection of a Grecian urn,
deaf yet to Darien, Homer a closed book –
burst open to 'La Belle Dame Sans Merci'.
This night my thoughts return
to that seeming simple-as-a-song ballad, to what it took
to have me come to poetry.

My joy forever? My truth and terror too.
This was the Cuban Missile Crisis, October '62.
In English, last week we'd finished *St Agnes' Eve*.
Next week, nuclear obliteration is due
unless there's a Khrushchev climb-down they don't believe
will happen. Countdown to doom.
Mr Valentine read us 'La Belle Dame' and into the room
came yon knight at arms, so haggard and so woe-begone
with the lily's pale anguish on his brow,
on his cheeks the rose fading, withering like our *Now*.
Was it to be all over and done
our nineteen-sixties sweetness scarce begun,
my warmed jewels never to be unclasped one by one,
my fragrant bodice never loosened, nor by degrees,
my unbuttoned garments fall rustling to my knees?
Oh I longed as I had never longed before
for my wild eyes to be closed, just once, with kisses four.

I couldn't sleep that night.
For next week we might
we really might, like you, poor dear John Keats, be dead.
I remember this so vividly I'm *there*

feeling again that middle-of-the-night deep dread,
standing looking out that window in the hall to where –
perhaps soon to be just *gone, not here* –
under the blueish lamplight our ordinary street
lay weirdly stilled and strange, like a Magritte
out of that art book off the school library shelf.
In my parents' room someone else not sleeping stirs –
we're all scared but you've to keep it to yourself.
Though day by day I see those wee *tells* betray their fears,
how they'd looked at each other, nothing said,
when Kennedy addressed his Nation. A *blockade*.
Now, hourly, when the news comes on I know
by their clenched attention to the radio . . .

It didn't happen. I am still alive,
still hunger for poetry, for life.
You never got to take sweet, silly, loving Fanny Brawne to wife,
John Keats, while I, who never thought to survive
into my beldame-years, must needs be stoical at seventy.
My Tom, dear husband of my heart, taken from me
and from this life he loved, an astonishing ten years ago.
I'm here. Birds still sing. Sometimes. I know, I know
I must try not to yearn
for all the sweetnesses gone and past return.

THE SPACES BETWEEN
for Leslie McGuire

The boy is ten and today it is his birthday.
Behind him on the lawn
his mother and his little sister
unfurl a rainbow crayoned big and bright
on a roll of old wallpaper.
His father, big-eyed, mock-solemn, pantomimes ceremony
as he lights the ten candles on the cake.
Inside her living-room
his grandmother puts her open palm to the window.
Out in the garden, her grandson
reaches up, mirrors her, stretching fingers
and they smile and smile as if they touched
warm flesh not cold glass.

More than forty thousand years ago
men or women splayed their fingers thus
and put their hands to bare rock. They
chewed ochre, red-ochre, gritted charcoal and blew,
blew with projectile effort that really took it out of them,
their living breath.
Raw gouts of pigment
spattered the living stencil
that was each's own living hand
and made their mark.
The space of absence
was the clean, stark picture of their presence
and it pleased them.
We do not know why they did it
and maybe they did not either but
they knew they must.
It was the cold cave wall
and they knew they were up against it.

The birthday boy is juggling.
He has been spending time in the lockdown learning
but though he still can't keep it up for long
his grandmother dumb-shows most extravagant applause.
She toasts them all in tea
from her *Best Granny in the World* mug, winking
and licking her lips ecstatically as,
outdoors, they cut the cake,
miming hunger, miming
prayer for her hunger to be sated.
The slim girl dances
and her grandmother claps
and claps again, blinking tears.
Another matched high-five at her window.

Neither the blown candles nor the blown kisses
will leave any permanent mark
– unless love does? –
on them on this the only afternoon
they will be all alive together on just this day the boy is ten.

CHIMNEY-SWEEPERS

Maytime and I'm
on a fool's errand
carrying home this bunch of the dandelion clocks
which Shakespeare called chimney-sweepers
and a friend tells me his wee grand-daughter
in the here-and-now calls puffballs.
I'm holding my breath, and them, this carefully
because I want to take them home and try
to paint them, although
one breath of wind and in no time
I'll be stuck with nothing but a hank of
leggy, limp, milky pee-the-bed stalks
topped with baldy wee green buttons, for
golden lads and girls all must
as chimney-sweepers come to dust.

On daisy hill by the railway bridge
one lone pair of lovers laze in the sun.
A little apart from her, he lounges
smoking a slow cigarette and waits
smiling, half-watching her weave a bluebell chain
that swings intricate from her fingers, hangs heavy
till she loops it, a coronet upon her nut-brown hair.
I'm wondering is this to be her something blue?

She calls out to me, I to her,
as folk do in these days of distancing
and I can hardly believe it when she says
she never in all her childhood
told the time by a dandelion clock.

She's up to her oxters in ox-eye daisies, this girl.
The ones my mother, Margaret,
always called *marguerites* but never

without telling me again how my father
writing to her from France before Dunkirk or after D–Day
always began his letters *Dear Marguerite*.

The saying goes that a maiden
crowned by bluebells can never tell a lie
the girl informs me, solemn as she
crosses her fingers, each hand held high.
The smoke from her lover's cigarette is
almost but not quite as blue as
the frail blooms – time, truth and a promise – that
she's braided together on this their one-and-only
sure-to-be-perfect summer's day.

Oh *Marguerite   Margaret   my Mum*
who never got to be as old as I am today
did you ever hear tell of this proverb?
Oh Mum how much I wish I could ask you
this and so many other
small and silly things, but
golden lads and girls all must
as chimney-sweepers come to dust.

FOUND POEM FOR THE POLLEN SEASON

Slender foxtail grass
silvery hair grass
silky bent grass.

Meadow soft grass
sweet vernal grass
loose sedge.

Blue moor grass
sea hard grass
glaucous sweet grass
bearded couch grass
common quaking grass
switchgrass also known as
great panic grass
perennial rye grass
pendulous wood sedge.

Yorkshire fog
floating club rush
barren brome grass.

Marram grass
mountain melick
great panicled sedge so
easily
mistaken
for japanese blood grass.

Lyme grass
wood millet grass
sheep's fescue
wall barley
wild oat
darnel.

OCTOBER EQUINOX

Wild,
wild weather, that ragged crow blown across the road like
a scrap of ripped old black binbag and every time the wind drops
the air full of the roar of the rut, each maculate leaf
a leopard changing its spots

WINTER WORDS

brave snowdrops on the ground
scant snowdrops from the sky
a wishbone on the windowsill

GLOOMY DECEMBER

These are the shortened days
and the endless nights.
— Carol Ann Duffy, from Mean Time (1993)

Gloomy December.
The doldrum days of the dead of winter.
These are the shortest days
and the endless nights.
So wish for the moon
and long for the light.

Chill winds. Relentless rain.
Dark to go to work in, darkness home again.
But, given just one fine day of sun and sharp, clean frost,
our lost, maybe long-lost
faith – if for nothing more than the year's turning –
comes back like the light comes back.
A promise in our bleak midwinter yearning
once in a rare and clear blue noon
if we wish for the moon.

Till then, the light's soul and spirit
is locked in its absence,
and our longing for it.

Whether you believe with the Magi in their miracle –
Three Kings bow down low before the Child of Light –
or whether we think them Wise Men on a fool's errand,
their gifts useless, magnificent, precious,
who came following one star and its faltering gleaming
till they came to the place,
it was a brave as well as a cold coming.
Yes.

And whether it was a refugee waif

or the Saviour that was born,
whether some shepherds on the night shift
saw angels, or a meteor storm,

believe in the light's soul and spirit
that's in its absence
and our longing for it.

THE BACKSTORY

This woman, she's about seventy-ish,
mibbe even seventy-four or five.
I think her name is Arlene.
Yes, she's Arlene, that feels right.

Well, Arlene got married
married far too young, to Malc
way back at the end of the sixties.
Arlene hasn't seen Malc –
not face to face,
since they got divorced way back in 1977.
None of a family, thank God,
bad enough splitting up without the complications.

Back then Malc was in a band –
lead guitar and vocals.
Malc *was* the band.
That voice of his
so distinctive.

The solo career
after the band split up a
couple of years later didn't
really take off as predicted, though.
But it was
a successful band at the time – very,
all over the UK and in America
not just here in Scotland.
A kind of country-rock crossover
with, they liked to say, Celtic roots.
A band that was always on the road.

When Arlene came down this morning
The Herald was on the table open at the page.

Her husband Tony,
her husband of the best part of forty years,
Tony must have left it open like that for her
when he left early this morning
for his regular Thursday golf with the cronies
he's been doing every week since he retired.

So this morning Arlene read the
Obituary of Malcy Torrance of
iconic Scottish Seventies rock band Lovers Leap.
And she found herself going up the stairs,
getting her notebook out.
She's always kept one – even way back.
Malc even used to pinch wee lines out of Arlene's notebook,
muck about a wee bit with them here and there,
turn them into the lyrics of the songs he wrote with the band.

Not that she got the credit.
Not that she ever minded.

Over the years, Arlene's
scribbled down a lot of stuff.
This and that – just putting into words
odd wee things that've struck her.
Who knows where they are now, half
these old notebooks of hers, and, no, she never
meant to stop writing things down,
but, recently, somehow
she's just not had the time.
Granted she has been busy with the grand-weans –
although, actually, Arlene's glad
for the pair of them be asked to do
what Tony's always saying is
a good bit mair than their fair share of the looking-eftir.
Anyway, this morning Arlene's got
her old notebook and biro out

and I can just see her now,
still in her pyjamas,
her coffee getting cold and her not caring,
scribbling away with hardly any scoring out.

Some people write Country and Western songs? Well,
I suppose this is what you could call a
Country and Western story.
And it goes something like this:

Once upon a time and it wisnae yesterday
his pals aw thought I was a catch
and my maw and all my aunties
thought I'd really won a watch
and we looked each other in the eye
sure we'd really met our match.

Oh, if we could only mind how right it was
before it went so wrong
this would be a song with a story
and this'd be the story of that song.

Our split
never hit the headlines – didn't require the *National Enquirer*
to speculate on the reasons
why it all went adrift with the shift of the seasons.
wasn't a Doesn't-Count-on-Location –
tho shit happens on the road.
It wasn't about what you put your dick up
or what you put up your nose
wasn't like the penny dropped when
you got out the van with a sheepish smile
and that single red rose . . .
wasn't as if I threw your guitar out the window
or cut up your clothes

no, I never packed your suitcase

and left it in the hall
called time on us and called a lawyer –
no that wasn't it at all.

Oh, if we could only mind how right it was
before it went so wrong
this would be a song with a story
and this'd be the story of that song.

Wasn't about what we were open about
or what we – wisely – kept hid.
Doesn't-Count-on-Location?
I think you'll find it did.
But we
never ever accused each other of
only wanting each other
on our own terms.
Wasn't as if we didn't know an open marriage
was an open can of worms.
Wasn't as if we stopped trying –
we tried constantly.
You never hit the bottle
you never hit me.
Wasn't as if we stopped talking.
We never lost it in bed.
But something 'bout us being together
really fucked with my head
and whatever it was stopped me wearing my wedding ring
whatever it was it wasn't
the usual thing
and I suppose I'll always remain in the dark
about what threw me into the arms of that guy at work.
Oh, it wasn't that, not any of that,
but this much is true
I'd never forgive myself if I couldn't
forgive me and you.

For if I could only mind how right it was
before it went so wrong
this would be a song with a story,
and this'd be the story of that song.

THE DIRTY DIVA – THOUGH KNOCKING ON A BIT THESE DAYS –NEVERTHELESS ATTEMPTS TO INVENT A NEW DANCE CRAZE

Can't get my socks on
can't get my rocks off
but that loss of libido
that everybody talks of
is yet to kick in.

Let's do the Salsa Geriatrica –
It's no sin.

Jeepers creepers
The Grim Reaper
for crying out loud
he's cutting a cruel swathe
through the Old Crowd.
he's on the rampage!
so what we gonna do
with our Late Middle Age

except the Salsa Geriatrica –
It's no sin?

There are those
God knows
think at Our Age it's
Not Right
never ever play
their 'Lay, Lady Lay',
their Marvin Gaye
nor their Barry White . . .
I say c'mon, c'mon, c'mon give it a spin –

let's try the Salsa Geriatrica –
it's no sin.

Try it on with
some septuagenarians and they go:
Gie's peace!
They're like: *I'm glad I'm past it, it's*
A Merciful Release.
Me? I'm still like:
Get ready, get set, begin

the Salsa Geriatrica!
It's no sin.

Had we but world enough
and time
pro-crastination
were no crime . . .
But
unless the whole idea's
totally horrendous – or (worse!) *risible* –
delay is inadvisable.
At our age.
Are we on the same page?
What else we gonna do with our
Late Middle Age?

DON'T GO DOWN THE BASEMENT

PROLOGUE

The Festival Theatre, Edinburgh. A touring musical.
Cheap seats, Girls' Night Out, no bad at all . . .
OK, *The Buddy Holly Story* wasnae the greatest ever told
but the songs are good, and watching it unfold
the audience are all wishing we could avert disaster
and somehow Buddy could rave on wi his Stratocaster
and play the morra night's gig in Mason City.
Not to be, and more's the pity.
Raither than thole
another four-hundred mile
in an auld school bus wi nae heater
Buddy charters yon plane, a rickety four-seater.
True, thon 'Winter Dance Party Tour' was the Tour from Hell,
but when bad-stuff happens, we ken very well
The protagonist aye brings it on hissel.
Thus, in a white-out in a cornfield in Iowa, there came a cropper
Buddy Holly, Ritchie Valens and the Big Bopper.

PART ONE

Aye, we were all like: Don't do it!
Buddy, just don't get on that plane
Can you no take a telling?
Well, I'll no tell you again.

The young wife tellt you to *think on*, Buddy
so could you no have bloody thunk?
It was snawin like fuck, the propeller fell aff
and the pilot was drunk.

If your name happens to be Kennedy
remember who you are
and dinnae go bowling doon boulevards in Dallas
in an open-top car.

A beautiful, beautiful white boy
with a beautiful black-man's voice, that was Elvis.
With one swivel of your blue suede shoes,
with one thrust of your pelvis

sex enters, on TV, the living rooms of America.
Pure Sex – that's the song you sing!
It's vital, it's whole, it's rock and roll
and Elvis you're the King.

But oh, Elvis! Your doctor in Graceland
was a bloody disgrace.
You ended up, forty-two year auld, ballooned, bloated
dead on the toilet – but still off your face

on *pre-scription* drugs. Oh no! Don't
go to the chemist. Don't let them fill
that bloody prescription the bastard wrote you
DO NOT TAKE THAT PILL

it's probably worse than street heroin –
Pills Will Kill . . . So many, before and since.
I'm thinking: Judy Garland, Marilyn,
Jim Morrison, Michael Jackson . . . Prince –

but hey, if a girl wants to be a *Princess*
deal is: become some Royal's wife.
But if he sniggers and says *whatever 'in love' means*
run for your life;

for that's not an auspicious beginning
for the so-called *stuff of fairytales.*
It'll jist get worse and worse till it's divorce
for the Prince and Princess of Wales.

And PS – Diana and Dodi, if you will deny
the bloody paparazzi their photae
mibbe a speed-freak drunk an coked oot his heid
isnae the best chauffeur to go tae?

PART TWO

The Greeks said Tragedy was jist like the thing
whereas Comedy required the bending
of the plot as it unravelled
to an – unlikely – happy ending.

In his *Poetics*, Aristotle said: *Our fear and pity*
for the tragic hero and tragic action
calls up the cleansing horror of Catharsis
and brings a certain satisfaction

as Hubris leads inevitably to Nemesis –
aye, when it came to the bit
thae Greeks aye had a word –
or two – for it.

But enough of all thae technical terms.
I cannae be annoyed
thinking up *whit's the Scots*
for schadenfreude? –

Oedipus, did your Maw nor your Paw no tell you
to body-swerve the Oracle? Oh dear,
Oracles very seldom tell you
whit you wanted to hear . . .

Ariadne, by all means snog Theseus
afore he goes into the Labyrinth to kill the Minotaur.
Somethin tae put a bit o heart in the boy?
But dinnae go too faur

an betray your mither an faither
wi thon fatal ball o wool
'n then forget to cheynge the black sails tae white!
Ach, Theseus 'n Ariadne? Not cool!

Jason, don't underestimate Medea.
She'll make you wish you'd never been born
faur less ever bairned her.
Hell had nae fury like *that* wummin scorned . . .

PART THREE
Aye, there's minny a fond attraction
proves fatal, push comes to shove.
Romeo an Juliet,
dinnae fall in love.

Plus there's poor auld King Lear
who's no aw there.
Three daughters?
Ends up oot on his ear?

Then there's the wan where pure evil Iago manipulates
poor jealous Moor o Venice, Othello.
There's the wan wi the pushy wife that kills the King –
you're no supposed to say his name out loud! Scottish fellow . . .

But of all Shakespeare's protagonists
to whom tragic fate did befall
surely Hamlet, Prince of Denmark
was the daddy of them all?

Eftir what his Feyther's Ghost revealed, you'd think
revenge would be . . . in with a shout?
Naw. Procrastinating Hamlet *would* gie everything
the benefit of the doubt.

Nor can we ignore how, in all Elsinore
from commoner to king,
every bugger could be depended upon
to dae exactly the wrang thing –

not only embark on a dodgy course of action,
but go oan wi it jist to keep up a front.
Gertrude, dinnae mairry Claudius,
the man is a cunt.

Ophelia? Oh, of course he did!
Mair than wance, then blamed it on you.
You were too young, too busy pickin flooers
to ken that's jist whit men do.

Polonius, your platitudes are tedious.
You're mibbe tryin tae be helpful, but, please,
if you will hide and eavesdrop ahint the arras
don't bloody sneeze.

OK, a Feyther's murder demands Revenge.
But, Laertes, dinnae hotfoot it back fae France
or you too will end up deid-er
than Guildenstern or Rosencrantz

whit wi yer sister Ophelia droonin hersel
when the pair sowell was no the full shilling
an then the hail thing escalating intae
a pure orgy o killing

wi first of all Hamlet's Mammy Gertrude drinking,
accidentally, from thon poisoned cup –
oh, and Laertes, if you will also poison yer sword-tip
don't get yer foils mixed up.

But at least you clyped on Claudius furst.
And that was the end. Finished.
Hamlet, dying, forced him to drink the dregs, ran him through with
       his sword,
till at last he expired, his villainy punished.

Hamlet, you did think – and think again – afore acting.
Did it help you? No wan bit.
Mibbe if shit is determined to happen, it will?
This is it.

THE CARER'S SONG

*Lyrics written early in Covid pandemic lockdown 2020, to be sung by Glasgow's
Carol Laula in honour of the nurses, auxiliaries and care-home workers from all over
the UK, and, especially, in loving memory of John Prine, the great songwriter and
chronicler of blue-collar America who died of the disease that year. It borrowed the
tune of Prine's 'Angel from Montgomery'.*

I am just a wummin   who works as a carer
wish life was fairer   but God knows it's no.
I've aye been a grafter   it's ma job to look after
them that's never had nuthin, or were Really Somebody no long ago.

I'm no an angel   I'm no a hero
tho yez clap on a Thursday till your hauns are aw sair.
Every day I face up to what we're aw feart o
just respect me   protect me   mibbe pey a bit mair?

I don't make a fuss   I just get on two busses
for I live in a hoose, aye   but I work in a Home.
I've to no think twice   jist follow th'advice
from thae bliddy clowns that it's hard to take it from.

Thon lot? Don't start me   it would break your heart, see
wi even less PPE   than the NHS
they think it's just fine   that we're on the front line
ach, it is what it is.   An what it is is a mess.

I am no an angel   I am no a hero
yez clap oan a Thursday till your hauns are aw sair.
Every day I face up to what we're aw feart o
so respect me   protect me   mibbe pey a bit mair?

Ach, you're all right, ma honey   let's get you comfy,
clean you up lovely   ma darlin, OK?
Please test us for Covid – I'm just bliddy livid
– Are 'dignity' and 'humanity' just empty words they say?

I am no an angel   I am no a hero
tho yez clap oan a Thursday till your hauns are aw sair.
Every day I face up to what we're aw feart o
so respect me   protect me   mibbe pey a bit mair?

Mibbe think first, eh?   Worst comes to the worst
it'll be me that has your loved one's dying hand to hold.
Should they require us   to fight this virus
wi nothin but a binbag apron and a perra Marigolds?

I am no angel   I am no hero
that yez clap oan a Thursday till your hauns are aw sair.
Every day I face up tae what we're aw feart o
so respect me   protect me   mibbe pey a bit mair?

Respect me   protect me   mibbe pey a bit mair.

Respect me   protect me
mibbe pey a bit mair.

A RARE TREAT

for Brian O'Sullivan

'Had a good morning this morning,' says Brian, 'I wrote a song.
The Young Man's Mother sings it to him,
I think it's OK. It moves the plot along.'
'Like any song worth its salt in a musical?' say I,
Wondering will he sing me it?
He smiles, explains it's actually too high
For him, scored as it is for the Young Man's Ma –
But, though he's not got *all* the last verse yet,
Here's the story so far . . .
I'm not getting any vibes from him of
Fools and bairns should never . . .
Which is how I get to be this song's first audience.
Ever.

My talented pal!
A musical!
Music and Lyrics – *and* he wrote The Book.
It's from *The Clouds* by Aristophanes,
Some Old Comedy he took,
Adapted.
This song?
The Loving Mother Character sings her son's name,
Again, again
'Pheidippides! Pheidippides!'
And these odd Greek syllables
Somehow make the catchiest refrain!
Brian my pal, sing me, please, the bit
That's not quite ready yet
In lyricist's *ham and eggs*?
Because it's obvious just how brilliant it is going to be.
This song has legs.

A HANDSELLING FOR ALICE'S REAL WEDDING

for Alice Marra and Colin Reid

Who is it walks you down the aisle, Alice?

Love, love walks you down the aisle,
the love that's loved you
since you were the wee-est girl.
So smile!
Smile, Alice – all this wedding's tears
are have-no-fear tears,
are mere tears of joy
to see the best girl marry exactly-the-right boy.

Who waits with you, Colin,
as you wait for your bride?

Love. The love that's loved you always
stands by your side
so stand by it, Colin, stand
and wait till love, your Alice,

comes to take your hand.

THE WORD FOR MARILYN

In memory of Marilyn Imrie, 1947–2020.

When you come to me in dreams, Marilyn,
as sometimes since you died you do but always
in dreams exactly as you were in life.

And whatever mad incoherent
other stuff might've gone on in that dream with its
chaotic constant metamorphosing cast
and drenching emotions entirely inappropriate for
whatever seemed to be happening
in its daft ever-shifting surreal dream-plot
if
I had a dream last night and you were in it,
Marilyn,
when I wake up I'm sad of course
but beyond that the
continuing calming comfort of your presence
pervades my day.

We were exactly the same age as each other
with wintry birthdays only one month apart
and today already it's the second birthday
you didn't get to celebrate.
Oh Marilyn,
our friendship goes back to our early thirties
and I can't remember what work thing it was
cemented our friendship –
something at the BBC at Queen Street for radio
and it won't have been a play, not then
not in the very early, early eighties – but whatever it was
that friendship was as
instantaneous as it was deep and firm and true.
Yes, we were over thirty,
Marilyn,

Women of the World and Girls About Town
searching for something we didn't know
if we believed was even possible –
a lasting love, a
till-death-do-us-part love.

Before the decade was over – but barely –
for each of us such a love
found us.

Whenever I'd think of those
spare, short, six lines
by Raymond Carver:
Late Fragment: And did you get what
You wanted from this life, even so?
I did.

And what did you want?
To call myself beloved, to feel myself
Beloved on the earth.

In my mind, Marilyn, I'd hear
you say these words
because I know you could have, would have, said these words
and meant them.
And this was the best comfort I could get
as I'd berate myself about how these
last few weeks I've been
looking out of windows, not thinking
just waiting for it to come to me,
please, the just-one-word
that'd sum up Marilyn as together
we all remember her.

Most days I'd get nothing –
another dreich skyline
or another gorgeous pink-striped winter dawn to gawp at
and still coming up with nothing –
but finally it came to me, it's
lovingkindness, Marilyn.
Yes, it's lovingkindness all-one-word, no-hyphen.
That's you. That'll do.

And of course it probably wasn't
a poem by Raymond Carver –
although indeed it says it all.
It was what it was – maybe it'll have been
a *late fragment* someone will have
found among his papers, titled it in all honesty,
and simply typed it up?

When anyone asks me
How long was it you and Marilyn Imrie
were such good friends?
I'll try and use a little lovingkindness as –
leading by example in the Marilyn manner –
I'll try to gently correct them, I'll
change past to present tense as I answer
Oh, Marilyn and I,
we've been friends for over forty years
and counting.

ASHET

On yon Zoom
the ither day a wee bit friendly argie-bargie stertit up
aboot whit exactly *wis*
an ashet
when it wis at hame? Well, some wid huv it
it wis a muckle-great delft platter for servin,
say, a hail gigot o mutton roastit wi aw the trimmins
an ithers insistit naw it wis nuthin but a
humble enamel pie-dish
sich as ye'd mibbe mak a shepherd's pie in or yaise
for reheatin (o aye, in a gey hoat oven!)
yesterday's left-ower stovies or day-afore-peyday pan-haggis
(never ever cryin that *skirlie*, nut ata,
no here in Glesca, no in the West).

There's monie wouldnae gie houseroom
to this shabby aul chrome-platit slottit-spoon
wi hardly a scrap o rid or black pent left on its widden haunle, but –
it was ma mither's – I haud it in ma haun wi ma
heid fu o mince an reminiscence, thinkin
how *a clock* could be a clock or a black beetle
how *a sair heid* is a sair heid but *a sair haun* is
a piece an jam
as lang's the slice o white breid's as thick as a doorstop
an the jam strawberry or rasp (the blood, the bandage) an I'm
wonderin
– since the press in ma kitchen contains
baith a chippt bog standard wee white pie-dish an thon
oval antique art-nouvea *losol-ware tulip* servan-dish
I got for a shillin in a kirk jumble-sale in the sixties –
pie-dish or *platter*? Which is the classic ashet?

Och, *settle an argument with a friend*, wee bit o
elementary detective work in a dictionar, an here it
turns oot it's *no*   either/or   but baith/and
which is even better – for *mair* is ayeweys mair than *less*
in ma book, eh no?

An I'll tell ye wan thing for shair: ma brand-new winterdykes
I ordered online an that arrived the day fae Amazon
might no be made o wid but raither
o clean plastic an lightweight metal
an huv an awfy well-designed an nifty wey
o foldin doon tae nuthin to store gey neatly in the loaby press
or o openin oot lik wings
and takin a loat mair claes than ma pulley ever could
but they'll aye be ma
winterdykes.

FROM BEYOND THE GRAVE

Jenny Clow, young maidservant to Nancy McLehose & frequent bearer of secret letters between Clarinda and Sylvander, delivers a heartfelt if anachronistic '#Me Too' to Robert Burns . . .

'What luxury of bliss I was enjoying this time yesternight! My ever-dearest Clarinda, you have stolen away my soul: but you have refined, you have exalted it; you have given it a stronger sense of Virtue, and a stronger relish for Piety . . .'

Robert Burns to Mrs Agnes McLehose, his Nancy, early in their passionate, if physically unconsummated, love affair, Edinburgh, January 1788

'—I, as I came home, called for a certain woman – I am disgusted with her; I cannot endure her! I, while my heart smote me for the profanity, tried to compare her with my Clarinda:

'twas setting the expiring glimmer of a farthing taper beside the cloudless glory of the meridian sun. Here, was tasteless, insipid vulgarity of soul and mercenary fawning; there, polished good sense, heaven-born genius and the most generous, the most tender Passion . . .'

Robert Burns to Mrs Agnes McLehose, on his reunion with Jean Armour, Mauchline, 23ʳᵈ February 1788.

'Jean I found banished . . . forlorn destitute and friendless . . . I have reconciled her to her fate, and I have reconciled her to her mother . . . I have taken her a room . . . I have taken her to my arms . . . I have given her a mahogany bed. I have given her a guinea and I have fucked her till she rejoiced with joy unspeakable and full of glory. But, as I always am on every occasion, I have been prudent and cautious to an astonishing degree. I swore her privately and solemnly never to attempt any claim on me as a husband even though anybody should persuade her she had such a claim (which she had not), neither during my life nor after my death. She did all this like a good girl, and I took the opportunity of some dry horse litter and gave her such a thundering scalade that electrified the very marrow of her bones. Oh, what a peacemaker is a guid weely-willy pintle! It is the mediator, the guarantee, the umpire, the bond of union, the solemn league and covenant, the plenipotentiary, the Aaron's Rod, the Jacob's Staff, the sword of mercy, the philosopher's stone, the Horn of Plenty and Tree of Life between Man and Woman.'

Robert Burns to his younger Edinburgh friend, Robert Ainslie, 3 March 1788.

Great lover? Rab, you wrote your ain reviews!
Did you believe in a wummin's right to choose?
For aw we ken t'wis never in Jean's gift to refuse
Thon 'electrifying scalade'.
She micht have got up, rolled her een, an hauf-amused
Muttered, 'no bad'.

Floored, there's minny a lass discovers
The brute hard-at-it buck rootin above her's
Quite shair he's the last o the rid-hoat lovers,
God's gift! –
Tho the delusion he's th'greatest o earth-movers
Be frankly daft!

An wha kens whit Jean Armour was feelin?
Mibbe aw yon 'ecstatic' yelping and squealin
In rising crescendo, had raither been revealin
No pleasure but pain?
Desertit, eight-month gone, long past concealin . . .
An *twins*. Again!

Rab, you dearly lo'ed a bit o posh an chose
Your 'Clarinda', the *married* Mistress McLehose
Frae 'mang Edinburgh's those-and-sich-as-those.
Tho you persisted –
(Poems, promises, billets doux) – tried *everythin*, God knows,
Still she resisted.

Silly, camp, fause names! I suppose I do admire
Th'attempt at secrecy? Why the hell tho did she require
Me to 'await the response' she was on fire
To receive from 'her Sylvander'.
Mair than his hauns, his pent-up desperation an desire
Did wander . . .

Ach, minny a swain faced thus wi nothin-doin
Indulges elsewhere in expedient rough-wooin
While some random other recipient o what's ensuin
Accepts her fate
An for the moment he disnae care if wha he's screwin
'S a mere surrogate.

He was mad wi lust for my chaste mistress. Nothing worse.
Really wanted her, she wouldnae. I did. My curse?
I thought he fancied me. Quite the reverse
I fear.
Jist made for his 'guid willy-pintle' a handy silk purse
O my soo's ear.

Twentieth-century folk thought 'twas their invention,
Birth-control! And granted Rabbie an exemption –
But afore Dutch caps, rubber johnnies, no to mention
Game-changin pills
There existit an obvious method o prevention
As auld's the hills . . .

Nae wey o avoiding pregnancy? Oh please!
Tell that tae the birds an bees
Minny a lover and his lass took post-orgasmic ease
'Mang th' hermless spatters
O a skillfu cocksman blessed wi expertise
In country matters.

I had to keep Mum 'boot Sainted Rabbie
Wha fucked like a poet, in Standard Habbie.
Quick, staccato an jab-jab-jabby
Then – oof, past carin
Let fly, an left me – is yon no jist fab, eh? –
Haudin the bairn.

He made promises that meltit like snaw
Clarinda got the song, I got hee-haw
'Cept the bairn, a faitherless yin an aw –
Rab, you could've easily,
If you cared aboot a lass at a
Have got aff at Paisley!

A ROOM O MY AIN, 1952

The King Is Dead, Long Live the Queen.
Little children should be seen
and not heard
in nineteen fifty-two

I'm four year-auld – we've just got word
we've got a *Scottish Special* house
the three of us –
Me, my Dad and my Mum –
oh they've been waiting and waiting
thought they'd still be waiting till kingdom come
for their ain hoose
for a hoose o their ain.

At first it was *none of a family yet*
then *jist the wan wean, an aye she's an Only One*
now at last their life has just begun –
been eight long year since
in my granny an granda's front room
they *got married in uniform, nae honeymoon*
(it's a story I've heard before
about the *no-picnic* that was the war) –
now life will never be the same
in Mum 'n' Dad's *first-ever married hame.*

Nae mair jammed, nae mair crammed
in wi the inlaws, one set
then the ither, *sharing a kitchenette*
steyin in the wan back room
wi nae room to swing a cat
imagine that
one room –
haw, how come
I'm four year-auld and still sleeping in a cot

when baby I am not?
Oh, I'm over the moon we'll be oot o here soon,
my Mum 'n' Dad've said
I'll get *my own room* and *my own double bed*
just like theirs, three cheers –
now we're *maw, paw and the wean*
we've got a house an it's a brand-new one
a hame o our ain.

God bless
the lovely emptiness
it's bare and spare but it's *absolutely super*
with the walls still too new, too damp, to wallpaper
but, ach, there's aye *stippling* an ither temporary decoration –
this *hale place'll be a palace*
by the time of the Coronation!

Anaglypta, artex, emulsion, eggshell, full gloss,
inch-tape, shade-card, formica, formica, formica . . .

A hale lifetime
since that room was my lifeline –
been mair than seventy years
since I got oot from ahint that cot's prison bars
an slept all night by mysel in thon big double bed
below the yellow candlewick bedspread
an the golden counterpane
that I had when I was a wean
in my ain room
in that room o my ain

Lulling me into the loneliness of sleep
every night either Mum or Dad would read to me . . .
A Child's Garden of Verses, terrifying *Tanglewood Tales,*
The Dragon's Teeth, Peter Pan and Wendy,
an oh, I loved them all.

An when they crept away and left me,
they'd aye have to leave the light on in the hall . . .

Little Women, the *Woman, Woman's Own*,
The Chalet School, Jane Eyre,
True Confessions, auld movie magazines,
the anything at all
that year in, year out, ower the years
I lay in that big bed and read to mysel.
The Broons Annual, The Famous Five, The Secret Seven,
Wuthering Heights, a Woolworths' half-a-crown classic
only slightly abridged, oh yon was heaven –
getting allowed
to take the big Burns book to bed
to learn to say 'To a Mouse' off by heart and out loud
an *Tiger, Tiger* . . . an *I remember, I remember*
the house where I was born, the
little window where the sun –
d'you mind the auld-fashioned, foosty pleasure, eh,
of *Palgrave's Golden Treasury?*
the *Beano*, the *Girl's Crystal*, the *Topper*
the *Children's Newspaper* an the *Reader's Digest* –
but a really good library book, that was the best.
I mind forbidden *Peyton Place*
and the Penguin *Lady Chatterley's Lover*
in below my pillow in a brown paper cover.

Lie on that bed again, be heavy as heavy
an make your eyes go all squinty
till you're up in the air
an the lampshade on the ceiling
is now a bucket on the flair
an through the door that's now a high window
might climb Ginger and Astaire.
They might shimmy on the ceiling –
oh, I still like this feeling

like to imagine I'm back in this room
where I still like being on my own
being all alone
where I can really go to town
wi seeing things in my own way
upside down.

MEMO FOR SPRING

(1972)

REVELATION

I remember once being shown the black bull
when a child at the farm for eggs and milk.
They called him Bob – as though perhaps
you could reduce a monster
with the charm of a friendly name.
At the threshold of his outhouse, someone
held my hand and let me peer inside.
At first, only black
and the hot reek of him. Then he was immense,
his edges merging with the darkness, just
a big bulk and a roar to be really scared of,
a trampling, and a clanking tense with the chain's jerk.
His eyes swivelled in the great wedge of his tossed head.
He roared his rage. His nostrils gaped like wounds.

And in the yard outside,
oblivious hens picked their way about.
The faint and rather festive jingling
behind the mellow stone and hasp was all they knew
of that Black Mass, straining at his chains.
I had always half-known he existed –
this antidote and Anti-Christ, his anarchy
threatening the eggs, well rounded, self-contained,
and the placidity of milk.

I ran, my pigtails thumping on my back in fear,
past the big boys in the farm lane
who pulled the wings from butterflies and
blew up frogs with straws.
Past thorned hedge and harried nest,
scared of the eggs shattering –
only my small and shaking hand on the jug's rim
in case the milk should spill.

POEM FOR OTHER POOR FOOLS

Since you went I've only cried twice.
Oh never over you. Once
it was an old head at a bus window
and a waving hand.
Someone's granny, a careful clutcher of her handbag
and wearing a rainhat despite the fact
it wasn't raining. Yet
waving, waving to grandchildren already turned away
engrossed in sweets she had left them.
Old head. Waving hand.

> Oh she wasn't the type to expose herself
> to the vagaries of weather
> (a rainhat in no rain)
> Yet waving, waving to those who had already
>   turned away.

Then once it was a beggar by the pub doorway
and his naked foot.
Some drunk old tramp,
player of an out-of-tune mouth organ
and begging. Instead of his cap,
his boot for alms.
His playing was hopeless,
his foot bare in the gutter in the rain,
his big boot before him, empty, begging.
Oh it was a scream. I laughed
and laughed till I cried.

It was just his poor
pink and purple naked foot

out on a limb

exposed.
And how (his empty boot) he got nothing
in return.

HOW HAVE I BEEN SINCE YOU LAST SAW ME?

Well,
        I've never been lonely
        I've danced at parties,
        and drunk flat beer
with other men;
        I've been to the cinema and seen
        one or two films you would have liked
with other men;
        I've passed the time in amusement arcades
        and had one or two pretty fruitless
        goes on the fruit machine;
        I've memorised the patterns
        of miscellaneous neckties.
Indifferent, I
        put varying amounts of sugar
in different coffee cups
        and adjusted myself to diverse heights
        of assorted goodnight kisses, but
my breasts (once bitten)
            shy away from contact
I keep   a curb
            on mind and body
Love?   I'm no longer
             exposing myself.

ON MIDSUMMER COMMON

On Midsummer Common
it's too good to be true,
backdrop of cricketers,
punts on the river,
the champ of horses
and mayflies in June
mere Midsummer Commonplace.

Not in midsummer,
but with the real rain of more normal weather
putting a different slant on things,
my hard-edged steel town
seen through the blur of bus windows.
Saturday afternoon streets crammed
with shoppers laden under leaden skies.
Out of the constant comedown of the rain, old men
in the final comedown of old age
file into public libraries to turn no pages.
Saturday. My town
can't contain itself.
Roars rise and fall,
stadiums spill
football crowds in columns
in the teeming rain.
Saturday buses are jampacked with football rowdies
all going over the score.
I am overlapped by all the fat and laughing losers
that pour from bingo parlours.
Outside cinemas, steadies
queue steadily to buy
their darkness by the square foot.
The Palais and troc are Choc-full
of gaudy girls dressed parrot fashion.
Saturday's all

social clubs, singers, swilled ale.
So much is spilt –
the steel clang, the clash of creeds,
the overflow of shouts and songs,
the sprawl of litter,
the seep of smells,
the sweat, the vinegar, the beer –
so much slops
into that night nothing goes gentle into,
not even rain.
Such a town
I feel at home to be at odds with.

Here on Midsummer Common
on a midsummer Saturday
you, this day, this place and I
are just exchanging pleasantries.
Oh, it's nice here, but
slagheaps and steelworks
hem my horizons
and something compels
me forge my ironies from a steel town.

FRAGMENTARY

Twilight (six o'clock and
undrawn curtains). It's as if

                                upstairs

                                        from me

lives some crazy projectionist
running all his reels at once.
Pub-sign neon scrawls credits on the sky that's
cinemascope for him. He
treats me to so many
simultaneous
home movies, situation comedies, kitchen sink dramas
I can't make sense of them –
just snippets, snatches with the sound gone,
mouthings in a goldfish bowl.

THE VISIT

We did not really want to go,
not very much,
but he said it was our Christian Duty
and anyway he had already booked the bus.
So we went
despite ourselves
dreading, half hoping to be horrified.
Through corridors with a smell,
bile greenish-yellow unfamiliar smell
of nothing *we* knew,
but of oldness, madness, blankness,
apathy and disinfectant.
We grinned.
We did not know what else to do.
A grimace of goodwill and Christian greetings,
hymn books clutched in sweaty palms.
We are the Church Youth Club to sing to you,
bring you the joy we have never felt.
We passed on through the strange men –
complex simple faces
so full of blankness you would not believe it –
bowing, smiling, nodding they ignored us,
or acknowledged us with sullen stares.
A tall orderly came towards us
with eyes that couldn't keep still
and a nervous twitch.
I wonder had he always been like that,
the watcher, the keeper-
calm of what prowled his cage?
We sang. The minister shut his eyes
and prayed from unironic lips
with easy phrases.

For me, only an orderly
who prayed with his eyes skinned.
Just the flick of eyes
which *can't* be everywhere at once.

AFTER A WARRANT SALE

I watched her go,
Ann-next-door
(dry eyed,
as dignified
as could be expected)
the day after they came,
sheriff court men
with the politeness of strangers
impersonally
to rip her home apart,
to tear her life along the dotted line
officially.

On the sideboard that went for fifteen bob,
a photograph.
Wedding-day Walter and
Ann. Her hair was lightened,
and her heart with hopes.
No one really knows
when it began to show –
trouble, dark roots.

It was common knowledge
there were faults on both sides,
and the blame,
whether it was over drink
or debt no one seems to know,
or what was owing to exactly whom.
Just in the end the warrant sale
and Ann's leaving.

But what seemed strange:
I wondered why,

having stayed long past the death of love

and the ashes of hope,
why pack it up and go
over some sticks of furniture
and the loss of one's only partially
paid-for washing machine?

Those who are older tell me,
after a married year or two
the comforts start to matter
more than the comforting.
But I am very young,
expecting not too much of love –
just that it should completely solve me.
And I can't understand.

PHOENIX

When crowsfeet get a grip on me
I'll call them laughter lines
I'll think of burnt-out romances
as being my old flames.

DAFT ANNIE ON OUR VILLAGE MAINSTREET

Annie
with your euphemisms to clothe you
with your not all there
    your sixpence short in the shilling
with your screw loose
your crazy tick tock in the head
your lurching pendulum
                      slightly unbalanced
with your plimsolls in winter
with your big-boots in summer and
    your own particular unseasonal
    your unpredictable weather.

Annie
out of the mainstream
mainstreet Annie
down at the cross
with your religious mania
singing Salvation Army choruses
to all on Sunday.
Annie
with your unique place
    your pride of place
in the community –
how
to every village
its doctor and its dominie
its idiot.

Annie
with the village kids afraid of you
with your myth of witchery
with your mystery
    your big raw bones

and your hamfisted face.
with your touching every lamp-post
    your careful measured paces down mainstreet
clothed in euphemisms
and epithets.
Daft Annie
    your epitaph.

OBITUARY

We two in W2
walking,
and all the W2 ladies, their
hair coiffed and corrugated come
with well-done faces
from the hairdresser's.
We together
laughing,
in our snobbery of lovers,
at their narrow vowels
and strange permed poodles.
Locked too long in love, our eyes
were unaccustomed to the commonplace.
                    Seems silly now really.

We two in W2
walking
down Byres Road
passing unconcerned
a whole florist's
full of funerals,
the nightmare butcher's shop's
unnumbered horrors,
the hung fowls
and the cold fish
dead on the slab.
We saw ourselves duplicated
by the dozen in the chainstore
with no crisis of identity.
Headlines on newsagents' placards
caused us no alarm
Sandwichman's prophecies of doom
just slid off our backs.
The television showroom's window

showed us cities burning
in black and white but we
had no flicker of interest.
An ambulance charged screaming past
but all we noticed was the funny old
Saturday street musician.
                    Seems silly now really.

We two one Sunday
at the art galleries
looking only at each other.
We two one Sunday
in the museum –
wondering why the ownership of a famous man
should make a simple object a museum piece –
and I afraid
to tell you how
sometimes I did not wash your coffee cup for days
or touched the books you lent me
when I did not want to read.
Well, even at the time
                    that seemed a bit silly really.

Christmas found me
with other fond and foolish girls
at the menswear counters
shopping for the ties that bind.
March found me
guilty of too much hope.
                    Seems silly now really.

MORNING AFTER

Sad how
Sunday morning finds us
separate after all,
side by side with nothing between us
but the Sunday papers
held like screens before us.
        Me, the *Mirror*
reflecting only on your closed profile.
        You, the *Observer*
encompassing larger, other issues.
Without looking up
you ask me please to pass the colour section.
I shiver
while you flick too quickly
                too casually through the pages, with
                too passing
                an interest.

INVENTORY

you left me
>   nothing but nail
>   parings orange peel
>   empty nutshells half-filled
>   ashtrays dirty
>   cups with dregs of
>   nightcaps an odd hair
>   or two of yours on my
>   comb gap-toothed
>   bookshelves and a
>   you-shaped
>   depression in my pillow.

GRANDFATHER'S ROOM

In your room in the clutter of pattern
you lie.
Sunlight strains through lace curtains,
makes shadow patterns
on wallpaper's faded trellises,
on fat paisley cushions,
on the gingham tablecloth.
On the carpet, rugs
layer on layer like the years,
pattern on pattern,
cover the barest patches.
Geometric, floral, hand-made rag rugs,
an odd bit left over from the neighbours'
new stair carpet –
patterns all familiar
from other people's houses,
other people's lives.

In a clutter of patterns
you lie
your shrunken head
frail as a shell or a bird skull
peeps from the crazy-paved
patchwork quilt.

Above your bed
in his framed death, your son,
my Uncle Robert that I never knew.
They say
he was well known for his singing at weddings
and was a real nice lad, killed
in the war at twenty-one.
His photo, hung so long in the same place, has
merged with the wallpaper,

faded into the pattern.
(But it can't be moved now,
it has left its mark.)
Uncle Robert in a uniform
above your bedside tabletop, the
medicines, the bright and bullet-shaped pills,
nothing in the angle of his smile
nor in the precise tilt of his cap, hinting
how soon, how suddenly he was to die.

There he is in black and white, believable.
Oh yes, he smiled and sang.
His sudden death stopped short
a slower certain dying, change.
While the other wall holds up
a scrap of nineteen thirty-three,
maintains it's true.
A photo of the family (or so they say) –
that flop-haired boy my balding father?
and you, grandfather, tall and strong,
smouldering in a landscape of shut pits and silent chimneys?
It's framed like a fact,
set fair and square but has less weight
is less real
than those faint patterns traced
by a weak sun through lace curtains.
Pale shadows, constantly changing.

FOR MY GRANDMOTHER KNITTING

There is no need they say
but the needles still move
their rhythms in the working of your hands
as easily
as if your hands
were once again those sure and skilful hands
of the fisher-girl.

You are old now
and your grasp of things is not so good
but master of your moments then
deft and swift
you slit the still-ticking quick silver fish.
Hard work it was too
of necessity.

But now they say there is no need
as the needles move
in the working of your hands
once the hands of the bride
with the hand-span waist
once the hands of the miner's wife
who scrubbed his back
in a tin bath by the coal fire
once the hands of the mother
of six who made do and mended
scraped and slaved, slapped sometimes
when necessary.

But now they say there is no need
the kids they say grandma
have too much already
more than they can wear
too many scarves and cardigans –

Gran, you do too much
there's no necessity.

At your window you wave
them goodbye Sunday
with your painful hands
big on shrunken wrists.
Swollen-jointed. Red. Arthritic. Old.
But the needles still move
their rhythms in the working of your hands
easily
as if your hands remembered
of their own accord the pattern
as if your hands had forgotten
how to stop.

POEM FOR MY SISTER

My little sister likes to try my shoes,
to strut in them,
admire her spindle-thin twelve-year-old legs
in this season's styles.
She says they fit her perfectly,
but wobbles
on their high heels, they're
hard to balance.

I like to watch my little sister
playing hopscotch,
admire the neat hops-and-skips of her,
their quick peck,
never missing their mark, not
over-stepping the line.
She is competent at peever.

I try to warn my little sister
about unsuitable shoes,
point out my own distorted feet, the callouses,
odd patches of hard skin.
I should not like to see her
in *my* shoes.
I wish she could stay
sure footed,
        sensibly shod.

SOMETHING I'M NOT

familiar with, the tune
of their talking, comes tumbling before them
down the stairs which (oh I forgot) it was my turn
to do again this week.
My neighbour and my neighbour's child. I nod, we're not
on speaking terms exactly.

I don't know much about her. Her dinners smell
different. Her husband's a bus driver,
so I believe.
She carries home her groceries in Grandfare bags
though I've seen her once or twice around the corner
at Shastri's for spices and such.
(I always shop there – he's open till all hours
making good.) How does she feel?
Her children grow up with foreign accents,
swearing in fluent Glaswegian. Her face
is sullen. Her coat is drab plaid, hides
but for a hint at the hem, her sari's
gold-embroidered gorgeousness. She has
a jewel in her nostril.
The golden hands with the almond nails
that push the pram turn blue
in this city's cold climate.

POEM ON A DAY TRIP

It's nice to go to Edinburgh.
Take the train in the opposite direction.
Passing through a hard land, a pitted
and pockmarked, slag-scarred, scraped land.
Coal. Colossus of pit-bings,
and the stubborn moors where Covenanters died.
Hartwood, Shotts, Fauldhouse, Breich –
something stirs me here
where the green veneer is thin,
the black-gut and the quarried ash-red
show in the gashes.
But the land changes
somewhere in the region of West and Mid Calder,
greener and gentler, rolling Lothians.
Edinburgh. Your names are grander –
Waverley, Newington, Corstorphine,
never Cowcaddens, Hillhead or Partick.
No mean city,
but genteel, grey and clean city
you diminish me –
make me feel my coat is cheap,
shabby, vulgar-coloured.
You make me aware of your architecture,
conscious of history and the way it has
of imposing itself upon people.
Princes Street.
I rush for Woolworth's anonymous aisles,
I feel at home here
you could be anywhere –
even in Glasgow.

OVERHEARD BY A YOUNG WAITRESS

Three thirty-fivish women met one day,
each well glossed against the others' sharp eyes for flaws.
Old school friends apparently – they slipped
with ease into the former conspiracy of dormitories,
and discussed over coffee and saccharine, the grounds
for divorce. All agreed love made
excessive demands on them,
wondered how long it must be missing
before it could be
                    Presumed Dead.

NOTES ON THE INADEQUACY OF A SKETCH

at Millport Cathedral, March 1970

Fields strung out so, piece-
meal on a crude felt-tip line
in real life revealed ribs
where the plough had skinned them alive.
My scrawl took the edge off the dyke.
Sure. But omitted to mark how
it held together, the gravity
of the situation (it being
a huddle of rough stone forms in a cold climate)
how it was set to hump across hills, or at what
intervals over which stones exactly
snails had scribbled silver.
I jotted down how fence
squared up to dyke (but nothing of
the wool tufts caught on random barbs)
how it bordered on that
ridiculous scrap of grass
(but failed to record its precise
and peculiarly Scottish green).
I made a sheer facade
of the cruciform cathedral, stated
only that the rectory garden
slanted towards an empty greenhouse
on the graveyard's edge.
For gravestones, I set mere slabs right-
angling to a surface I took at face value.
(I did not explain how at my feet
sprawled a rickle of rabbit bones
ribcage and spine in splinters,
skull intact.) I probed no roots.
I did not trace either gravestones'
legends or their moss (it let me read
between the lines the stones' survivals).

I selected what seemed to be essentials.
Here, where wind and rain
made a scapegoat of a scarecrow, my pen
took it for an easy symbol. But it's plain
setting down in black and white
wasn't enough, nor underlining
certain subtleties. This sketch became
a simile at best. It's no metaphor.
It says, *under prevailing conditions*
smoke from a damp bonfire was
equal in tonal value to the sea.
So what?
       Today on the empty
summer's sand the March rain needled no one.
(My sketch mentions no rain
neither how wet it was nor how straight
it fell nor that seagulls tried to call a halt
to it.) From my quick calligraphy of trees
no real loud rooks catcall the sea's
cold summersault.

LETTER FROM NEW ENGLAND

from a small town, Massachusetts, summer 1970

I sip my Coke at the counter
of the Osterville soda-fountain
that is also the Osterville news-stand &
I watch Nothing Happening
out on mainstreet
of this small New England town.

just
the sun &
white clapboard houses with trees in between &
certain cottonclad &
conservative spinsters nod at nodding acquaintances &
occasional rocking chairs nod on front porches &
old men in panamas hail each other loudly &
mothers compare feeding methods &
the parson posts a letter &
some highschool kids are perched on the fence
     of the Pilgrim Fathers' Museum
     (open only on Sundays)
     practising real hard at sitting on fences so
     as to grow up to be
     realgood New Englanders &
cars purr past, each containing
     one pale lady in sunglasses
     behind a smoke-tinted windscreen
     in transit between
     Ideal Home
     and beautyparlour &
what-looks-to-me like a farmer
     puts a Big Box
     in the back of a Ford &
my-bike-without-a-padlock
     sits for hours outside the library

because you can Sorta Trust Folk
in a small New England town
where no one locks their doors.

business is slow, says the soda-jerk,
like molasses in janu-werry &
I buy myself a *New York Times*
at the Osterville news-stand
(that is also the soda-fountain)
just to remind me that
This is America &
America has Problems
       pollution &
       recession &
       escalation &
       de-escalation &
       women's liberation &
       racial integration
       which
is not-to-speak-of Unspeakable Problems like
Spiro T. Agnew
& not-to-mention Problems
like odorforming bacteria & horrid
halitosis
which as each &
every ad would warn us are
ever-ready to engulf us.

And I feel I should be somewhere else
like
       a be-in, or
       a love-in, or
       learning how the American Election System works, &
       How To Make A President &
       what is the difference between a

Republican & a
Dem-o-crat?

I should be
   spectating at a looting, or
   sightseeing in some ghetto, or
   marching civil-righteously, or
   rioting on campus &
   striking matches
   for people burning draftcards &
   sticking pink bubblegum
   on every seat in the senate
   as a last-ditch attempt
   at Nonviolent Action, or
   out in California
   getting genned-up generally
   on the Voice of Youth's current (& ∴ correct)
   attitudes
   to the kinds of Grass & Peace & Love
   different from the grass & peace
   you get for free in New England with
   No Attitudes Necessary.

I should be somewhere else –
   not
      practising Non Involvement
      (& taking a slow suntan)
      eavesdropping on the Silent Majority
      (& eating hot butterscotch &
      ice cream sundae
      with marshmallow sauce vanilla
      cream and double nuts)
at the Osterville soda-fountain
that is also the news-stand
in this small New England town.

GETTING BACK

I was to ring you, remember,
the minute I got back. (Your number
among all those American addresses that came since.) I look
it up where you wrote it, something special in my book.
Four months. Four thousand miles apart and more. Keeping in touch
with us both on the move and all, no fixed addresses, was too much
to ask of us. From the Acropolis to the Empire State
it's a far cry. Then, between San Francisco and Istanbul, late
August burned and the distance grew.
That close and now at odds. You
had done with the sun by the time I got round to it.
You woke up, I sank into sleep, worlds away. We moved in opposite
directions in the dark about each other's days.
Now, I only lift the telephone and the operator says
she's trying to connect us. Between us four miles, no distance,
it's a local call – I should get through for sixpence.

But I just got back. No small change. I forgot
to check on it. I push a quarter in the shilling slot,
pips stop (my heartbeat) you reply to my small and civic dishonesty.
I jingle my pocket – nickles, dimes, meaningless currency –
and try to picture you at the receiving end, moustache at the mouth-piece
unless you've changed a lot. I take a breath 'And how was Greece?'
We namedrop cities into silences, feel the distance grow
find no common ground to get back to. I know
in my bones, nothing's the same anymore.
Don't you remember the girl I'm a dead ringer for?

BOX ROOM

First the welcoming. Smiles all round. A space
for handshakes. Then she put me in my place –
oh, with concern for my comfort. 'This room
was always his – when he comes home
it's here for him. Unless of course,' she said,
'he brings a Friend.' She smiled. 'I hope the bed
is soft enough? He'll make do tonight
in the lounge on the put-u-up. All right
for a night or two. Once or twice before
he's slept there. It'll all be fine I'm sure –
next door if you want to wash your face.'
Leaving me 'peace to unpack' she goes. My weekend case
(lightweight, glossy, made of some synthetic
miracle) and I are left alone in her pathetic
shrine to your lost boyhood. She must
think she can brush off time with dust
from model aeroplanes. I laugh it off in self defence,
who have come for a weekend to state my permanence.

Peace to unpack – but I found none
in this spare room which once contained you. (Dun-
coloured walls, one small window which used to frame
your old horizons.) What can I blame
for my unrest, insomnia? Persistent fear
elbows me, embedded deeply here
in an outgrown bed. (Narrow, but no narrower
than the single bed we sometimes share.)
On every side you grin gilt edged from long-discarded selves
(but where do I fit into the picture?) Your bookshelves
are crowded with previous prizes, a selection
of plots grown thin. Your egg collection
shatters me – (plover, robin, songthrush, magpie,
wren, assorted seabirds) labelled carefully, sucked dry
years ago – that now you have no interest

in. (You just took one from each, you never wrecked a nest,
you said.) Invited guest among abandoned objects, my position
is precarious, closeted so – it's dark, your past a premonition
I can't close my eyes to. I shiver despite
the electric blanket and the deceptive mildness of the night.

SONG FOR COMING HOME

I browsed among the dress shop windows
(The town, the sun, the styles were new.)
I was looking for something lightweight for summer
And picked on you.

But what was less than love in summer
Autumn turned to almost hate.
So now I leave our bed of roses
With a hurt like a heavy weight.

I'm drinking beer in a speeding buffet
Along with some soldier I've met on this train.
My father will pick me up at the station
But I'll have to put me together again.

GEORGE SQUARE

George Square
idleness
an island
children splashing
in a sea of pigeons
pigeons strutting
pigeon-toed.

And we
city dwellers
sitting
separate
close together.
City dwellers
we only know
nature captive –
zoos and gardens
Latin-tagged.
We know no earth
or roots.
We see no slow
season shift
but sudden summer
blaze a concrete day
and catch us unawares.
We can find no sense
in traffic lights'
continual change of emphasis.

Nature captive:
this is a city
nature's barred.
But the flowers
bound and bedded
bloom
incurable as cancer
and as for fat old ladies'
flowery
summer dresses
my god they really are
a riot.

MAN ON A BENCH

This old man
has grown year-weary
no joy in changing seasons, just
another blooming spring
another sodden summer
another corny old autumn
and another winter
to leave him cold.

CARNIVAL

Glass roof holds down a
stale air of excitement,
bottles up noise.
It's all screams and legs
cutting prescribed arcs. We walk,
the lights revolve around you.
People spin at tangents,
swing limit-wards on chain end.
Collisions are less than inevitable.

The speedway is a whirlpool.
The waltzer reels out-of-time
to ten pop songs.
Pressures force skirts up, girls bare
their teeth and scream.
You say it's screams of pleasure.
The timid roll pennies.

Aunt Sally has ten men. They
grin and shake their heads.
I miss the point.
The hall of mirrors hints at all sorts
of horrible distortions, but
you're favourably reflected in my eyes.
We play the fruit machines.

I spin to a mere blur on a wheelspoke
about your axis. There is a smell of onions
and axle grease.
The ghost train has pop-up fears for fun,
makes me laugh off mine and try
octopus, big dipper, roller coaster.
(Single riders pay double fare.)

Here is no plain sailing, all bump
and jerk. Above the screams, the sound
of some clown laughing.
Showmen shuffle hoops, push darts.
Prizes are sheer trash, and every lady wins.

You buy me candyfloss and smile.
I sink my teeth into sweet damn all.

CLOAKROOM

Firstly
you girls who are younger
and therefore more hopeful,
thinking this is Woman's Own world
and that a dab of such and such
perfume behind the ears
will lure
a kid-gloved dream lover
who knows how to treat a girl
gently.
You think you can tangle him in your curls
and snare him with your fishnet
stockings.

Secondly
we girls who are older
and therefore – but is it wiser
to recognise our failure
reflected in succeeding Saturday nights?
Our eyes are blank
of illusions
but we automatically
lengthen lashes, lacquer hair
lipstick our lips for later
and the too easily faked closeness
of close-mouth kisses
which always
leave a lot to be desired.

THE CHOOSING

We were first equal Mary and I.
With same-coloured ribbons in mouse-coloured hair
and with equal shyness,
we curtseyed to the lady councillor
for copies of Collins' Children's Classics.
First equal, equally proud.

Best friends too Mary and I.
A common bond in being cleverest (equal)
in our small school's small class.
I remember
the competition for top desk
or to read aloud the lesson
at school service.
And my terrible fear
of her superiority at sums.

I remember the housing scheme
where we both stayed.
The same houses, different homes,
where the choices were made.

I don't know exactly why they moved,
but anyway they went.
Something about a three-apartment
and a cheaper rent.
But from the top deck of the high school
bus I'd glimpse among the others on the corner
Mary's father, mufflered, contrasting strangely
with the elegant greyhounds by his side.
He didn't believe in high school education,
especially for girls,
or in forking out for uniforms.

Ten years later on a Saturday –
I am coming from the library –
sitting near me on the bus,
Mary
with a husband who is tall,
curly haired, has eyes
for no one else but Mary.
Her arms are round the full-shaped vase
that is her body.
Oh, you can see where the attraction lies
in Mary's life –
not that I envy her, really.

And I am coming from the library
with my arms full of books.
I think of those prizes that were ours for the taking
and wonder when the choices got made
we don't remember making.

There was a bit of an upset
one afternoon. Well, waking
from an after-dinner nap (you get so tired) I
heard sounds, moans I suppose you would call them,
small cries, a kind of
whimpering.
That Miss Galbraith   it was her all right.
The curtains were well drawn but
hanging down
below their floral edge (they're no longer than bed-level)
her half
         -leg cut off just below the knee
and a nurse with forceps or something
at the stitches.
It was loose
around the bonestump, like leather folded under, gathered and
hamstrung with catgut.
The skin was a bit on the blue side, oh
                       her
                       shrieks   and   three
loud dark drops of bad blood
from where the clean thing had probed it.
Of course all this was none
too pleasant
for anyone concerned. But on the whole here
it's a well-ordered existence.
Daily
those of us who are up to it fix the flowers.
(Daffodils are in season   make a fine show for
the visiting hour).
There's not much to it to tell the truth
it's just a matter of the fresh ones
arranging them as best you can and
picking out the dead ones

then disposing of them in the polythene sack in the slunge
which smells a bit.
This is only natural.

I had my dressing changed today.
To be honest I had not thought to be flawed
so very visibly.
But when all is said and done, no matter.
Getting better is the main thing.

Up and about again. The world
shrinks to the size of the ward
and this dull day room.
Weak sun and one day much like
any other. We are on Christian name terms
in no time.
Newspapers come, full of nonsense
BLIND CLIMBING ACE TO WED
EX-ORANGE CHIEF ACCUSED.
We are recovering.
You could call this a breathing space,
a chance to catch up on last Christmas's
correspondence.

But for the most part
looking out of the window
at the stray sheep in the hospital grounds
making themselves ill
silly creatures
cropping in the rhubarb patch, is about all we are good for.
We all agree operations
fairly take it out of you.
There is a TV we don't watch much.
We cannot laugh / we are in stitches.
The way we feel
a sneeze would split us at the seam.   Oh,

but our wounds won't gape unless we are unwise &
overdo things.
We are reminded healing hurts.
We all have wounds
                              which will
get better through time, the marks
fade into ferns like fossils,
become old wounds.
All in all most of us are making good
recoveries. With luck we'll be home soon,
back to our loved ones
(oh and here's hoping)
because they love us they will also
love our scars.

OBJECT

I, love,
am capable of being looked at
from many different angles. This
is your problem.
In this cold north light it may
seem clear enough.
You pick your point of view
and stick to it, not veering much –
this
being the only way to make any sense of me
as a formal object. Still
I do not relish it, being
stated so – my edges defined
elsewhere than I'd imagined them
with a crispness I do not possess.

The economy of your line does not spare me
by its hairsbreadth.
I am limited. In whose likeness
do you reassemble me?
It's a fixed attitude you
force me into.
Cramp knots calf muscles;
pins and needles rankle in my arm;
my shoulder aches;
irked, I am aware of my extremities.
A casual pose, at first it seemed
quite natural. My features freeze.
A snapshot's decision would have demanded nothing
much of me in the way of endurance.
Perhaps your eye's lens, being selective, is more merciful?
It flicks
constantly between us, taking stock,

trying to see me in proper proportion.
I did not choose which face to confront you with.

As a diversion
my eyes are allowed just this
wedge of studio and window space
over your left shoulder
and above your head.

Over and over, indifferent,
my boredom records it, raw and formless,
studio clutter
the floorboards' irregularities
a knot or two
occasional splinters going against the grain;
Random spatters on the white wall –
cerulean, terre verte,
transparent golden ochre; black
dust on white ledge; chestnut tree's topmost
pale candles flickering beyond the sill,
cutting the clean edge of the attic opposite;
(once, over there, mirrored,
seen at several removes if I strained my eyes enough,
a woman in an overall
entering that dim room and
later leaving again, shutting out a square of light).
The thin wisps of smoke from those strange-shaped chimney pots,
the innumerable tones of grey
and green-grey merging, spring glimmering.

In this view of things
too much to take into account is what it amounts to.
But you, love,
set me down in black and white exactly.
I am at once

reduced and made more of.

WEDDING MARCH

Could I buy a white dress and hope for good weather?
Could I take something borrowed? Could we bind us together?
And while Visions of Sugar Plums danced in each head,
could we lie long content on the bed that we'd made?

No, I've not my own house in order enough
to ever make you a tidy wife.
Could I learn to waste not and want not –
make soup from bones,
save wool scraps, bake scones
from sour milk? Would I ask for more
than to lunch alone on what's left over from the night before?
Could I soothe our children's night time bad dream fear
with nursery rhymes, and never find my cupboard bare?
Imagine an old handbag full of photographs,
once in a blue moon I'd drag them out for laughs –
smiling at poses I once carefully arranged,
in hoots at the hemlines and how we've changed.

We'll try. It still is early days.
I'll try and mend my sluttish ways.
We'll give our kitchen a new look –
a lick of paint, a spice rack, and a recipe book.
I'll watch our tangled undies bleaching clean
in the humdrum of the laundromat machine.
I'll take my pet dog vacuum on its daily walk through rooms,
and knowing there is no clean sweep,
Keep busy still with brooms.

RIDDLE-ME-REE

My first is in life (not contained within heart)
My second's in whole but never in part.
My third's in forever, but also in vain.
My last's in ending, why not in pain?

is love the answer?

MEMO TO MYSELF FOR SPRING

April
April first you must fool me
I am no longer
anybody's fool.
I have danced with too many
velvet-tongued men.
I have seen too many
plaster effigies of saints
for faith to mean much.
Hope
is treacherous
and much to be guarded against in April.
I refuse to put out with
any more charity –
I won't be as mad as March in April.
April you confidence trickster,
you very practical
practical joker –
your clichéd burgeoning and budding
calculated
to set me wandering in a forest of cosmetic counters'
lyric poetry.
You urge me,
buy a lipstick
treat yourself to a new dress
try again.
But April first you must fool me.
April
I fear you
May.

ISLANDS

(1978)

OUTER

I.
Another life
we marvel at the tweeds
a bale by each gatepost.
This is the day the lorry will collect
granite-marl   green-lovatt
herringbone   houndstooth   rust and
heathermix.

From each dour house
always this always black
and white dog comes to stand stock still.
He's only ruffled by the wind.
He doesn't waste a bark. He's only
here to check we skirt his land.

Another life
each spare rib croft
each staggered drystane wall
that makes slicing up bare land
look next to natural.
Low houses   separate   strung across the hill
so far away from us –
the woman on the doorstep with a basin
that might be henmash
or monday washing
the man
shut in with the bare bulb
and the clattering in the blacktarred hut
where the weaving gets done.

Lambs home in
Two hard tugs
and they fasten onto each vague mother.

Absentmindedly it seems
sheep tug at the roots of everything
till it's all baldness, stones and droppings.
Hens scratch and pick.
The flagrant cockerel's let crow
from the boss-eyed skull of a rusted truck.
Bones, blackhouses, implements,
things fall to bits.
Sheep come apart in handfuls –
it's that time of year –
old cars in the salt air,
Far too many stones to ever clear.

What's not useful lies and rots.
Useless to say *ramshackle*
or to call it waste.
Nothing goes and leaves no trace –
just that here's a climate where
it's all meshed over, nettled, part of things
in no time. Absorbable.
Rain and mud and wind
will streak and fritter even this too-blue
plastic feedbag till it blends.

Even the weaving will go to the wall
(the hand-
loom's finished if this doublewidth comes in)
Shawbost, Breger, Arnol who'll
make ends meet?

For there's a bare living only
if even the godless can pass Sunday
decently idle in their stocking soles
and never cross the door.
If you use the otterboard to trick the fish
and without your nosey neighbour knowing

fit a motor that will turn your loom.
If you don't get caught.
If you can keep the sheep out
your patch might learn a smattering of growth.
Wind combs out wool wraithed
on nebulous, necessary fences.

2.
And so we go to Callanish to see the stones.
Another world entirely.
Chill at the bone
we walk the longest limb avenue of stones
all twice as tall as any man.
Nowhere on this island can you find this stone.
Who brought?
Hard and how far? Why?
Purpose a plain use our bones root to remember.
Long before Christ   precisely cruciform   a calendar
a seasons-map   magical
and more.
Human bones at the crux. A skull. A chamber
inside the certain circle of these standing stones.
Long before the solstice we'll be gone.
We won't see the silver giant
rise and walk at dawn.

3.
And when the butter wouldn't churn
there was a saying if you took a pan –
having first shut fast the windows and the door –
and gave some of that slow milk
a right good scald over the fire
the witch that was the one that cursed it

had to come.
It worked.
The auld bitch knocked my father said
and afterwards the village knew her.

Over our drink it seems
Dolidh will tell us – if she's pressed –
of the witches of Tolsta.

And och it's all nonsense
but then his mother's sister was supposed
when she was only young
to have been half-promised
before she thought the better of it to this lad.
Who could understand it?
It was she who did the jilting
but she lost every bit of colour
and every day she grew more thin.
Her mother sent her to the White Magic Man
six miles away. Herbs
and a prayer. He said walk back
but remember not to speak
before you cross your own doorstep.
And on the way
she met that lad's mother and was forced
to return her good-day.
She wasted. Still she got thin.
Until her mother sent her to the Man again.
He said
I told you not to talk.
Go back.
Once more as she was walking she met the lad's mother
This time she didn't answer.
She got better.
Later it was said

someone found a clay doll under running water.

Donald gives us more malt
Dolina pokes the fire.
Midsummer but we shiver
thinking of the slow wearing away of water.
She draws us closer in.

4.
wind hurts
old molar
hollow stump blunt tooth bare
round and round
this broch
will baffle still

stonewall
doublebluff
drystane

harshness of that winter
watched
and when the cry went up
walled in between
the dark invader
and the women young and beasts
between stone walls
was chance of surviving for these men.

dun carloway we
crawl the long ramp
between the inner and the outer
wall again.

5.
Golden Harvest.
The Girl Pat.
Eilan Glas.
Naturally sixteen has not much time
for all the old songs.
These two have dogged the Mod
this last afternoon, undone
the top three buttons, folded
shirt-collars open to a deep vee –
schoolgirls arm in arm
down by the harbour humming.
Arm in arm
on such high cork shoes they still
move easily
among oil and rope and smeared
rainbows of fishscales.

They giggle
or go blank
or bat back smart answers
to the young dogs (sealegs,
cuffed wellingtons) moving easily
among nets and hooks and weights.
Luminous floats,
wolf whistles.

Trouble is this town's too small.
They've twice trawled around the circuit
of mainstreet and back round church street,
sneered at every white-net Sunday hat with streamers
in the Pakistani draper's shop display.
In the autumn there's the nursing.

At Woolworths' beauty counter
one smears across the back of her hand

the colour of her next kiss.
The other nets in her wiremesh basket
Sea Witch.
Harvest Gold.

6.
Laura has gone in a clean white blouse
to Stornoway to sing Beginners Gaelic in the Mod.
Eeshy and Agnes-Mhairi
always laugh she says
and imitate the way incomers talk.
Let them she says.
living here she wants to learn.
Eleven years old,
she'd rather be here than Glasgow any day.
This is where she wants to stay.
She opens her book. She shines.
We stumble after her, repeat.

Is e seo tigh ban.
Is e seo tigh dubh.
This is a white house.
This is a black house.

INNER

1.
make a change
if you get the weather

yes the place we're staying in
is green

bracken comes out clenched
only unbends
in the company of many others.
rigid, sinister as soldiers,
won't let us pass.

need not-English –
don't want to know the silly pretty names
for wildflowers
when I look them up in Sarah's
book. starlike in wiry grass
Skye flowers are too wild to call
Seapink   Kingcup   Lady's Smock.
another language.
last week on Lewis
Jim said he'd found that Gaelic words for colours
weren't colours as he thought he knew them.
chrome-yellow red-spectrum unsayable
straight from the tube.
rather a word might mean
red or reddish-brown earthbound.
another black or deep or purplish –
the colour of the darkness.
blue a clearness.
takes time says Jim
to know exactly how to paint here.
such distinctions.

glàs
might mean green or even calm-sea grey.
more a chroma of the weather
colour of the mind.

2.
the birds
at first they bothered me
so big
so strange
their cries

just who
is that cuckoo
getting at all day?
the mechanical lark
on its yoyo string
the crossbow shadow of the hawk.

only took
two hooligan gulls
to chase that eagle round in circles
for half an hour before
they shot off yammering
to lord it at the tip.

big hoody
ugly bird
came down twice
sat square in the kitchen window
went caw caw
bashed his great horny beak twice hard
against the glass.

as if we were in an egg
big hoody was determined to smash.

but seems there's no omen in it.
hoodycrow's only
a bird
who's looking for a mate
and fallen for his own reflection
you know how people get.

3.
mail comes
sometimes we send postcards
hope this finds you
we are much the same

midges very bad in evenings
we have woken every morning for a week
under the tin roof
listening to the rain

walking by the sea
we find clean bones
cork floats tiny
coral branches
green glass cockleshells
driftwood a broken
copper sprinkler rose gone green
and botched and oxidised
smooth pebbles mermaid purses
things to pick.
a collage on the window ledge.
I'd like
an art that could somehow marry
the washed-up manmade
and the wholly natural
make a change

don't even know
if I like cities or small places

heart urchin
rare to find an unbroken one
perfect from the sea
smaller
than a salt cellar
frail container
some marine-motif something
star-like etched on the shell
shake it   you can tell
something small and dry and shrivelled is inside.

shake it and your page
is seasoned with smithereens of sand

heart urchin
something to hold in your hand.

LAUNDRETTE

We sit nebulous in steam.
It calms the air and makes the windows stream
rippling the hinterland's big houses to a blur
of bedsits – not a patch on what they were before.

We stuff the tub, jam money in the slot,
sit back on rickle chairs not
reading. The paperbacks in our pockets curl.
Our eyes are riveted. Our own colours whirl.

We pour in smithereens of soap. The machine sobs
through its cycle. The rhythm throbs
and changes. Suds drool and slobber in the churn.
Our duds don't know which way to turn.

The dark shoves one man in,
lugging a bundle like a wandering Jew. Linen
washed in public here.
We let out of the bag who we are.

This young wife has a fine stack of sheets, each pair
a present. She admires their clean cut air
of colour schemes and being chosen. Are the dyes fast?
This christening lather will be the first test.

This woman is deadpan before the rinse and sluice
of the family in a bagwash. Let them stew in their juice
to a final fankle, twisted, wrung out into rope,
hard to unravel. She sees a kaleidoscope

for her to narrow her eyes and blow smoke at, his overalls
and pants ballooning, tangling with her smalls
and the teeshirts skinned from her wriggling son.
She has a weather eye for what might shrink or run.

This dour man does for himself. Before him,
half lost, his small possessions swim.
Cast off, random
they nose and nudge the porthole glass like flotsam.

THE BARGAIN

The river in January is fast and high.
You and I
are off to the Barrows.
Gathering police-horses twitch and fret
at the Tron end of London Road and Gallowgate.
The early kick-off we forgot
has us, three thirty, rubbing the wrong way
against all the ugly losers
getting ready to let fly
where the two rivers meet.

January, and we're
looking back, looking forward,
don't know which way

But the boy
with three beautiful Bakelite
Bush radios for sale in Meadow's Minimarket is
button popping station hopping he
doesn't miss a beat   sings along   it's easy
to every changing tune.

Yes today we're in love aren't we?
with the whole splintering city
its big quick river   wintry bridges
its brazen black Victorian heart.
So what if every other tenement
wears its hearth on its gable end
all I want
is my glad eye to catch
a glint in your flinty Northern face again
just once. Oh I know it's cold
and coming down
and no we never lingered long among

the Shipbank traders.
Paddy's Market   underneath the arches
stank too much today
the usual wet-dog reek rising
from piles of old damp clothes.

Somebody absolutely steamboats he says on
sweet warm wine
swigged plaincover from a paper bag
squats in a puddle with nothing to sell
but three bent forks   a torn
calendar (last year's)
and a broken plastic sandal.
So we hadn't the stomach for it today.
We don't deserve a bargain then!
No connoisseur can afford to be too scrupulous
about keeping his hands clean.
There was no doubt   the rare   the beautiful
and the bugle beaded   the real antique   dirt cheap
among the rags and drunks
you could easily take to the cleaners.

At the Barrows everything has its price
no haggling   believe me
this boy knows his radios.
Pure Utility
and what that's worth these days.
Suddenly the fifties are fashionable
and anything within a decade of art deco
a rarity you'll pay through the nose for.
The man with the patter and all these curtain lengths
in fibreglass is flabbergasted at the bargain
and says so in so many words.
Jesus, every other
arcade around here's
a 'Fire Surround Boutique' –

and we watch the struggling families;
father carrying hearth home
mother wound up with kids.
All the couples we know fall apart
or have kids.
Oh we've never shouldered much.
We'll stick to small icons for our home –
as long as they're portable –
a dartboard   a peacock feather
a stucco photoframe.

We queue in a blue haze of hot fat
for Danny's Do-Nuts that grit
our teeth with granules of sugar
I keep
losing you and finding you –
two stalls away you thumb
through a complete set of manuals for
primary teachers in the thirties
I rub my sleeve
on a dusty Chinese saucer
till the gilt shows through.
Oh come on   we promised
we'd not let our affection for the slightly cracked
trap us into such expenditure again.
Oh even if it is a bargain
we won't buy.
The stallholder says we'll be the death of her
she says   see January
it's been the doldrums the day.

And it's packing-up time
with the dark coming early
and as cold as the river.
By the bus stop I show you
the beady bag and the maybe rosewood box

with the inlaid butterfly and the broken catch.
You've bought a record by The Shangri-Las
a pin-stripe waistcoat that needs a stitch
it just won't get and a book called *Enquire
Within – Upon Everything*.
The raw cold gets colder.
There doesn't seem to be a lot to say.
I wish we could either mend things
or learn to throw them away.

IN THE FRANCIS BACON ROOM AT THE TATE

in every picture
  every figure
(except
the figure of Van Gogh
in Francis Bacon's 1957
Study for a Portrait)
has a defined space he must inhabit.

Delineate.
Cold steel. Prosthetic.
Chromium or crowbar.
Hotel room neutral gloss
over suffering, over violence and loss.
Solid, marginally shifting walls enclose
all flesh.
Genitals, a curled rose.
Face a blur.
One limb a mere
stump. Gouge that tongue
plush soft and scarlet in its cage of teeth.
Look, where that knife-edged
shank-bone sinks beneath
that surface, is it ankle-deep
in fur rug
or barbed wire? Can't shrug
off normality, its terrible textures.
These pictures
bring it all home.
Every solitary figure is a loner.
Every smart pad frames its owner.

In the Francis Bacon Room at the Tate,
in every picture,
 every figure (except
the figure of Van Gogh in Bacon's
1957 *Study for a Portrait*)
has this boxed-in space he must inhabit.

But Van Gogh is a figure in a landscape that bleeds
On all sides from the picture edge,
flows from him all ways,
harshened under cruel sun
to acid scarlet and poison green.
Van Gogh is lonely, lumpen, out-of-place
being at one with the landscape.
He's rooted like an awkward tree,
tied to his own shadow, a black hole.
All there is to hem him is his hat
a slashed arc, burnt gold, sharp citrus.
Careful, it's a hat
and not a halo.
And it offers nor much shadow.
The only space Van Gogh has to inhabit
is this terrible landscape,
is the space beneath his hat.

THE GRIMM SISTERS

(1981)

I. THE STORYTELLER POEMS

STORYTELLER

she sat down
at the scoured table
in the swept kitchen
beside the dresser with its cracked Delft.
And every last crumb of daylight was salted away.

No one could say the stories were useless
for as the tongue clacked
five or forty fingers stitched
corn was grated from the husk
patchwork was pieced
or the darning done.

Never the one to slander her shiftless.
Daily sloven or spotless no matter whether
dishwater or tasty was her soup.
To tell the stories was her work.
It was like spinning,
gathering thin air to the singlest strongest
thread. Night in
she'd have us waiting held
breath, for the ending we knew by heart.

And at first light
as the women stirred themselves to build the fire
as the peasant's feet felt for clogs
as thin grey washed over flat fields
the stories dissolved in the whorl of the ear
but they

hung themselves upside down
in the sleeping heads of the children
till they flew again
in the storyteller's night.

2. THE FATHER

loving and bungling,
offending the evil fairy by forgetting
her invitation to the Christening,
or being tricked into bartering his beloved daughter
in exchange for the rose he only
took to please her – then compounding it all
by over-protectiveness and suppression
(banning
spinning wheels indeed
when the sensible thing would have been
to familiarise her from the cradle
and explain their power to hurt her).

But when she comes,
the beautiful daughter,
leading her lover by the sleeve, laughing –
'Come and meet my daddy, the King,
he's absolutely a hundred years behind the times
but such a dear.'
and she's (note Redeeming Kiss)
wide-eyed and aware.
Stirring, forgiven, full of love and terror,
her father hears her footstep on the stair.

3. THE MOTHER

is always two-faced
At best, she wished you
into being. Yes, it was she
cried at the seven drops of blood that fell,
staining the snow – she
who bargained crazily with Fate
for that long-awaited child as red as blood
as white as snow
and when you came true it was
she who clapped her hands merrily because
she was as happy as a queen could be.
But she's always dying early,
so often it begins to look deliberate,
abandoning you,
leaving you to the terrible mercy
of the Worst Mother, the one who married your father.
She doesn't like you, she
prefers all your sisters, she
loves her sons.
She's jealous of mirrors.
She wants your heart in a casket.
When she cuts the apple in two and selflessly
takes the sour green half
she's good and glad to see you poisoned
by the sweet red pulp.
Tell me
what kind of prudent parent
would send a little child on a foolish errand in the forest
with a basket jammed with goodies
and wolf-bait? Don't trust her an inch.

THE GRIM SISTERS

And for special things
(weddings, school-
concerts) the grown-up girls next door
would do my hair.

Luxembourg announced Amami night.
I *sat at peace* passing bobbipins
from a marshmallow-pink cosmetic purse
embossed with jazzmen,
girls with ponytails and a November
topaz lucky birthstone.
They doused my cow's-lick, rollered
and skewered tightly.
I expected that to be lovely
would be worth the hurt.

They read my Stars,
tied chiffon scarves to doorhandles, tried
to teach me tight dance steps
you'd no guarantee
any partner you might find would ever be able to
keep up with as far as I could see.

There were always things to burn
before the men came in.

For each disaster
you were meant to know the handy hint.
Soap at a pinch
but better nail varnish (clear) for ladders.
For kiss curls, spit.
Those days womanhood was quite a sticky thing
and that was what these grim sisters came to mean.

You'll know all about it soon enough.
But when the clock struck they
stood still, stopped dead.
And they were left there
out in the cold with the wrong skirt length
and bouffant hair, dressed to kill,

who'd been
all the rage in fifty-eight,
a swish of Persianelle
a slosh of perfume.
In those big black man-trap handbags
they snapped shut at any hint of *that*
were hedgehog hairbrushes
cottonwool mice and barbed combs to tease.
Their heels spiked bubblegum, dead leaves.

Wasp waist and cone breast, I see them yet.
I hope, I hope
there's been a change of more than silhouette.

THE FURIES

I. HARRIDAN

Mad Meg on my mantelpiece,
Dulle Griet by Brueghel, a Flemish masterpiece
in anybody's eyes. 'Well worth historical consideration'
was how I looked at it. The surrealist tradition
from Bosch to Magritte is such a Flemish thing!
Oh a work of great power, most interesting . . .
I chose it for my History of Art essay, took pains
to enumerate the monsters, reduce it all to picture planes.
I was scholarly, drew parallels
between Hieronymus Bosch's and Pieter Brueghel's Hells;
Compared and contrasted
Symbolism and Realism in the Flemish School;
discussed: Was Meg 'mad' or more the Shakespearean Fool?

The fool I was! Mad Meg, Sour-Tongued Margot,
maddened slut in this mass of misery, a Virago,
at her wit's end, running past Hell's Mouth, all reason gone,
she has one mailed glove, one battered breastplate on.
Oh that kitchen knife, that helmet, that silent shout,
I know Meg from the inside out.
All she owns in one arm, that lost look in her eyes.
These days I more than sympathise.

Oh I am wild-eyed, unkempt, hellbent, a harridan.
My sharp tongue will shrivel any man.
Should our paths cross
I'll embarrass you with public tears, accuse you with my loss.

2. SPINSTER

This is no way to go on.
Get wise. Accept. Be
a spinster of this parish.
My life's in shards.
I will keep fit in leotards.

Go vegetarian. Accept.
Support good causes.
Be frugal, circumspect.
Keep cats. Take tidy fits.
Go to evening classes.
Keep a nest egg in the bank.
Try yoga. Cut your losses.
Accept. Admit you're a bit of a crank –

Oh I may be a *bit* of a crank
but still I get by, frugally. Think positive.
I live and let live. Depend
on nobody. Accept.
Go in for self-improvement.
Keep up with trends.
I'll cultivate my conversation.
I'll cultivate my friends.
I'll grow a herbaceous border.
By hook by crook I'll get my house in order.

3. BAWD

I'll get all dolled up in my gladrags,
stay up till all hours, oh
up to no good.
It'll amaze you, the company I keep –

and I'll keep them at arm's length –
I've hauled my heart in off my sleeve.

I'll let my hair down,
go blonde, be a bombshell, be on the make,
I'll gold-dig, I'll be frankly fake.

I'll paint my face up, paint the town,
have carmine nails, oh
be fatal dame.
I've bold eyes, kohl sockets.
I'll look daggers, kill.
My lipstick colour's Merry Hell.

I'd frighten the French.
I'll be a torment, haunt men's dreams,
I'll wear my stockings black with seams.

I'll rouge my cleavage, flaunt myself, my heels
will be perilously high, oh
but I won't sway.
I'll shrug everything off the shoulder,
make wisecracks, be witty off the cuff.
Tell blue jokes in mixed company.

I'll be a bad lot.
I've a brass neck.
There is mayhem in my smile.
No one will guess it's not my style.

MY RIVAL'S HOUSE

is peopled with many surfaces.
Ormolu and gilt, slipper satin,
lush velvet couches,
cushions so stiff you can't sink in.
Tables polished clear enough to see distortions in.

We take our shoes off at her door,
shuffle stocking-soled, tiptoe – the parquet floor
is beautiful and its surface must
be protected. Dust
cover, drawn shade,
won't let the surface colour fade.

Silver sugar-tongs and silver salver,
my rival serves us tea.
She glosses over him and me.
I am all edges, a surface, a shell
and yet my rival thinks she means me well.
But what squirms beneath her surface I can tell.
Soon, my rival
capped tooth, polished nail
will fight, fight foul for her survival.
Deferential, daughterly, I sip
and thank her nicely for each bitter cup.

And I have much to thank her for.
This son she bore –
first blood to her –
never, never can escape scot free
the sour potluck of family.
And oh how close
this family that furnishes my rival's place.

Lady of the house.
Queen bee.
She is far more unconscious,
far more dangerous than me.
Listen, I was always my own worst enemy.
She has taken even this from me.

She dishes up her dreams for breakfast.
Dinner, and her salt tears pepper our soup.
She won't
give up.

THREE TWISTS

I. RAPUNZSTILTSKIN

& just when our maiden had got
good & used to her isolation,
stopped daily expecting to be rescued,
had come to almost love her tower,
along comes This Prince
with absolutely
all the wrong answers.
Of course she had not been brought up to look for
originality or gingerbread
so at first she was quite undaunted
by his tendency to talk in strung-together cliché.
Just hang on and we'll get you out of there
he hollered like a fireman in some soap opera
when she confided her plight (the old
hag inside etc. & how trapped she was);
well, it was corny but
he did look sort of gorgeous
axe and all.
So there she was, humming & pulling
all the pins out of her chignon,
throwing him all the usual lifelines
till, soon, he was shimmying in & out
every other day as though
he owned the place, bringing her
the sex manuals & skeins of silk
from which she was meant, eventually,
to weave the means of her own escape.
All very well & good, she prompted,
but when exactly?
She gave him till
well past the bell on the timeclock.
She mouthed at him, hinted,

she was keener than a TV quizmaster
that he should get it right.
I'll do everything in my power, he intoned, *but
the impossible* (she groaned) *might
take a little longer.* He grinned.
She pulled her glasses off.
*All the better
to see you with my dear?* he hazarded.
She screamed, cut off her hair.
Why, you're beautiful? he guessed tentatively.
No, No, No! she
shrieked & stamped her foot so
hard it sank six cubits through the floorboards.
I love you? he came up with
as finally she tore herself in two.

2. BEAUTY *&* THE

Beast
he was hot
he grew horns
he had you
screaming mammy daddy screaming blue
murder.
From one sleepy thought
of how like a mane his hair . . .
next thing
he's furred & feathered, pig bristled,
warted like a toad
puffed & jumping –
the green cling of those
froggy fingers
will make you shudder yet.
Then his flesh gone

dead. Scaled as a handbag.

He was that old crocodile
you had to kiss
yes, Rosebud, I
suppose you were right.
Better than hanging around
a hundred years for someone
to hack his way through the thorns
for the shoe that fits
for the chance to have you cough up
the poisoned apple
wodged in your gullet.
So you (anything for a quiet
life) embrace the beast, endure.

Three days & nights, three patient years,
you'll win I'm sure.
But who'd have guessed
paying your dues would mean
the whole wham bam menagerie?

Oh, but soon
(her hair grew lang her breath grew strang)
you'll
(little One-Eye for little Three-Eyes, the
Bearded Lady)
Yes, sweet Beauty, you'll
match him
horror for horror.

3. AFTER LEAVING THE CASTLE

On the first night
the lady lay in the dark with her lover
awake all night
afraid her husband would pursue her.

On the second night
the lady lay awake in the arms of her lover
her tongue and teeth idly
exploring the cold of his earring.

On the third night
the lady lay awake afraid
her husband would never come after.

On the fourth night
the lady thought as she drifted off to sleep
how monotonous it was going to be
to live on rabbit stew forever
& she turned a little away
from snoring, the smell of wild garlic.

When they passed him on the road
on the fifth day,
she began to make eyes at the merchant.

TAM LIN'S LADY

Oh I forbid you maidens a',
who wear gowd in your hair –
to come or go by Carterhaugh
for young Tam Lin is there.

So you met him in a magic place?
OK
But that's a bit airy fairy for me.
I go for the specific – you could, for instance,
say that when he took you for a coffee
before he stuck you on the last bus
there was one of those horrible congealed-on
plastic tomatoes on the table . . . oh don't
ask me
I don't know why everything has to be so sordid these days . . .
I can take *some* sentiment –
tell me how charmed you were
when he wrote both your names and a heart in spilt coffee –
anything except that he carved them on the eldern tree.
But have it your own way.
Picking apart your personal
dream landscape of court and castle and greenwood
isn't really up to me.
So call it magical. A fair country.
Anyway you were warned.

And if, as the story goes nine times out of ten –
he took you by the milk-white hand & by the grass-green sleeve
& laid you on the bonnie bank & asked of you no leave,
well, so what?
You're not the first to fall for it,
good green girdle and all –
with your schooltie rolled up in your pocket
trying to look eighteen. I know.

All perfectly forgiveable.
Relax.
What I do think was a little dumb
if you don't mind me saying so
was to swallow that old one about you being
the only one who could save him.

Oh I see – there was this lady
he couldn't get free of.
Seven years and more he said he'd sacrificed himself
and if you didn't help him he'd end up
a fairy for ever! Enslaved.

Or worse still in hell without you.

Well, well.
So he stopped you from wandering in the forest
and picking pennyroyal and foxgloves
and making appointments and borrowing money for the abortion.
He said all would be well
If only you'd trust him just this once
and go through
what he was honest enough to admit in advance
would be hell and highwater for you.

So he told you which relatives to pander to
and which to ignore.
How to snatch him from the Old One
and hold on through thick and thin
through every change that happened.
Oh but it was terrible!
It seemed earlier, you see,
he'd been talking in symbols (like
adder-snake, wild savage bear
brand of bright iron red-hot from the fire)
and as usual the plain unmythical truth was worse.

At any rate you were good and brave, you did
hang on, hang on tight.
And in the end of course
everything turned out conventionally right
with the old witch banished to her corner lamenting,
cursing his soft heart and the fact she couldn't keep him,
and everyone sending out for booze for the wedding.

So we're all supposed to be happy?
But how about you, my fallen fair maiden
now the drama's over, tell me
how goes the glamourie?
After the twelve casks of good claret wine
and the twelve and twelve of muskadine,
tell me
what about you?
How do you think Tam Lin will take
all the changes you go through?

SIX DISENCHANTMENTS

The mirror you
are tells me too often
I am not beautiful.

The warm room you were
once was a good place to be.
Oh catch me saying
the walls of the room were warm fingers stroking
but it was clean and decent,
it was the kind of place that let me warm myself.
I spent a lot of time in it
scribbling and humming, rearranging
at my leisure
the objects on the mantelshelf.

The rocket you are
still takes off occasionally
with a bump and a woosh in the night.
Always, it's always the surprise of my life
and I have to hang on tight.

You say the scissors I am
are too keen on cutting.

You say the teacher I am
is a terrible version of a cartoon schoolmarm
too straight lipped and square shouldered
all pinstripes and pencil skirt, spike heels, she's
strictly
too lewd to be true
and you can't be sure what punishment
she wants to exact from you.
So you thumb your nose and tell her
her boys will all grow up too soon

leave school and throw their schoolcaps
over the moon.

God
the brickwall you are these days
it doesn't even crack when you smile.
Believe me I spent a lot of time
working with my fingernails at mortar and lime
before I started to bash and
batter my head at it, that brick wall.
Now, even when I stop,
it doesn't stop hurting at all.

II. THE BELTANE BRIDE

THE BELTANE BRIDE

Yestreen the queen was wyce enough
To forswear all desire
From limerance and venery
She flinched as at fire.

She said she'd love to live with him
But she was not that kind
She'd raither lie in ironed silk
And in her right mind.

He pu'd the dress from her shooders
And a' the pins from her hair
And he easily undid her tidy life
But the ladye didna care . . .

'Tho' shairly I'm fond
Tho' they a' ca' me fool
I'll lie under this crazy quilt
wi' my Lord of Misrule.'

SONG OF SOLOMON

You
smell nice he said
what is it?
Honey? He nuzzled a soap-trace
in the hollow of her collarbone.
The herbs of her hair?
Salt? He licked
a riverbed between her breasts.

(He'd seemed
not unconvinced by the chemical
attar of roses at her armpit. She tried
to relax have absolute faith in
the expensive secretions of teased civet to
trust the musk at her pulse spots
never think of the whiff of
sour milk from her navel
the curds of cheese between the toes
the dried blood smell of many small wounds
the stink of fish at her crotch.)

No there he was above her apparently
as happy as a hog rooting for truffles.
She caressed him behind the ear
with the garlic of her cooking-thumb.
She banged shut her eyes
and hoped he would not smell her fear.

STOOGE SONG

How did I get here?
Out of my
street clothes & into
these sad spangles
having the silken flags of many countries
dragged from between my ears,
the perfect egg
coaxed from my cleavage,
it's undignified.
How did I get here?
The children chorus YOU VOLUNTEERED

& oh yes I
do
seem to remember myself
long ago
safe in the dark on the other side of the orchestra pit
laughing & munching
on those sweets I'd caught, that Buttons threw . . .
then I sort of recall
something about him leaning over the footlights
& me telegraphing furiously
CHOOSE ME CHOOSE ME

& it isn't as if I ever
liked him did I? Surely
I can't have been taken in
by his blackpatent hair & his permanent grin?

Shall I let you into a little secret?
Let me tell you what's what.
Can you keep it under your hat?

There is No Easter Bunny.
There.
Pure illusion & so are
(big gimmick)
those hawks he teases out of handkerchiefs
instead of doves.
It wasn't real claws
that made such short work
of my
long
kid gloves.

Right on cue
he takes my hand &
I stammer out that bit about
I HAVE NEVER SEEN YOU BEFORE YOU IN MY LIFE
but I must have my lines all wrong again,
all the people laugh.
& NOW, THE GRAND FINALE
THE LITTLE LADY WILL BE SAWN IN HALF

& oh (here we go again) truly
I have
never had my head so
effectively separated from my body.
Look I can wiggle my toes, can
wave tinkly fingers from
the four corners of the stage.
I volunteered. It was
all my own idea to come up here.

I smile & smile & smile to show my rage.

MIDSUMMER NIGHT

Was that a donkey braying in my dream?
Couldn't make head or tail of it but
it hawhawed itself blue in the face
whatever it was. Still, Confusion's clearly
what's called for in any comedy worth worrying about.
That and Chance
which certainly seems to be playing its part all right.
So we're laughing?
Get us, half enchanted and undecided
whether or not to give in to it,
wandering the wide woods on such a night like
the wrong pair of ill-met demi-
lovers we most likely are
in far too high a pollen count for
anybody's comfort. This is the
silly season though – you said so yourself –
surely a solstice is a time for going to extremes.
Have a heart though, I've always been
the equinox sort – white nights
and talking till birdsong
are as new a taste to me as the
piney retsina we sat late in the restaurant with,
till one. And still no real dark yet
to go home in.

Earlier, between
the World Cup and Wimbledon the blue
TV lights flickered from every douce house
in the solid suburbs we drove through to come
to such a shifting place.
Remember the horses
how silently they moved
from dark woods.

'Would you call this a green glade?' you
asking gravely with a glint,
the lilac haze and three rooks on the long meadow,
that russet shape that changed
we could swear it, and stretched
and lengthened to a fox and back to prick-eared
hare again. Nothing tonight could decide
what form to take.

We are good and strange to one another and no mistake.

BLUESHIRT

Halfway
into your blue
and white striped shirt you stop
and gather me up once more
against your dark
before you button yourself into the day.

Well break-
fasted I move alone and trusted
among your books and jazz
your photographs (horn-
players friends and trees)
I scribble at your table hang
my three clean shirts
in your closet am caught
in the cold cold stare of the tiger cat
I know was named by the lady
you say left long ago.
There's no snapshot of her taped up
not so much
as a hairpin in the bathroom cabinet.

An hour ago
you whistled off to work
leaving a kiss a spare key
and no conditions.
Like Bluebeard's wife
I stare at this key printed on my palm
its intricate notchings
then (absolutely clean

of charms or chicken bones) I
pocket it.
In your innocent ticking fridge
I might find the forbidden egg
crowned with blood.

THE HICKIE

I mouth
sorry in the mirror when I see
the mark I must have made just now
loving you.
Easy to say it's alright
adultery
like blasphemy is for believers but
even in our
situation simple etiquette says
love should leave us both unmarked.
You are on loan to me like a library book
and we both know it.
Fine if you love both of us
but neither of us must too much show it.

In my misted mirror
you trace two toothprints
on the skin of your shoulder and sure
you're almost quick enough
to smile out bright and clear for me
as if it was OK.

Friends again, together in this bathroom
we finish washing love away.

THE OTHER WOMAN

The other woman
lies
between us like a bolster.
When I hit out wild she's
insubstantial, a
flurry of feathers, a mere
sneezing irritant.
When my shaped and hardened words turn
machine-gun
against you she's rock solid
the sandbag you hide behind.

The other woman
lies
when she says she does not want
your guts for her garterbelt.
I send out spies,
they say relax
she's a hag
she's just a kid
she's not a patch
she's nothing too
she's no oil painting.

I'd know her anywhere.
I look for her in department stores, I scan
every cinema queue.
Sometimes suddenly in some downtown restaurant
I catch her eye
casting crazily around for me.

The other woman
lies
the other side of my very own mirror.

Sweet, when I smile
straight out for you, she
puts a little twist on it, my
right hand never knows what her left is doing.
She's sinister.
She does not mean you well.

LAST SUPPER

She is getting good and ready to renounce
his sweet flesh.
Not just for Lent. (For
Ever)
But meanwhile she is assembling the ingredients
for their last treat, the proper
feast (after all
didn't they always
eat together
rather more than rather well?)
So here she is tearing foliage, scrambling
the salad, maybe lighting candles even, anyway
stepping back to admire the effect of
the table she's made (and oh yes now
will have to lie on) the silverware,
the nicely al-
dente vegetables, the cooked goose.
He could be depended on to bring the bottle
plus betrayal with a kiss.

Already she was imagining it done with, this feast, and
exactly
what kind of leftover hash she'd make of it
among friends, when it was just
The Girls, when those three met again.
What very good soup
she could render from the bones,
then something substantial, something extra
tasty if not elegant.

Yes, there they'd be, cackling around the cauldron,
spitting out the gristlier bits
of his giblets;
gnawing on the knucklebone of some
intricate irony;
getting grave and dainty at the
petit-gout mouthfuls of reported speech;
'That's rich!' they'd splutter,
munching the lies, fat and sizzling as sausages.
Then they'd sink back
gorged on truth
and their own savage integrity,
sleek on it all, preening
like corbies, their bright eyes blinking
satisfied
till somebody would get hungry
and go hunting again.

III. HAGS AND MAIDENS

EVERYBODY'S MOTHER

Of course everybody's mother always and
so on . . .

Always never
loved you enough
or too smothering much.

Of course you were the Only One, your
mother
a machine
that shat out siblings, listen

everybody's mother
was the original Frigid-
aire Ice queen clunking out
the hardstuff in nuggets, mirror-
silvers and ice-splinters that'd stick
in your heart.

Absolutely everyone's mother
was artistic when she was young.

Everyone's mother
was a perfumed presence with pearls, remote
white shoulders when she
bent over in her ball dress
to kiss you in your crib.

Everybody's mother slept with the butcher
for sausages to stuff you with.

Everyone's mother
mythologised herself. You got mixed up
between dragon's teeth and blackmarket stockings.
Naturally
she failed to give you
Positive Feelings
about your own sorry
sprouting body (it was a bloody shame)

but she did
sit up all night sewing sequins
on your carnival costume

so you would have a good time

and she spat
on the corner of her hanky and scraped
at your mouth with sour lace till you squirmed

so you would look smart

And where
was your father all this time?
Away
at the war, or
in his office, or any-
way conspicuous for his
absence, so

what if your mother did
float around above you

big as a barrage balloon
blocking out the light?

Nobody's mother can't not never do nothing right.

THE ARIADNE VERSION

Of course Ariadne was in it
right up to here,
the family labyrinth – lush
palatial and stained with sacrifice.
Maybe money grew on trees
for Minos in summer Crete
but Ariadne, imagine it,
sizzling on the beach all day
with school out
or mooning around in that room of hers
tricked out chintzily
to her mother's fond idea of some sub teen dream –
all those Daedalus dolls dangling, for godsake.
Someone should realise at Ariadne's age
they were just not
amusing any more.
Oh they gave her arty crafty kits
for her birthday – balls
of silver filigree fingering
to keep her hands busy at any rate with
tatting or
crochet or some such crap.
No one would admit it.
It had burst inside her recently
like a bull in a china shop.
She was grown up.
She had to get the hell out, somehow.
But talking to them was
bashing your head against a brick wall,
when it came to unravelling anything
they just weren't interested.

Big Daddy would just do his Kingpin bit,
lay down the law.
And her moonstreaked mother had gone blonde again,
mincing around in that rawhide trouser suit,
all silicone and facelift – must be off again
after some big bronzed stud in the palace guard.
Her father was turning a blind eye as usual –
if he'd objected everytime she made him wear the horns
she'd only have dredged the past again
and hurled at him every nymph he'd ever
given the palmgrove treatment.
Ariadne lay wide awake listening
to the quarrelling leak through leadlined walls.
Worse was the love.
Some labyrinth.
It fitted them like a glove.

Ariadne lay on the silver sands
applying more Ambre Solaire
(she was browning nicely).
Ariadne decided
she'd be off like a shot with the first man
who looked halfways likely,
so she'd better
kill off her own brute bit
her best friend, her brother,
doll-up to the nines go ultra
feminine (one hundred per cent).
The sea roared and pounded.
Over the far horizon appeared a black sail . . .

MY MOTHER'S SUITORS

have come to court me
have come to call oh
yes with their wonderful world
war two moustaches their long
stem roses their cultivated
accents (they're English aren't they
at very least they're
educated-Scots).
They are absolutely
au fait with menu-French
they know the language of flowers
& oh they'd die
rather than send a dozen yellow
they always get them right & red.
Their handwriting on the florist's card
slants neither too much to the left or right.

They are good sorts.
They have the profile for it – note
the not too much nose
the plenty chin. The
stockings they bring have no strings
& their square
capable hands are forever
lifting your hair and gently
pushing your head away from them
to fumble endearingly at your nape
with the clasp of the pretty heirloom
little necklace they know their
grandmother would have wanted
you to have.
(never opals – they know
that pearls mean tears).

They have come to call & we'll all
go walking under the black sky's
droning big bombers
among the ratatat of ack-ack.
We'll go dancing & tonight
shall I wear the lilac, or the
scarlet, or the white?

GIRL'S SONG

My father
would warn of the danger. Eggs all
in one basket. Pride hurtling for its fall.
One swallow does not make a summer,
he'd have me remember.

I'm seven, I'm
over the moon.
I've a brand-new coat of bright red stuff.
My father asks me: is it warm enough?

I'm twenty four, I
go over the score.
In my father's eyes I'm all but lost.
I want magenta and pentecost.

This letter
is from my father. He forwards mail
and drops a quick line in his careful hand.

How am I for money? Am I sure I've enough?
Father forgive. Though it's hard to read
you sign with love.

THE CAILLEACH

Bitter winter
won't let up
never stop
the old stranglehold.

Bluemoon
crystalgazer's
done her stint of wintering.
High-handed
hard-bitten
her rigour
will outlast
austere
dogstar's
deathwatch stringencies.

Brittle sun
spiking light's just
grist
to winter's mill.
She's all set to put us through it.

She'll crack down
old Mama Iron Heel
she'll make us rue it.

POPPIES

My father said she'd be fined
at best, jailed maybe, the lady
whose high heels shattered the silence.
I sat on his knee, we were listening
to the silence on the radio.
My mother tutted, oh that it was terrible,
as over our air
those sharp heeltaps struck steel, rang clear
as a burst of gunfire or a laugh
through those wired-up silent streets around the Cenotaph.
Respect.
Remembrance.
Surely when all was said
two minutes' silence in November
wasn't much to ask for, for the dead?
Poppies on the mantlepiece, the photograph
of a boy in a forage cap, the polished
walnut veneer of the wireless,
the buzzing in the ears and when
the silence ended the held-fire voice
of the commentator, who was shocked,
naturally, but not
wanting to make too much of it.

Why did she do it?
Was she taken sick – but that was no
excuse, on the radio it said,
couldn't you picture it?
how grown soldiers buttoned in their uniforms
keeled over, fell like flies
trying to keep up the silence.

Maybe it was looking at the khaki button eye
and the woundwire stem

of the redrag poppy
pinned in her proper lapel
that made the lady stick a bloody bunch of them
behind her ear
and clash those high heels across the square,
a dancer.

THE LAST HAG

The last hag I have her
nailed. Corndolly, a hank of straw, old
spindle shanks
dried up. A relic.
The last word in the folksy bit
bunched in her dirndl with sticky
burrs with poppypods'
deathrattle.
I've cut her down to size at last,
old hasbeen
always at me with
her witchy whispering
saying daughter, successor –
so much sales talk
for all that growing stuff.
I stopped my ears.
I strung her up above my high wide bed.
She'll shrivel, I'll sleep
solo curled and small but sound. Seems right.
Could be good
to go underground a while.

I want to winter a bit,
honestly.
Take pleasure as I move
in empty rooms
arrange dry grasses.
Sweet to see my own stored pulses
shelved.
Bottling plenty – oh you'd not believe
the goodies I've got
salted away.
Take each day
one in front of the other.

hayfoot strawfoot that's how.

And in my own good time
I'll let rip again.

DREAMING

FRANKENSTEIN

(1984)

WHAT THE POOL SAID, ON MIDSUMMER'S DAY

I've led you by my garrulous banks, babbling
on and on till – drunk on air
and sure it's only water talking –
you come at last to my silence.
Listen, I'm dark
and still and deep enough.
Even this hottest gonging sun
on this longest day
can't white me out.
What are you waiting for?
I lie here, inviting, winking you in.

The woman was easy.
Like to like, I called her, she came.
In no time I had her
out of herself, slipping on my water-stockings,
leaning into, being cupped and clasped
in my green glass bra.
But it's you I want, and you know it, man.
I watch you, stripped, knee-deep
in my shallows, telling yourself
that what makes you gasp
and balls your gut
is not my coldness but your own fear.

– Your reasonable fear,
what's true in me admits it.
(Though deeper, oh
older than any reason.)
Yes, I could
drown you, you
could foul my depths, it's not
unheard of. What's fish

in me could make flesh of you,
my wet weeds against your thigh, it
could turn nasty.
I could have you
gulping fistfuls fighting yourself
back from me.

I get darker and darker, suck harder.
On-the-brink man, you
wish I'd flash and dazzle again.
You'd make a fetish of zazzing dragonflies?
You want I should zip myself up
with the kingfisher's flightpath, be beautiful?
I say no tricks. I say just trust,
I'll soak through your skin and
slake your thirst.

I watch you. You clench,
clench and come into me.

AN ABORTION

The first inkling I had of the beast's agony
was the something not right
of her scrabbling, scrabbling
to still not quite find
all four feet.
Sunk again, her cow-tongue lolled
then spiked the sky, she rolled
great gape-mouth, neck distended
in a Guernica of distress.
That got through to me all right
behind glass as I was
a whole flat field away.
It took an emblem-bellow
to drag me from my labour
at the barbed words on my desk top.

Close to, green foam flecked her muzzle
and drizzled between the big bared brown teeth.
Spasms, strong, primeval
as the pulsing locomotion of some
terrible underwater creature,
rippled down her flank
and her groan was the more awesome
for being drier, no louder than a cough.
When she tried to rise again
I saw it.
Membrane wrapped, the head of a calf
hung out and the wrong-looking bundle
of a knuckle. Then her rope-tail dropped
and she fell back on it, steamrollering it
under her.

When the summoned men came,
buttoning blue coveralls over
the Sunday lunches and good-suit waistcoats,
the wound string around one man's knuckles
meant business and the
curt thank-you-very-much of the other
dismissed me.

Shamed voyeur, back at my notebooks again
my peeled eyes caught the quick hoick
of the string loop, the dead thing flopping
to the grass, the cow on her knees and
up again, the men leaving, one
laughing at some punchline.

The thing is this. Left alone,
that cow licking at those lollop limbs
which had not formed properly
with her long tongue,
that strong tongue
which is a match for thistles
and salt-lick coarse as pumice stone
tenderly over and over again at
what has come out of her and she is responsible for
as if she can not believe it will not
come alive,
not if she licks long enough.

Outside she is still licking, licking
till in the blue dusk
the men in blue come back again
and she turns, goes quietly with them
as if they were policemen
and she knew exactly what she were guilty of.

DREAMING FRANKENSTEIN

for Lys Hansen, Jacki Parry and June Redfern

She said she
woke up with him in her head, in her bed.
Her mother-tongue clung to her mouth's roof
in terror, dumbing her, and he came with a name
that was none of her making.

No maidservant ever
in her narrow attic, combing
out her hair in the midnight mirror
on Hallowe'en (having eaten
that egg with its yolk hollowed out
then filled with salt)
as a spell to summon up her lover
– oh never one had such success as this
she had not courted.
The amazed flesh of her
neck and shoulders nettled
at his apparition.

Later, stark staring awake to everything
(the room, the dark parquet, the white high Alps beyond)
all normal in the moonlight
and him gone, save a ton-weight sensation,
the marks fading visibly where
his buttons had bit into her and
the rough serge of his suiting had chafed her sex,
she knew – oh that was not how –
but he'd entered her utterly.

This was the penetration
of seven swallowed apple pips.
Or else he'd slipped like a silver dagger
between her ribs and healed her up secretly

again. Anyway
he was inside her
and getting him out again
would be agony fit to quarter her,
unstitching everything.

Eyes on those high peaks
in the reasonable sun of the morning,
she dressed in damped muslin
and sat down to quill and ink
and icy paper.

2. WHAT THE CREATURE SAID

The blind man did not hate me.
I saw him through the window,
through the rippling circle my own
hot breath had melted
in the spiky flowers of the frost.

I was exhausted,
imagine it. Midwinter. Mountains.
Forest. Dragging my bad leg
over iron ground, impossible passes,
pained by that fleshwound where
that villager's silver bullet
grazed me.

There he was, bent
above the hot soup, supping
his solitude from a bone spoon.
And when my single rap
at the glass spun him full face
towards me, mild as a cat,

my heart stopped but oh
he did not flinch.

Then I saw his
milky eyes stared right through me,
unblinking, and he fumbled
oddly forward to meet me at the latch.
I lifted it and entered,
sure that I found a friend.

3. SMIRNOFF FOR KARLOFF
for Marilyn Bowering and Bessie Smith

So you're who's been sleeping
in my bed. Well, hello there.
Long time no see.
So you're my Big Fat Little Secret
stretched out cold,
just between you and me.

Between you and me and the bedpost
it's getting a little crowded in here.
Roll over, let me whisper sweet zeroes
in your Good Ear.
Open up your Glad Eye.
Oh my! I'm going to make you.
Going to make you sit up.
Going to make you.
Going to take you to bits.
Going to take you to the cleaners.
Going to make you look cute,
going to let you roly-pole all over me
in your funeral suit –
the one you wear to weddings. Yeah.
With the too-short drainpipe trousers

with the brothelcreeper boots with the
tyre-track soles
and the squirt-in-the-eye trick carnation
in your button-hole.

You know, Matron,
it takes more than hospital corners to keep
a good man down, oh
yeah. Everything
in apple pie order.
All present
and correct. Shipshape. Aye-aye.
He got all my wits around him
his extrasensory senses and his
five straight limbs.
Yes sir,
you'll be up and about again
in no time.

What wouldn't you
give to love me. An arm, and a leg?
Going to make you.
make you sit up,
sit up and beg. Hey, Mister, Mister
can your dog do tricks?
Going to make you,
going to put you to the test,
make you give your all six
nights per week and on Sundays
going to take the rest.

Sure, you can smoke in bed.
It's a free country.
Let me pour you a stiff drink.
You're shivering.
Well, you know what they say, if you

can't take the cold then get outta
the icebox. What's that?
Smirnoff?
Well, you know, Mr Karloff,
I used to think an aphrodisiac was some
kinda confused Tibetan mountain goat
with a freak-out hair-do until I
met my monster and my monster
met his maker.
Oh yeah.

That's who been sleeping in my bed.
Same old surprise. Oh goody.
Long time no see.
Ain't going to let nothing come between
My monster and me.

SMUGGLER

for Susan Musgrave

Why she loved him, she said, was for
his black pirate's heart.
Get her, adrift in his
brass bed, half seas over, stared awake
by the match box she found last night
balanced on the bed head.
Contents: one single scarlet fingernail.

Love?
She explains it another way.
In a heatwave between the wars,
her maiden aunt once told her,
high in the Campsies (they had cycled
from Glasgow, they were fourteen, with
packed lunches in the baskets between the horns
of their handlebars) they skinnydipped and sunbathed
naked, she and her sister, and she slept.
She woke up later to a cloud and a bird like
a hawk circling and Nettie, her sister, her twin,
the one who died of TB at the time of Munich,
leant over her and bit her nipple off.

She explains it another way.

PAGE FROM A BIOGRAPHY

When she was seventeen she left home, secretly,
and lived rough amid the Axminster:
Became clever as Caliban at knowing the most
nourishing morsels among the jewel-berries she filched from
    the chintz.
Left alone she'd sample every tipple in the drinks cupboard
(topping up the jungle juice with tapwater).
She learned to name her poison
and know her true enemies.

She'd left no note but as they
did not seem to notice she'd gone she never
heard the dee-jay appeal for her return
or at least a postcard, no need for an address,
to set their minds at rest.

As for the weasel, well there was no sign of one
and this family wasn't cocktail cabinet class
but occasionally she thought she glimpsed
something furry and honey coloured with Christ knows
what kind of jaws and teeth slink behind the radiogram
and lie there limp as a draught excluder.

She poked the odd clandestine crust at it
flattering herself that Trouble was her middle name.

THE PEOPLE'S POET

for Edwin Morgan

Under the blue moon of this
whole silly business
really working for once, the people's poet
is reading to us from his most recent work.
Natty in tattersall,
boyish and fifty on the bare stage
under the blue light –
if the sidespots have rose-coloured filters,
well that won't wash with him –
listen,
his quick light voice not tripping ever
over his own peppery rhythms, the sibilants
and little silver sparks of spittle.
At first,
it was him blinking
into the black at the audience
and us wondering
had we backlit him too harshly, bungled it again?
Imagine encouraging him to
leave his Antartex and his looseleaf
in the anteroom
and then him having to tiptoe
through all those ladies doing yoga
in helanca, stretching breaths,
just to rescue his poems!
He was nice about it,
nice about
the coffee we were sorry
not to be able to offer in the interval
and the low ticket sales.

Into his second poem
he seems in his element.
On the orange bucket-chair behind him
his wad of hardbacks and pamphlets.
That's all. The wall's
aerosol maze is ours,
the empty bottle,
painted guitar, and
at his feet somebody's rainbow scarf
a serpent
straight off a snakes-and-ladders board and
maybe it is a game
for him?
Certainly there is fun in it –
didn't the six
particle poems tickle us pink?
Then there was a witch, a cat, a broomstick
a sort of story for
Hallowe'en which it isn't,
though it was while he read it; there was
a mummy in need of urgent repair;
those transcripts of tapes from outer
outer space.
Yes. The woman pissing in Central Station
he wouldn't let us look away from
for one minute, our confusion, the celebration,
the celebration
(Callas, Nabokov, Bolan, Presley, Lowell)
of the loved lately dead. The Dance
that danced them off is not
what he ever praises (though
who can ignore it?)

Outside the buses throb and topdeck
passengers slide past at eye-level, almost touchable,
Children shout clean into the cold.

The light from the public lavatory
catches the hurrying moon-
face of one girl and she's gone.
Taxis tick on
at possibly terrible cost.
But the winter city won't
stay locked shut
and that's what he sings out about.
It's choc-a-block with life
and lives we can make for.
(As next door
each yoga lady breathes
towards 'the new me'.)
Listen.
A Second Life.
Instructions to an Actor –
it's mostly resurrection
he calls up in us.
There is no comfort in it.
Except the odd moment,
the ridiculous and the marvellous –
speaking with tongues to the hard of hearing
just for the hell of it
this poet is playing with pure sound
('there is no meaning in any ordinary sense.')
Listen,
the mad particles dance
stanza by stanza
the poem is becoming more miraculous
more clear.

CONSTRUCTION FOR A SITE:
LIBRARY ON AN OLD CROQUET LAWN,
ST ANDREWS
Nine Approaches

1.
Step down
into the silence, a green
pool.

2.
Forget
the sea is here.
From where you are
you cannot see
the sea.
Stop your ears.

3.
Swim
the length of this empty
pool, slowly.
Turn, anchor yourself dead centre.
Measure yourself one minute
against four green walls,
the domestic slant of the kitchen garden,
the perfectly right-
angled clipped box-hedge
and you're sunk.

4.
On the old croquet lawn
blackbird bounces

at his killing game.
On the site of the new library
accurate blackbird extracts
fat facts of worms.
Wink
back at him, he'll
zig off waggling
the tail-end of an idea.

5
Listen,
chilly birdsong
sprinkling icewater
over the garden, a tap
turning on and off again.
Library silence.

6.
This is the lie of the land.
This is the house.
This is the staggered line of trees, Maytime
still struggling to bloom in a sea wind,
daisies snatching shut-eye in the shade,
bluebells bruising blue, the late
late primroses on the cold slope.
This is the ironwork of the old gate.
It does not open.
It does not remind you of a prison.
This is the garden laid out for a gentle game
and when the garden grows
this is the wall that shelters.
This is the cut-out crowstepped arch
that frames the savage castle.

Don't

let history frame you
in a pretty lie.

7.
When
imaginary Alice in flimsy
muslin shivers slightly in
a heatwave in Nineteen Ten and
Hugh does a handstand on the barbered grass, hurrahs
as Frederick's mallet chips
a perfect one through oh refuse
to pretend to remember
the flavour of those
last of the raspberries that
Rab (cap-off) the gardener's
boy brought over (and which he did not taste).
Refuse to pretend to remember
how he and very decorated Frederick would both
be fattening worms in France
not six years later.
Freeze them in sepia.
Refuse to pretend to remember.

8.
the garden as mirror of man's logical scientific and ordered mind.
the library as garden.
the library as mirror of man's logical scientific and ordered mind.
the garden as game.
the game as mirror of man's logical scientific and ordered mind.
the game as mirror.
the mind as mirror of man's logical scientific and ordered garden.
the library as game.
Play the garden.

9.
The Formal Garden
(as the mind in the library) turns
in on itself. Croquet
and contemplation put us
through hoops. Consider.

FOURTH OF JULY FIREWORKS

The guests are gathered.
Boston-Irish Nancy, half in huff
says, 'Better help yourselves,
you all know Mister's timing well enough.'
Aside at me she mutters,
'Millionaires can afford to let things wait.
Honest-to-God Mister would be late
for his own funeral.' Cigarstore Indian,
I hide behind my apron, wait and drink in all I can.

(We don't exist. They pick our trays,
Tom Collinses, Martinis and canapés.)

Oh horror, New England night,
when I fetched the ice down and that snake
looped my feet in the kitchen garden! I still shake.
'Harmless,' says Nancy.
I hear her hiss, 'Some host!
That beggar'll only get here when he's sure he's last.'

Fourth of July. Cape Cod. Dead on cue,
last-man Mister comes running to his barbecue.
Arms flailing like a cricketer's across the lawn
from his 'so English' house with a flame-red shirt on.

It's the cocktail hour. The air is still.
Mister gets busy on the charcoal grill.
Social-kissing women, backslapping men
has failed to break the ice. But then
Missiz appears like magic from the dusk.
Cool, ten years his junior, she smells of musk
and *Madame Rochas*. Two small spots of anger
high on her cheekbones linger.

When Mister says it's done enough
the guests spread ketchup on the fatted calf.
The night hots up. Liquor flows. Listless
couples come alive. A bit apart, restless,
Missiz sways gently on her own
to Glen Miller on the gramophone.
All eyes are on the soignée cling
of this year's leisure favourite, velvety stretch towelling
for patio-party wear. Those purples and electric pinks
'Just far too hectic altogether,' Nancy thinks.

(Ten years with Missiz, Nancy's face
is quite professional, impervious.)

Ice melts in the Martini tray. Midges
drown. The whole night edges
to a thunderstorm. Maybugs big as golfballs thud
as screendoors bounce them. But, after our blood,
divebombing mosquitoes dodge the mesh and slide
in down their own thin whine.
They bite despite insecticide.

All at sea,
white and dayglo orange fins spinnaker the bay.
Music blares
from the jazzed-up clubhouse round the Cape, Cotuit way.
The whole damn town is two thirds empty after Labour Day.
These summer people
migrate to Florida, lock, stock and barrel.
Tonight their parked cars sprawl the drive and trail
behind those his-and-hers coupled custom Cadillacs
like a comet trail.

(Oh I can see it all quite clearly, feeling small
and stone-cold sober. But I do not count at all.)

Out on the lawn the sprinklers, oddly luminous,
sputter like Roman Candles, ominous
as the sudden snap of queer clear light
from one weird streak unzips the dark.
The German Shepherd guard dogs bark.
A wind gets up. These beach-house boards
are flimsier than playing cards.

(Over the bay, like flares
odd rockets go up with a shock of stars.)

Mister drags off his box of fireworks to the shore.
Missiz drains her drink and hits the floor
with someone half her age. His snake-arms slur
around her waist. Eyes glaze. Sentence endings blur.
Missiz ('mutton dressed as lamb')
comes in slowly as the false-calm
lead-slow sea that slicks the beach. Sinatra sings.
The tide ravels up slowly, shelving things.

Raindrops big as bullets dent the roof we all stand under,
watching Canute's fireworks out-rage the storm,
try to steal its thunder.

THE CARNIVAL HORSES

All along Hudson they are sanding down
the carnival horses.
Outside antique shops, so many, so
slender young men bend attentively
at the curlicued flanks, their
eyes and noses almost closed to dust,
the noxious effects of chemical paintstripper.
That mercenary bitch next door
brasso-ing the handles on a hope-chest
is nothing to them.
Like grooms with curry-combs
plying their wire-brushes
around the tossed head and
always wild eyes, whisking
the ears clean of paint-layers,
the gummed-up old notes of the hurdygurdy,
exposing the perfect quotemarks of the nostrils.
What is it
(Falada, Falada)
we wish that he would say?

Later when he's
skewered in a loft
somewhere in NoHo
silhouetted with his flung hooves and tassel-tail
re-gilded against prettily exposed brick
he'll make each
new owner who paid through the nose for him imagine
he feels the long slide down the sticky pole,
that he could ride again
the perfect carousel at the fair he never
ever went to
on his favourite chosen beast
he never even for a dime possessed.

ONTARIO OCTOBER GOING WEST

The wilderness tells the eye you won't
get very far with me says
tangle scribble says
pawmark and leafprint stippling layer
on layer says fernstitch herring-
bone   rusted wirewool to lie on   whisk-ear
blackthorn.
says strewn silky pillow-stuffing   burst
milkweed.   says nudging
blunt bullrushes   (brown velvet)   fishhooked burr
bramble barb   vast feathery colourlessness.

The trees scream jaundice
canary   orange peel   adultery
oxblood   magenta.
the single drowned birch shrieks
fingerbone.
the lake says frankly this is
a very old trick   it's all
done with mirrors.

The barn *(see my*
ancient white hex sign in a circle) says
I'm twice as big and
beautiful as any house.
Winters like these   believe me
I have to be.

The railway says east west.

The prairie   when you get to it
says keep going.

NEAR QU'APPELLE

for Liz Allen

But then love   she said
is almost always
surely   she said
a strange country?
She had pale
seafarer's eyes that girl
there was ocean-glass
there were bits of seashell
on the windowledge
and outside the flat
colourless flat miles and miles
as far as what looked
very nearly blue but
was really only distance
and more of it.
You will recognise our house
she'd said.
It is the one up on—
jeez the prairie   couple of
years here you learn to call
almost anything a hill.
First year   more   I thought
I would go mad   the wind!
But then I'd married him
it was either that or go crazy.

She grinned
and sunburn wind-
burn it did not matter which –

the long-ago
little-girl delicately hand-tinted
certainly still

recognisable photograph of her
in her own her other country
hanging behind her on the wall.

IN ALBERTA

We have stopped by these
great big grain elevators marked with logo-wheat
stencilled Cargill   stamped Alberta Pool.
The boxcars
are just as clearly labelled
with destinations & capacities
numbers   warnings *(do not hump*
no climbing on roof).   Stopped
flat & nothing for it but for ten minutes
to examine the forged & intricate
ball & socket   ironwork   loop & pin hand
fastened   engineered
male & female couplings between the cars &
exactly
how they work
how often they break I honestly
don't know sweetheart.
In Alberta
there are oilwells like
loony mechanical chickens
dipping guzzling
& the man in the next seat says
in Alberta
everybody's applying for a divorce
says pair next door
common-law five years & then
the ceremony but she
goes off on this so-say holiday
in Salmon Arm next thing
divorce.   He says no
it's not just the young ones
in Alberta
he says his brother

just damnwell

turned himself over in the dirt machine
lucky to be alive
lucky to survive.
Says he knew a man once
got squashed to nothing nobody
could recognise.
Says there's lots of big machines
could crush a man
in Alberta.

SAILING PAST LIBERTY
for Rick Shaine

The first time I, well I think it was
that weekend, remember,
you'd gone to that
wedding in the Mid-
West, I was waiting it out with your
fat cat in Manhattan. I must
have already decided my darling you
were worth waiting for . . .

Early summer dust
on hot SoHo pavements, neon
scrawls New Wave on street cafés,
me walking holes in my five-dollar
ropesole sandals – Little Italy
Chinatown, the Bowery, Wall
Street and Battery Park in a loud
bright bubble that was like assault
so the Staten Island Ferry seemed
the best of twenty-five-cent bargains
(for tourism
was all I'd any reason then to think it was,
oh baby).
Then sailing past Liberty –
that string-quartet on the first deck
struck up for the fun of it, giving
us Vivaldi, and that fabulous skyline.
That great green
Harbour Lady, blank
containerships, gloomy hooters,
and one full-sail schooner.

Or maybe it was . . .
anyway, months later,

twilight and very nearly winter
it felt out on that deck together
you saying it wasn't
what you gave up but what you gained,
the collar of your leather-
jacket up, you
sheltering me from the cold, no
we'd sailed
long past Liberty by then,
those same bell-buoys rang eerily
that once rang in the new for
every immigrant who ever
entered Ellis Island hopefully.
(Dark eyes, I imagined
your grandfather in sepia
seeing this, holding tight
his little sister's hand.)

That was September, and
now I am here and
you are there
but that is neither here nor there
as far as what we feel
or what, together,
we will make happen.

And that white-card
cut-out of Liberty you sent
her graces my sister's Glasgow mantel-
piece, the week before her wedding.

2. TWO BIRDS

on each of these two
cards from you blue-

tacked to the wall above
my writing table.
on
torn-edge Japanese hand-
made wood-paper flecked
with gold
two
big-winged black-tipped wild
geese are caught in perfect
mid-flight assymetry on the blue
getting there.
and yet there's effort in it too,

the master artist does not deny it
– as on this cracked Valentine
we found at the market stall, all
lovey-dovey these two
conventional circa
nineteen-ten bluebirds, one with
flower, one with billet-doux
above linked hands entwined
through hearts, a pretty
ditty about Constancy

that made us smile.
hearts are not
pretty frames for anything, all
rococo forget-me-nots of cloying
Edwardiana.
they're raw and red
they jump, we know they do.

I say still: birds can be airmail blue
and hearts can be true.

3. MY HOUSE

is now also your house
because you stayed in it too.
its walls have been printed
with your shadow.

coming home
there is still a faint
something of cigar
and a nickel that must have
fallen from your pocket.
and my bed
remembers your weight
as easily as my fingers do your hair.

Friday night and
the springs of the mattress
give an almost groan
not quite accepting me on my own.

4. INTER-CITY

Hammered like a bolt
diagonally through Scotland (my
small dark country) this
train's a
swaying caveful of half-
seas over oil-men (fuck
this fuck that fuck
everything) bound for Aberdeen and
North Sea Crude.
Empty beer cans of
spun aluminium roll like ball-bearings
underfoot and

sloshing amber's a
storm in a whisky glass or two.
Outside's all
black absolutely
but for fizzing starbursts
of weird blue or orange streetlights
and lit-up grids of windows.
Only bits of my own blurred
back-to-front face and
my mind elsewhere.
The artsy-fartsy magazine I'm
not even pretending to read
wide open
at a photograph called *Portrait of Absence*.

5. IN THE CUTTING ROOM

Working together (this
late) & below us with its
car chases
its sirens & sex
symbols the real
city flickers.
The Ramrod all-male cinema
and the twenty-five-cent peepshow girls.

Here mister moviola you share
your high strange place
of stacked flat cans & numbered
glistening strips liked pegged
filmy stockings on a bathroom line
you are at work on them
in your small corner,
I in mine.
Chaste on Broadway, we moved

our privacy through the public streets.

The Brill elevator clanked us up through forty floors,
a water beetle big as a man's fist
scrabbling its corner.

You run it
over & over
forward back – one
dizzy whirr her scream shuts
& the woman in the white
nightgown jerks herself backward
to the bed the nicely
glossed over
bad black sex.
Under the light of the
anglepoise I am
(beauty & the beast) at my business
of putting new twists
to old stories.

Working together & we seem
to love each other (but
that too is an old story)
yet not one of those fine few skills
(loops of language
spliced syllables of movement) we
have learned to curse but labour at
together   separate

No love is not a Steenbeck
a heart is not
an editing machine – we can cut
out nothing   ignore everything
except what we want to see.
Ribbon of dreams,
have we put together too much
from scanty footage?

SHIPS

for John Oughton

We were
talking of ships, you
should have been there, you
would have seen them too.
Silent, slow, they slid their great bulks along the window
blocking half our light, coming
steaming in at tree-height
they anchored at the edge of everyone's vision.
This was not
ships that go bump in the night, absolutely
no boats bobbing in bathtubs but
big ships
with cargoes of portent.
Four poems, four ships, imagine.
My black sail:
the moon as a ghostly galleon:
Michael's 'wild ships of loon': and (for me)
it's mainly your imaginary icebreaker
I think of, ploughing
the white line up Hepbourne Street,
churning up the tarmac outside your house
and us adrift in your bed
wound in the sound of foghorns.

Once
for me to think of ships was to admit shipwreck,
maroon,
those utter inevitable deserted islands.
(The worst ships I saw,
did I ever tell you?
Were those grey battleships in the half-light.
Menace, an unending
fleet of shapes glooming past

that balcony on the Bosphorus
all night the Night
Before the War Began.)

Don't think of them.

At every launching
there is held breath, wide eyes,
that glide
into a new watery world.
We don't need champagne to celebrate it.

Take this message.
It's ocean-worthy,
it is a small ship in a bottle.
All night I have been tinkering with intricate riggings,
pulling threads,
to try and make it sail for you.

HAFIZ ON DANFORTH AVENUE

There are no nightingales in this lunchroom, but
I have all these presents wrapped in that cheap
Christmas paper printed with those cardinals
you said sang out too loud.
Waiting for the
last of the breakfast specials I fish out
from the bottom of my handbag your father's
copy of Hafiz you lent me. Old ink
on the flyleaf, the name
that is also your name, the date
and where he bought it.

No place
for a lady here at eleven a.m.
in bitter mid December on the Danforth – all these
Greek men at the counter
on their rooted stools, sallow
under astrakhan, brindled moustaches,
the clack of worrybeads, I catch
a flash of amber and tassels.
A toothpick, a gold filling –
Tonight I gonna finish one gallon of wine.
Tony makes it great. Forget
the mortgages, the pressure, tonight
if my wife she drives me I can get loaded.

A laughing winecup, a tangle
of knotted hair I tingle
remembering us side by side – I am reading
your old Hafiz, you the New Divan I
brought with me, somehow linking
Glasgow to Toronto to Teheran.

Later you stretch out,
the book is closed on the carpet
a spiral of tangerine peel on the cover.

In the photograph you showed me Sunday
you are twelve, it is the year
you lived in Baghdad, you
are jug-eared, a proper cropped
North American boy.
There are two Iraqi taxi drivers,
a big Yankee car with
dangling charms of Islam. I can
smell the heat and the petrol.

The morning breeze is the messenger of Love . . .
The beloved
is sometimes the seller of sweetmeats,
the poet an eloquent sugarloving parrot.
And today's snowflakes
muffle the mounds of Best Canadian
pumpkins and hubbardsquash outside
next door's greengrocery.
Here, through chromium and steam
the sugar dredger, a plate of lemons,
jellies, sherbert-coloured wedges
of chiffon pie.

The beautiful black waitress
wears a white beanie.

They've written Merry Christmas with glitterdust
on the mirror here in Motorama
beside the poster which says
Cold, Beautiful
Milk.

The young lovers
holding hands under the next table
play on the jukebox
'You don't bring me flowers.'

And to tell you this is easy,
scribbling this was as simple
as the shopping list it jostles
on the next page of my notebook.
Love, as well as bread and coffee
it says eggplants, olive oil
don't forget
the nutmeg and cinnamon.

A GIFT

When you come sometimes in what feels like secret
bringing a quick kiss
& a cargo of poems & photographs
(bringing in black & white
an armful of scratchy trees – those
typed soft words like desire & foghorn)
bringing yourself you bring me
the problem of acceptance.
What's this I say?
I've always been the one
giving
& guzzling & suffering with this love stuff.
I've been the one struggling at the words
I wanted written, not said.

So looking at your lines again
I melt & want to tell you I'm not jealous,
I know they're caused by loving.
& looking at your lines again (your body
stretched on my bed) the light
catching the surprising lines on your face
that show your age & I know are caused by laughing
I see
when well-meaning
other lovers brought you their gifthorses of nightmare &
self-hatred you somehow stayed unscathed.

READING THE SIGNS

never in my wildgoose dreams
before I came here
(once there was the wildest
car chase only it was on
sort of skates in a strange changing
hill/cityscape & I
was winning not
that I had had to even find my feet on them
but they were brand-new blades
& I
was sailing)
not even then did I imagine this
the ease of say
we're going somewhere by favourite train
by car   there's music
or idle eavesdropping to be done
& anyway I can just sit
reading the signs
WINTERIZE NOW
MIDAS MUFFLER KING
loving the landscape looking
at you alternately not
much bothered which

& across the wide skies of Ontario
which are new but not strange are strung
the words of others
the notes of jazz are strung
lights and trees
these straggled vees of geese stay
threaded invisibly together like
Orion
or you & me

FLITTING

Your place or mine, many a midnight
sees us shacked up somewhere and whose
bed is the better bet depends
whether we'd rather
tonight's permanent island
on a sea of chaos that's dis-
mantling itself or one
putting itself slowly together.

This summer I'm
splitting at the seams, I'm
full of it, my every
suitcase has its
teeth into this move. You've
spent a small fortune
on your big house.

It's either my Victorian reticules those
Biba fringes I'm going to throw out
dripping beads in the dark cramped round us,
or else your dead old lady's
velvet roses that
breathe the heavy weather and
'Miss Otis Regrets' outside your open window.

Either way
someone's used a strange toothbrush
and not sure it's wisdom
except we're at each other's throats all night
in blind tenderness
and in either
exact same other country we're dead easy.
You can make head and tail of me.

In the morning, a cause-
way to negotiate to whichever kitchen's
sketchy breakfast. You call me *sunshine*
which only goes to show
how little you know.

A GIVEAWAY

I cancelled out the lines that most let on
I loved you. One week after I thought that it was done
and perfect, practically in print – here goes again
more of this that amateurs think of as tampering.
The tripe that's talked at times, honestly –
about truth and not altering a word,
being faithful to what you felt, whatever
that is, the *First Thought's Felicity.*
I have to laugh . . . the truth!
You and me and no reason
for me to imagine I know the half of it.
I've said it time and time again,
listen, you've got to be ruthless,
if the rhythm's not right, it's not right,
it's simple
you've got to cut and cut and cut.
Rewrite.

Today's fair copy skips the scored-out bit.
And all the better for it. That verse
set in the bedroom spoilt the form
and was never the issue anyway. Irrelevant.
At any rate I've gone to town on it all right
with black biro, blocked it out – hay
fever sneeze spill and kiss are all
the words even I can make out of it now.
Never could cancel with a single stroke!
Oh maybe it is a giveaway but don't
please be naive enough to think I'd mind
your knowing what I might invent of what I feel.
Poets don't bare their souls, they bare their skill.
God, all this

long apprenticeship and still
I can't handle it, can't
make anything much of it,
that's my shame.

It's not an easy theme.
But finally I've scrubbed it, faced it, I know
the whole bloody stanza was wonky from the word go.

HEARTBREAK HOTEL

Honeymooning alone
oh the food's
quite good (but it all needs salting).
Breadsticks admonish,
brittle fingers among formality – bishops' hats,
stiff skirts, white linen, silver implements.
This dining room
is all set for a funeral, an anatomy lesson,
a celebration of communion
or a conjuring trick – maybe someone
will be sawn in half,
or a napkin could crumple
to an amazing dove.
Except
it's all empty
though I eat my helping
under a notice that says: *This Place
is Licensed for Singing and Dancing.*

Go to your room.
What more lovely than to be alone
with a Teasmade, a radio and a telephone?
Loose end? Well, this is what you find
when you take the time off to unwind.
Empty twinbeds
and the space all hanging heavy
above your neat spare shoes
in your wall-to-wall wardrobe
underneath the jangling wires.

Honeymooning alone
can't get to sleep without the lights on,
can't swallow all that darkness on my own.
Syrup from the radio's

synthetically soothing late-night show
oh remember, remember
then I reach to pop one of those press-stud pills
I keep under the pillow so
my system will still tick next week
on the blink
a little crazily for you. I can't sleep –
it's as livid as a scar
the white neon striplight
above my vanity bar.

Mirror, Mirror on the wall
does he love me enough,
does he love me at all?
Should I go back
with that celebrated shout?
Did my eyebrows offend you?
Well I've plucked them out.
Oh me and my mudpack,
I can't smile
my face will crack.
I'll come clean.
I've made good new resolutions
re my skincare routine.
Every day
there's a basket of blossomheads,
crumpled Kleenex to throw away.
As if I found it easy to discard.
Think hard.
I've got a week to think it over
a shelf full of creams, sweet lotions
I can cover,
smother all my darkness in, smooth it over.
Oh it'll take more than this aerosol
to fix it all, to fix it all.

CHINA SONG

for Janice and John Gow, 1980

We are sitting pretty on our saucers.
Empty headed, not a thought
in our delicate trepanned porcelain
skulls, eggshell blue.
Admiring our own gold-bands, just like you
will be wearing in a day or two. And
when we say Wedding China
we want you to know we mean best bone
scarcely serviceable for every day.
And if you'd think
there'd be rather more
earthenware dished out these days
with so many marriages never winning
the tinfoil anniversary far less the wooden wedding,
still, we're glad to be wished-for, special,
nestled here in rustled tissue
beside the crystal you cannot see the future in.

WHY I GAVE YOU THE CHINESE PLATE

for Kenny Storrie

I know how you feel
about ladies that dark and slim
and quiet and unlike me.
And chinoiserie.

I'm not sorry.
Neither are you what
I'd have thought I wanted.

In a landscape somewhere else
under a surface finely crazed with cracks
the silks of this painted girl instead
of all the dark girls you'll never have
as long as you keep wanting me to love.

Goldgreen, plum and jade
a nice glaze.
So choose
where you'll hang it
on the wall we might tear down.

OLD NOTEBOOKS

Because she honestly
thought she'd like to learn to bake
good bread they
lugged the flour home
stone-ground from the flaxen mill.
Wanting to be whole
she pictured aprons sprigged with print
country kitchens
them sipping out of stoneware
a real couple
cutting, buttering another slice.

They tried to keep some always on the go –
yeast creaming itself in cups
something in a warm place rising
under a clean cloth (if they had one)
and but for the odd
leadballoon loaf it worked.
Telling themselves that
every batch got better
they cooked up good smells.
The tapped crust gave the proper
hollow sound.

Hard to remember
when they gave up the bran and went
back to bad habits grabbing
a quick sandwich at work and
forgetting to phone –
the apron all
balled up in the bottom of the laundry
for months with knotted strings.
So that now
opening old notebooks finding

recipes written in the hand
that was hers but no longer
slants quite the same she
does not sigh to think
they might have stripped the cupboard's pine
perhaps revealed a pleasing grain. Ah well
the half-hundredweight
sack of wholemeal slumped
like a corpse in the cubbyhole . . .
She shrugs, says
it soured we had to throw it out.

FIN

I know it's the end.
I can see it coming. I'm
like those women in the cinema who make you mad
fumbling for gloves
elbowing themselves into coats, buttoning up –
such a final snapping shut of handbags
the minute it looks like it's all over
but a change of mood and music.
So you demand response do you
right to the bitter end, you like
to see the credits roll?
I'm off.

THAT SUMMER

What you said before you upped and left
landed as splat as that
out-of-the-blue fat sheep at the
bottom of the cliff, the whole
heavy bellyful.
On my walk between the cottage
and the phonebox
I saw it disintegrate predictably
the pretty hooves
its only visible
bright eye dull and ooze
the usual moving
iridescence of bunched flies
on the matted pelt that was
nothing like the fireside sheepskin
we'd once been so smug about.
The whole sodden mess
gradually felted itself
flat and mashed into the long grass
among the cuckoo-slobber
and this was high summer.
The milled edge
of my tenpence piece
rasped at the slot
as I dialled the number of the flat
thinking of things growing fur
in the fridge, it ringing and ringing,
no one answering.

WEST KENSINGTON

Wound-
up swaddled in your sleeping-bag in the living room
with stitched together thighs.
Shrugging it off
was shimmying out of a mermaid suit.
Thanks a bundle but
all the well-meant
extra blankets only
ended in a useless mound.
I've my own
manhandled luggage by me.
A sourish mouth from last night's Duty Free

Suddenly I can visit your bathroom and not question
whose eyebrow tweezers, why female shampoo.
You said to help myself and I did, but
had to watch I didn't wake you,
likely still well out of it two doors away,
what with the brassnecked kettle whistling
in the face of a brand-new day.
I tiptoed with my toothbrush to the cold tap,
stirred bitter instant in a rinsed-out cup,
snapped your sofa back
to a seated position.

And the funny thing was it didn't
seem funny.
I was fine
except your cats
came on to me all night.
Apart from that I slept all right.

As always. Any time,
any time, remember, I'd do
the same for you.

THE EMPTY SONG

Today saw the last of my Spanish shampoo.
Lasted an age now that sharing with you,
such a thing of the past is.
Giant Size. The brand
was always a compromise.
My new one's tailored exactly to my needs.
Nonspill. Protein-rich.
Feeds Body, promises to solve my problem hair.
Sweetheart, these days it's hard to care,
But oh oh insomniac moonlight
how unhoneyed is my middle of the night.
I could see you
far enough. Beyond me
how we'll get back together.
Campsites in Spain, moonlight,
heavy weather.

Today saw the end of my Spanish shampoo,
the end of my third month without you.

NOISES IN THE DARK

The four a.m. call to the faithful wakes us,
its three-times off-key harmony of drones and wails.
Above our heads I snap the light cord but the power fails
as usual leaving us in the dark. Tomorrow takes us
who knows where. What ruins? What towns? What smells?
Nothing shakes us.
We touch and today's too painful sunburn sticks and sears
apart again. Faithful to something three long years,
no fear, no final foreign dark quite breaks us.

Hotel habitués,
the ritually faithful wash their feet. Old plumbing grumbles.
The tap-leak in our rust-ringed basin tickles
irritant, incessant, an itch out of the dark. Whitewash crumbles
from the wall where the brittle cockroach trickles.
Fretful, faithful, wide to the dark, can we ever forget
this shabby town hotel, the shadow of the minaret?
Human or bird or animal? What was it cried?
The dark smear across the wall still unidentified.

A LETTER

Your handwriting. A letterbomb
potentially. Blank side upmost on my mat
to turn it over was to trigger what
could blow my pieced-together calm.

In day thoughts a grey ghost,
livid in dreams. Damn you, I'm not blind
to the shock of your writing, its cockeyed slant, my mind
flips blank side uppermost.

What can you possibly want to say?
It fell so quietly I did not hear it drop.
White and flat and foreign, the envelope
does not give anything away.

Once letters flew like birds
between us. I'd read and read again, stuff
your spilling pages behind every clock and photograph.
They were full of everything but words.

This'll be the usual. The job's still fine,
I suppose? You'll ask me how are John and Di,
has Doreen had her baby, how am I
how's he and this new life of mine?

You talk of your new loves. Plural. Wild oats
at your age. Jesus, you should know better.
I'm mad at my own tears, but not enough to rip this letter.
Recently I've burnt nothing but my boats.

Though I confess that bitter confetti of the last one.
But that was in passion – these days it's far too late
for anything except to (eventually) reply to it –
the past that isn't dead enough to stuff a cushion.

SUNDAYSONG

its about time
it came back again
if it was going to.
yes   something's nesting
in the tentative creeper scribbling
kellygreen felt tip
across our bedroom window.
hello.
its a lovely morning.   we've got
full french roast for the enamelled yellow coffee pot.
there'll be transistors in the botanics
and blaring notes of blossom.
let's walk.   let's talk.
let the weekend watch wind down.
let there be sun
let first you and me
and then breakfast and lunch be
rolled into one.

THE LEGEND OF THE SWORD & THE STONE

I wish I wish we'd stopped before
It wasn't making love any more.

I had this trust. It broke.
Who was that lady . . . ? It's no joke.

But I dare you. Unzip my dress.
Turn me into an enchantress.

Enter with me on this act,
I will not give you back intact.

I am not flesh and blood and bone –
You are embedded deep in stone.

I know what witches know.
I won't free you, won't let you go.

Oh, but it was easy, withdrawing.
Smile on your lips, faraway look in your eye.
Oh how you whistled
as you knotted your necktie.
Wounding me
you left no scar
but bore away Excalibur.
New love. New War.

RAINBOW

Listen you said
you never listen to a word I say
let alone the music.
This song you said
is beautiful. It's just about the finest thing
you ever heard. Listen to the cadences . . .
that chord . . .
Meanwhile the song rose and fell around us as
indifferent as rainfall
(it was pouring at the time) and all
that got through to me
was I heard you grow alternatively
labial and gutteral
as I watched your lips move
(and fell more and more in love)
and waited for a convenient lull
to put something a bit more in my line
on the record player.

Look I said
architect! You never use your eyes.
Colour I said
is just incredible. I'd go so far
as say it is the main thing. Well . . . maybe
form is
for you purists. But see that colour sing,
the daffodils against that goldy thing,
those oranges in that pink plate.
What the *impressionists* . . .
And in the clear light of that very moment
(the rain had just stopped)
the colour shimmered from the walls
and it buzzed, you couldn't pin it down.

Walls couldn't keep it flat or matt
on their simple surfaces.
It bounced from everything, it was
all around us.
And as I opened my mouth to say
so there and something about
form can't contain colour, you
kissed me on the nose
you laughed, you said
The way you look when you get het
up about something – oh
the colour you go!
Sweetheart you're vivid when you're livid.

Just then a convenient romantic rainbow
arched itself across our horizon.
It was a perfect one while it lasted –
it reached out for real roots
made for rainbow ends even.
Some colour! We couldn't
take our eyes off it for an instant
Hugged on the balcony
we were eavesdroppers on the whole hush.
And it hung there!

Then the gutters spilt liquid hilarity
from the full throats of their spigots like
a glockenspiel
We both heard it,
oh and we saw
odd drops from the window ledge make a
timpany of single notes,
each note shot with the spectrum.
Our rainbow arched and spread, grew
more and more vibrant until
it came to earth with a shock.

THE DOLLHOUSE CONVENTION

Come to our one-day fair.
I suppose you could call it almost a convention
of us miniaturists – the intricacy
of jewellers is absolutely
not wasted on us.
With base metals we can create
for instance this plaited replica
of an exact thumbnail breadloaf,
this tiny tray of taffy apples.
Aren't they sweet?

Loves, we must have such stuff to fill
our dollhouses with.
Bring your daughter, don't
bring her, we have stopped pretending
it's only for the children we put on a show.
So if a setpiece says
Edwardian drawing-room scene,
whole family grouped round piano.
or modern ranch house circa 1970 –
note father figure on a scaled-down Barcalounger
with miniaturized Playboy magazine –
remember
we have sweated blood
worked with needles of astonishing thinness
in cloth and lace and real hair,
in paper and ceramic and spun glass
we tried to get the details right.

For what?
Is it for the mere satisfaction of seeing
into every room at once, even
the ones as children we were locked out of,
that we reduce

what we most deeply fear might be trivial
to what we can be sure
is perfectly cute?

IN THE DREAMSCHOOL

you are never the teacher.
The history lesson
goes on for ever.

Yammering the always
wrong answer to the hardest question
you stand up in nothing but
a washed-in vest.

In the dreamschool nothing can be covered up.
Fleeced, yellowing
you never learn.

Teacher is big-eyed behind
awesome bifocals
and his teeth are green.
An offered apple will only tempt the snake
curled under his chalkstripe jacket. Loch-
gelly, forked tongue, tawse.
Bug-eyed bullies drag you towards
the terrible lavatories.

Sawdust soaks up sour mistakes.

2. THE TEACHERS

they taught
that what you wrote in ink
carried more weight than what you wrote in pencil
and could not be rubbed out.
Punctuation was difficult. Wars
were bad but sometimes necessary
in the face of absolute evil as they knew only too well.

Miss Prentice wore her poppy the whole month of November.
Miss Mathieson hit the loud pedal
on the piano and made us sing
'The Flowers of the Forest'.
Miss Ferguson deplored
the Chinese custom
of footbinding but extolled the ingenuity
of terracing the paddyfields.
Someone she'd once known had given her a kimono
and a parasol.
Miss Prentice said the Empire had enlightened people
and been a two-way thing.
The Dutch grew bulbs and were our allies in
wooden shoes.

We grew bulbs on the window sills
beside the frogspawn that quickened into wriggling
commas or stayed full stop.
Some people in our class were stupid,
full stop.
The leather tawse was coiled around the sweetie tin
in her desk beside the box of coloured blackboard chalk
Miss Ferguson never used.

Miss Prentice wore utility smocks.
Miss Mathieson had a moustache.
If your four-needled knitting got no
further than the heel you couldn't turn
then she'd keep you at your helio sewing
till its wobbling cross-stitch was specked with rusty blood.

Spelling hard words was easy when you knew how.

3. THE PRIZE

For Perfect Attendance was an easy one to win.
Bible stories for girls.
Martha and Mary on the coloured frontispiece.
Your Sunday name in the Superintendent's copperplate.

It only meant being there, not 'paying attention'.
The Redemption hymnbook proved
the Devil did not possess every best tune.

Red ticks like flyaway
flocks of birds sprigged the best exercise books.
Gold stars were favours given seldom as boiled sweets
in crinkled cellophane. Xs were kisses
and kissing was wrong as all my sums.
Being first was top desk.
The doltish and dirty shared front row
with one sent- down clever chatterbox in easy reach
of the teacher's ruler.

That September the squirrel
on the Shell country calendar wasn't on the wall
before Mattie won first death.
The weather chart said: *Today it is Cloudy*
and my Top in General Knowledge
came of knowing the name for such a cloud
was Cumulus. We had to all turn over our jotters
and go over and over once again
till we knew by heart the Highway Code.

THE OFFERING

Never in a month of them
would you go back.
Sunday,
the late smell of bacon
then the hard small feeling
of the offering in the mitten.
Remember how the hat-elastic cut.
Oh the boredom,
and how a lick of spittle got purple dye or pink
from the hymn-book you worried.
Maybe your neighbour would
have technicoloured pictures of
Jesus curing lepers
between the frail tissue pages of her Bible
or she'd stroke you with the velvet
of a pressed rosepetal
till someone sucking peppermint
and smelling of mothball
poked you and hissed that you weren't to fidget.
Remember the singing
(with words and actions)
and how you never quite
understood the one about Nic-
odemus Coming to the Lord by Night.

Sunday,
perhaps an auntie
would visit with a cousin. Every Sunday
everyone would eat ice cream
and your mothers would compare you,
they'd stand you by the doorstop
and measure you up.

Sunday, maybe later in the evening
there'd be a Brethren Meeting.
Plain women wearing hats to cover
uncut hair. And
singing, under lamp-posts, out in our street!
And the leader
shouted the odds on Armageddon, he
tried to sell Salvation.
Everybody turned their televisions up.

Never in a month of them
should you go back.
Fond hope.
you'll still find you do not measure up.
The evangelist still mouths behind glass unheard.
You'll still not understand
the singing, the action or the word.
Ice cream will cloy, too sweet, too bland.
And the offering
still hard and knotted in your hand.

LEGENDARY

1.
And if he was guilty then it was of glibness.
He thought he could just whistle
but what he picked was too simple a song
(though an old one).
The North Knight found his lady fair –
toothsome smile
fifties glamour, tirling
a cheerleader's ponytail –
The outlandish knight courted his lady fair
siller kaims for gowden hair
and no he never noticed
the hammered-home nine mother-cursed combs of care.

Where had she come from?
He thought he saw it all.
The trick mantle seemed transparent enough.
He was dazzled.
Fishnet and what he took for spangles
but were fishscales (rapidly losing lustre)
from the day they dragged her
from the far Atlantic.
Certainly she fulfilled the conditions
coming neither clothed nor naked
neither riding or walking, and
carrying what was at once undoubtedly a gift
and yet nothing he should be grateful for.

Her wisecracks whipped him on.
It became a kind of contest.
When he set her impossible tasks
such as sew him a shirt without any seams or needlework
she laughed, sent home to mother for a copy
of *Dressmaking Made Easy* and *McCalls' Pattern Book*.

It was not
that she refused to recognise the magnitude of her problems,
just that for any real heroine
nothing is too menial –
at any rate in fairytales.
She knows inevitably she will come into her own.

So she turned his riddles inside out easily
like someone flyping pairs of socks
and threw them back at him.
Right at the start she told him
Death is colder than clay.
Poison greener than grass.
The Devil worse than any woman.
He just stood there straddling the road
in all that clanging antiquated armour
turning brick-red
coming slowly to his awful conclusion.
His blood sang out
She is Fit Mate.

2.
Easy for any outsider
to see they should have known better.
Even if it weren't for all the dipping they'd done
into all the legends which all went on at length
about this kind of catastrophe and carnage –
well, their own open eyes should have told them.
Bodies lay all around them
in the bonny broom, mutilated hideously.
And other versions of themselves
differently tinted
lay stiff and flat and parched
in photograph albums of former lovers.
The landscape was in an awful state.

But they went ahead with it.
They made the effort.
He was a deadeye marksman
but some of the silky things he brought home limp
she hadn't the stomach to make stew of.
When she scrambled the eggs he'd so carefully collected
purely to contemplate Creation Myths
he had to swallow it, say nothing.

She bought a Bendix. Had babies.
A pigeon pair.
Above all she wanted to be worthy.
he knew she confided to her diary
her honest malison and her good grudge
as she swelled monstrously, or was suckled at.
But she would sit there,
smoothing her gingham,
grimacing and knitting.
He knew she had it in her.
He wanted to shake her.

Soon he had to hunt further.
He had these three mouths that fed from him.
Sometimes he dreamed of them, sucking, accusing.
So often he left them all week
deep in the greenwood.

'What bluid's that on thy coat lap husband, husband?
Tell me the meaning of this stain I've found.

'Hawks' bluid was ne'er sae red, husband
lipstick that pink
whore's rouge that scarlet,
make my bed separate
make my bed soon
I'm weary wi living and fain wad lie doon.'

Next morning over plates of flakes
though too young to understand
the goshawk and the turtledow
spooning it in
could not but notice how
strange their parents had become.
Stiff figures. Playing cards.

And meeting her a month later
to discuss formalities, financial things,
the North Knight was struck by a commonplace pain.
My wife is a handsome woman
I can never love her again.

I have no idea what goes on inside her head.

One week later she was dead.

3.
And if a lily grew from her grave
round him he grew a briar.
And if a lily grew from her grave
and twined towards his breast
he would have none of it,
it was too like a mouthpiece
and its stalk
was too like a hotline down to her.
He tore at the roots of it.
He refused to talk.

And so he went on
living quietly
taking care of the children
buying them Clark's sandals
checking their fillings.

We do not know
whether in dreams
as in the legends
she comes as a birch

and with the jawbone of a salmon
and with the teeth of a pike
and her own yellow hair
a harp is made.

But if in the evening he should feel like a tune
and reach his fiddle down
it will never utter against him,
its strands are catgut
and the bow is not
a singing bone.
He is dry eyed,
says tears are not worth their salt.
And he owns
the voice he hears repeating, over and over, I am guilty.
Not guilty. Guilty. Not guilty.
It's not my fault.

FETCH ON THE FIRST OF JANUARY

Nae time eftir the Bells, and the
New Year new in wi the
usual crowd, wi whisky, cheers and kisses –
Ah'd aboot managed the windaes shut
some clown had thrown wide
hopin tae hear the hooters on the Clyde
when the door went.
Well, well,
who'd've though Ah'd be staunin there
tae first foot masel?

This some kinnuffa Huntigowk for Hogmany?
Hell-mend-ye, ye're
a bad penny, Jimmy –
Mister Ne'erdy Ne'er-do-Weel
sae chitterin ill-clad for the caul
sae drawn an pale,
oh, wi the black bun burnin a hole
in yir poackit an the coal
a Live Coal.

'Gawn, get' – Ah should shout it,
should shake a stick or ma fist,
oh but Ah should hunt ye, by Christ,
they wey you chased that big black tyke
that dogged ye wance, mind? –
aw the wey fae Hope Street hame.

Ah'll no let ye near me,
don't make me laugh,
got a much better
Better Half.
Och, aye tae glower at each other
was tae keek in a gey distortin mirror,

yet ye've the neck to come back again
wi yir bare face, Jake Fetch,
the image o my ain.
Ice roon yir mooth when ye kiss me
the cauld plumes o yir breath
Ah'm lukkin daggers
You're lukkin like Death.
Ah'm damned if ye'll get past ma door,
nae fear!

Come away in, stranger, Happy New Year.

MIRROR'S SONG
for Sally Potter

Smash me looking-glass glass
coffin, the one
that keeps your best black self on ice.
Smash me, she'll smash back –
without you she can't lift a finger.
Smash me she'll whirl out like Kali,
trashing the alligator mantrap handbags
with her righteous karate.
The ashcan for the stubbed lipsticks
and the lipsticked butts,
the wet lettuce of fivers!
She'll spill the Kleenex blossoms,
the tissues of lies, the matted
nests of hair from the brushes'
hedgehog spikes, she'll junk
the dead mice and the tampons
the twinkling single eyes
of winkled out diamante, the hatpins,
the whalebone and lycra,
the appleblossom and the underwires,
the chafing iron that kept them maiden,
the Valium and initialled hankies,
the lovepulps and the Librium,
the permanents and panstick and
Coty and Tangee Indelible,
Thalidomide and junk jewellery.

Smash me for your daughters and dead
mothers, for the widowed
spinsters of the first and every war
let her
rip up the appointment cards for
the terrible clinics,

the Greenham summonses
let her rip.

She'll crumple all the
tracts and the adverts, shred
all the wedding dresses, snap
all the spike-heel icicles
in the cave she will claw out of –
a woman giving birth to herself.

VYMURA: THE SHADE CARD POEM

Now artistic I ain't, but I went to choose paint
'cos the state of the place made me sick.
I got a shade card, consumers-aid card, but it stayed hard to pick.
So I asked her advice as to what would look nice,
would blend in and not get on my wick.

She said, 'Our Vymura is super in Durer,
or see what you think of this new shade, Vlaminck.
But I see that you're choosy . . .
Picasso is newsy . . . that's greyish-greeny-bluesy . . .
Derain's all the rage . . .
that's hot-pink and Fauve-ish . . .
There's Monet . . . that's mauve-ish . . .
And Schwitters,
that's sort-of-a *beige*.'

She said, 'Fellow next door just sanded his floor
and rollered on Rouault and Rothko.
His hall, och it's Pollock an he
did his lounge in soft Hockney
with his cornice picked out in Kokoshka.

'Now avoid the Van Gogh, you'll not get it off,
the Bonnard is bonny,
you'd be safe with matt Manet,
the Goya is *gorgeous*
or Chagall in eggshell,
but full-gloss Lautrec's sort of tacky.
So stick if you can to satin-finish Cézanne
or Constable . . . that's kind of a khaki.
Or the Gainsborough green,
and I'd call it hooey to say Cimabue
would never tone in with Soutine.

If it looks a bit narrow when you splash on Pissarro
one-coat Magritte covers over.'
She said, 'This Hitchens is a nice shade for kitchens
with some Ernst to connect 'em at other end of the spectrum
Botticelli's lovely in the Louvre.'
She said, 'If it was mine I'd do it Jim Dine.
Don't think me elitist or snobby
but Filippino Lippi'd
look awfy insipid,
especially in a large-ish lobby . . .'

Well,
I did one wall Watteau, with the skirting Giotto
and the door and the pelmet in Poussin
the ceiling's de Kooning
other walls all in Hals
and the whole place looks quite . . . cavalier,
with the woodwork in Corot –

but I think tomorrow
I'll flat-white it back to Vermeer.

THE SUZANNE VALADON STORY

I could've been a laundress,
a soft-soaped hopeless scrubber –
I could've been a waitress –
and lived to serve anothair?
I could of been a housemaid
and stayed upon my knees –
but instead of these
because *Moi* sans chemise
was certain to please,
until I used my noddle
I was the Bohemienne
Comedienne
who is an artist's model!

I'd be flat on my ass still
if I hadn't seized zee pastel
I was just a girl who couldaint say *Non!*
Now I am the artiste, Suzanne Valadon.

Mon affaire with Renoir
deed not go very far
and Lautrec, although nice
seemply could not reach my heights.
Édouard Manet – he canny.
(Quel *type*, what a creep!)
But Dégas,
ooh-la-la
he drew me in ink and he etched me on zinc
until some bloody Fauve went and painted me mauve
and Seurat stippled me pink.
Oh they did me in oils
till I came out in boils
but when I asked them for a crayon,
oh they turned me Van Gogh's ear!

I'd be posing noon till ten still
If I hadn't snatched zee pencil
I was the girl who couldain't say *Non!*
Now I'm an artiste, Suzanne Valadon.

Then I'd climb in zee sack
for the price of a cognac
oh life in Bohemia
Could not 'ave been more seamier.
but I'd have slept with them for sables –
zee brushes not zee furs!

I was well on my way
to the Salon des Refusés
I was just a girl who couldain't say *Non!*
Now I'm la Grande Artiste,
Suzanne Valadon.

Oh, I was seeck, seeck, seeck
being scribbled, screwed or blitzed
at the Moulin de la Galette
so I told them what to do with
zee impressionist palette.
I got off the dais,
I covered my ass,
snapped his charcoal stick in two
and I drew
wizout a fuss
Aha!
said Renoir
I see you're One of Us.
And Lautrec (I'll always *lov* heem)
said wiz out a doubt Suzanne
you can be dronk in charge of a charcoal line

as good as any man.
Dégas said I was a genius
and on further inspection
put heez monnaie where his mouth was.
And bought mes pictures
to grace heez great collection.

I'd have ended in zee guttair as a clapped out lush
if I hadn't seized mon courage and a number seven brush
I was the girl who couldaint say *Non!*
Now I am la Grande Artiste
Moi!
Suzanne Valadon.

THE LIFE OF MRS RILEY

I was eighteen year old in sixty-four
another three years till the key-of-the-door,
my mammy said.
when I smell Pink Camay I can picture it yet,
John and Paul on my Dansette
jumbo rollers in my hair and nothing in my head,
my daddy said.

My da said no one was good enough –
rockers were mental and Mods were tough
in sixty-four.
And I giggled at Problem Page Advice,
and I sappled through my nylons and kept myself nice,
wore panstick, wore mohair, I wore angora
In sixty-four.

There was this lawyer bloke who took a notion –
my auntie said he would go far.
Apparently he was articled
and a . . . sorta trainee at the Bar.
You often wonder, don't you?
But what's for you won't go by you
you often wonder why you –
but mibbe I should thank ma lucky star?

Because when – I don't know what it was –
in the clinch, his winching made me ill.
Couldny put ma finger on it, but I thought it was
the caked-on Clearsil, the cavalry twill
and – in The Beatle-era –
he'd lard mair than a smeara
Brylcreem on his crowning glory –
well, to cut a long story –

stood up this Kenneth went on a blind date
turned out to be Frank, I thought he was great,
I couldn't wait
for the life of Mrs Riley.

For ma Christmas he gave me an H. Samuel locket
engraved *F R loves J D*
said I'd find somethin nice in his pocket
– a packet of three.
And for him well I went for
a lovely charcoal jumper
that I got out Marks and Spencer
and wrapped it round the Hollies' new LP.

When emdy asked us was it getting serious
we laughed and said we had no future plans.
But Hogmanay saw Frank and me delirious.
On five Pernod and blackcurrants plus four cans
of Special plus a snakebite
we didny know how to make right
and we arsed a bottle of Bacardi
at Jessie Pearson's party.

We kissed and we kissed till we couldny resist –
totally pissed! We were in no fit state –
but I couldn't wait
for the life of Mrs Riley.

We switched the radio up till full volume
and jammed a chair below the handle of the door.
It was Jessie Pearson's wee brother Paul's room
there was, I think, another couple on the floor . . .
Frank said everything would be all right,
Luxembourg announced A-mami night
and Horace Batchelor's Infradraw –
it didny work at aw –

by Valentine's Day I was five weeks late,
I couldn't keep doon a thing I ate
and I couldn't wait
for the life of Mrs Riley.

My mammy said I was too easily led,
better call the banns cause we'd made our bed
we'd have to lie . . .
I wore a lemon tent dress down the aisle,
when I look at the photys I have to smile –
to say we could have done any different, Frank and I
we'd have to lie.

Well, we've been very happy – nothing great
but I doubt if I would hesitate –
'cos I couldn't wait
for the life of Mrs Riley.

FAVOURITE SHADE

She's getting no more black, her.
I goes, you've got bugger all bar black, Barbra.
Black's dead drab an' all.
Dreich. As a shade it's draining.
Better aff
somethin tae pit a bit a colour in her cheeks, eh no?

Black. Hale wardrobe fulla black claes.
Jist hingin therr half the time, empty.
On the hangers, hingin.
Plus by the way a gloryhole
chock-a-block with bermuda shorts, the lot.
Yella kimono, Ah don't know
whit all.
Tropical prints.
Polyester. Everything Easy-Kerr. Bit naw, naw
that was last year, noo
she's no one to give
nothing coloured
houseroom. Black.
Black.
Ah'm fed up tae the back teeth lukkin at her.
Her feyther says the same.

Wance yir workin ye cin weer whit yi like.
No as if yiv nothin tae pit oan yir back.
Black!
As well oot the world as oot the fashion.

Seen a wee skirt in Miss Selfridge.
Sort of dove, it was lovely.
Would she weer it, but?

Goes: see if it was black
if it was black
it'd be *brilliant*.

LOOK AT US

Can't you see us in the movies?
Can't you see us play our part?
You as Charlie Chaplin
and me as the World's Sweetheart.
Hearts and flowers and baggy pants
in flickering black and white
my dumbshow love and cupid's-bow –
but the captions don't read right.
Can't understand what's happening
imagine how it feels
to be stuck in a Saturday serial –
and someone's switched the reels.
And I'm bound and gagged on the Railway Line –
is this the final shot?
The piano's playing overtime
to catch up with the plot
and the train is getting nearer
my wide eyes open and shut
surely this can't be quite right –
should someone not shout: CUT!

Oh look at us,
don't we look ridiculous?

In the musicals of the thirties
we make the Perfect Pair.
We click together in any kind of weather
like Rogers and Astaire.
Fine Romance or Ziegfeld Folly?
Tap shoes, top hat and tails –
oh you look real cute in your morning suit,
and I'm polished to the nails.
As Just One of the Chorus
good timing's all you need

oh I'd be fine if you hadn't gone and pulled me out of line
to dance your female lead.

Oh look at us,
don't we look ridiculous?

I saw this forties' movie
now, that could have been 'bout us –
like he kissed her then she slapped him
then he gave her hair a muss.
'I've paid you your retainer –
now find him, that's your brief '
'Is that address you're nearly wearin
or a Lurex handkerchief?'
So let us drink to the long cool blonde
and the lonely private dick
who conversed in whiplash wisecracks
that cut them to the quick.
There was a loner and a
lady schoolmarm, and she turned gangster's moll.
But in the end they solved it –
so it wasn't like us at all.

So, pour me another bourbon,
I'll drink to all we did,
though outside it's still raining,
here's looking at us, kid!

Oh look at us
don't we look ridiculous.

I WOULDN'T THANK YOU FOR A VALENTINE

I wouldn't thank you for a Valentine.
I won't wake up early wondering if the postman's been.
Should ten red-padded satin hearts arrive with sticky sickly
    saccharine
Sentiments in very vulgar verses I wouldn't wonder if you meant
    them.
Two dozen anonymous Interflora roses?
I'd not bother to swither over who sent them!
I wouldn't thank you for a Valentine.

Scrawl SWALK across the envelope
I'd just say 'Same Auld Story
I canny be bothered deciphering it –
I'm up to here with Amore!'
This whole Valentine's Day thing is trivial and commercial,
A cue for unleashing cliches and candy-heart motifs to which I
    personally am not partial.
Take more than singing telegrams, or pints of Chanel Five, or
    sweets
To get me ordering oysters or ironing my black satin sheets.
I wouldn't thank you for a Valentine.

If you sent me a solitaire and promises solemn,
Took out an ad in the *Guardian* personal column
Saying something very soppy such as *Who Loves Ya, Poo?*
I'll tell you who, I do, Fozzy Bear, that's who!
You'd entirely fail to charm me, in fact I'd detest it,
I wouldn't be eighteen again for anything, I'm glad I'm past it.
I wouldn't thank you for a Valentine.

If you sent me a single orchid or a pair of Janet Reger's in a heart-
    shaped box and declared your Love Eternal
I'd say I'd not be caught dead in them they were politically suspect
and I'd rather something thermal.

If you hired a plane and blazed our love in a banner across the skies
If you bought me something flimsy in a flatteringly wrong size –
Och, if you sent me a postcard with three Xs and told me how you
     felt,
I wouldn't thank you, I'd melt.

MEN TALK

Women
Rabbit, rabbit, rabbit, women
Tattle and titter
Women prattle
Women waffle and witter

Men talk. Men talk.

Women into girl talk
About women's trouble
Trivia 'n' small talk
They yap and they babble

Men talk. Men talk.

Women gossip. Women giggle.
Women niggle, niggle, niggle
Men talk.

Women yatter
Women chatter
Women chew the fat, women spill the beans
Women ain't been takin
The oh-so good advice in them
Women's magazines.

A man likes a good listener

Oh, yeah
I like a woman
Who likes me enough
Not to nit-pick
Not to nag and

Not to interrupt cause I call that treason
A woman with the good grace
To be struck dumb
By my sweet reason. Yes –

A man likes a good listener
A real man
Likes a real
good listener

Women yap, yap, yap
Verbal diarrhoea is a female disease
Woman she spread she rumours round she
Like Philadelphia cream cheese.

Oh,
Bossy women gossip and
Girlish women giggle
Women natter, women nag
Women niggle, niggle, niggle

Men Talk.

Men
Think first. Speak later
Oh, yeah?
Men Talk.

CONDENSATION

After two-and-a-half years with his mother
We were no longer love's young dream
When me him and the weans got a hoose o wur ain
In a four-in-a-block in this scheme.

But – somewhat to our disappointment –
When we turned the key in the door
It was very Sanderson, very substandard,
When it came to the decor.

Tell tale black marks roon the cooker and sink,
Toadstools on the ceiling
And the back bedroom was boggin wi damp
(It gave you a clammy feeling).

Plus the bathroom had been invaded
By a sort of a fungussy thing
That looked quite a lot like it was part of a plot
From a horror book by Stephen King.

Of course we complained.
We complained again. And – eventually – the Corporation
Sent a couple of fellas who were quick to tell us
'If it's any consolation
The water that's runnin down your walls
Isn't dampness, it's con-densation.'

'Oh,' says I, 'I see,' says I,
'Whit's that when it's at hame?'
Seems dampness comes in, oot the ootside,
But if it's condensation we're to blame.

Well, taking baths in the bathroom
Or boiling kettles in the kitchenette

Or shutting-up windaes in winter to keep the heat in
Or warming up rooms with paraffin
It all causes steam, don't forget.

Well, pardon us for breathing, (I was really seething)
We complained again. Then complained-again again.
The woman said, 'Now please don't be abusive
I can assure you you've nothing to gain.'

She came she saw she tutted.
She said, 'I see what you mean . . .
Yon's murder on your Laura Ashley
And it's awfully hard to keep clean.'

She was very sympathetic
I have to admit she was *nice*.
But short of hopin we'd keep the windaes wide open
And the fire oan full blast
And breathe shallow and fast
She was very short of advice.

Well, it's the same the whole world over
It's the poor what gets the blame
And the rich that gets the . . . central heating.
Isn't that a blooming shame?

Well, what do we expect with this government's
Distribution of wealth -
They wish to get back to Victorian values
And Dickensian standards of health.

BAGPIPE MUZAK, GLASGOW 1990

When A & R men hit the street
To sign up every second band they meet
Then marketing men will spill out spiel
About how us Glesca folk are really *real*
(Where once they used to fear and pity
These days they glamorise and patronise our city –
Accent-wise once they could hear bugger all
That was not low, glottal or guttural,
Now we've 'kudos' incidentally
And the patter's street-smart, strictly state-of-the-art,
And our oaths are user-friendly).

It's all go the sandblaster, it's all go Tutti Frutti,
All we want is a wally close with Rennie Mackintosh putti.

Malkie Machismo invented a gismo for making whisky oot o
        girders
He tasted it, came back for mair, and soon he was on to his thirders.
Rabbie Burns turned in his grave and dunted Hugh MacDiarmid,
Said: It's oor National Thorn, John Barleycorn, but I doot we'll
        ever learn it . . .

It's all go the Rotary Club, it's all go 'The Toast Tae The Lassies',
It's all go 'Holy Willie's Prayer' and plunging your dirk in the
        haggis.

Robbie Coltrane flew Caledonian MacBrayne
To Lewis . . . on a Sunday!
Protesting Wee Frees fed him antifreeze
(Why God knows) till he was comatose
And didnae wake up till the Monday.

Aye it's retro time for Northern Soul

and the whoop and the skirl o the saxes.
All they'll score's more ground glass heroin and venison Filofaxes.

The rent-boys preen on Buchanan Street, their boas are made of
     vulture,
It's all go the January sales in the Metropolis of Culture.

It's all go the PR campaign and a radical change of image –
Write Saatchi and Saatchi a blank cheque to pay them for the
     damage.

Tam o'Shanter fell asleep
To the sound off airy laughter
Woke up on the cold-heather hill side
To find it was ten years after
And it's all go (again) the devolution debate and pro . . . pro . . .
     proportional representation.
Over pasta and pesto in a Byres Road bistro, Scotland declares
     hersel a nation.

Margo McDonald spruced up her spouse for thon Govan by-
     election
The voters they selectit him in a sideyways left defection,
The Labour man was awfy hurt, he'd dependit on the X-fillers
And the so-and-sos had betrayed him for thirty pieces of Sillars!

Once it was no go the SNP, they were sneered at as 'Tory' and tartan
And thought to be very little to do with the price of Spam in
     Dumbarton.
Now it's all go the Nationalists, the toast of the folk and the famous
– Of Billy Connolly, Muriel Gray and the Auchtermuchty
     Proclaimers

It's all go L.A. lager, it's all go the campaign for an Assembly,
It's all go Suas Alba and winning ten-nil at Wembley.

Are there separatist dreams in the glens and the schemes?

Well . . . it doesny take Taggart to detect it!
Or to jalouse we hate the Government
And we patently didnae elect it.
So – watch out Margaret Thatcher and tak tent Neil Kinnock
Or we'll tak 'the United Kingdom' and brek it like a bannock.

THE COLOUR
OF BLACK
& WHITE

(2003)

THE UNKNOWN CITIZEN

How to exist
except
in a land of unreadable signs and ambiguous symbols
except
between the hache and the ampersand
except
between the ankh and the ziggurat
between the fylfot and the fleur de lys
between the cross and the crescent
between the twinned sigrunes and the swastika
or the sauvastika its mirror image, its opposite –
meaning darkness/light whichever –
with a blank page for a passport

except
under some flag
some bloody flag with a
crucially five
(or a six or a seven)
pointed star?

THE MAN IN THE COMIC STRIP

For the man in the comic strip
things are not funny. No wonder he's
running in whichever direction his pisspoor
piston legs are facing
getting nowhere fast.

If only he had the sense he was born with
he'd know there is a world of difference
between the thinks bubble and the speech balloon
and when to keep it zipped, so, with a visible fastener.
But his mouth is always getting him into trouble.
Fistfights blossom round him,
there are flowers explode when the punches connect.
A good idea is a lightbulb, but too seldom.
When he curses, spirals
and asterisks and exclamation marks
whizz around his head like his always palpable distress.
Fear comes off him like petals from a daisy.
Anger brings lightning down on his head
and has him hopping.
Hunger fills the space around him
with floating ideograms of roasted chickens
and iced buns like maidens' breasts the way
the scent of money fills his eyes with dollar signs.

For him the heart is always a beating heart,
True Love –
always comically unrequited.
The unmistakeable silhouette of his one-and-only
will always be kissing another
behind the shades at her window
and, down-at-the-mouth, he'll
always have to watch it from the graphic
lamplit street.

He never knows what is around the corner
although we can see it coming.
When he is shocked his hair stands perfectly on end.

But his scream is a total zero and he knows it.
Knows to beware of the zigzags of danger,
knows how very different from
the beeline of zees that is a hostile horizontal buzzing
of singleminded insects swarming after him
are the gorgeous big haphazard zeds of sleep.

IN THE BLACK AND WHITE ERA

for Ian McMillan

'Hitchcock,
there was a Hitchcock on,' he said. '*Lifeboat.*
I'd harped on about it that much that Dad and I
had stayed up late to watch it.
Cocoa, and there we were, father and son in
nineteen-fifties checky dressing gowns and striped pyjamas.
Mum was up late too, footering with the packing
because next day we were going on our holidays.
The big black and white TV
was a boiling box of cruel grey sea,'
he said, 'when the door went.
We were normally such a family of early bedders too,
and my mum was all for not answering –
the time of night and us going on our holidays tomorrow –
which wasn't a bit like her, not normally,
and obviously – door went again, and then again –
wasn't going to be on, now was it? So
when she changed her tune from
'Don't go, Jack,' to 'You better go, Jack,'
Dad tied his cord again tighter and went to answer it.

What I remember, and I do remember
whatever my mum says, and though my dad denies it,
is the man sitting there on our settee,
sitting there the way no visitor ever sat,
not normally, without so much as a cup of tea
and a biscuit, which was unheard of, with that big dog of his
wetly wolfing down the water my mother –
and this wasn't like her – had so very grudgingly
brought it in that flowered bowl I'd never seen before.

'I've never seen you before in my life,'
said my dad to the man. And, honestly
it wasn't like him to be blunt like that.
This was after the man looked long at him and said,
'I know you, you're Jack Jones, I was
on the same ship as you, *Ark Royal*, remember?'
My mum was wringing her hands and saying,
'A fine time of night this is to come to folk's door –
and here they're away on their holidays tomorrow too!
You with your shaggydog stories of walking to Hamilton
and needing a bowl of water for your dog.
The doorstep wasn't good enough for you, was it?'

The TV was still on. *Lifeboat*. Which, with
a visitor in, it wouldn't have been, not normally.
A Hitchcock I never saw the end of,
not that night,
and as far as I know has never been repeated.

IRA AND GEORGE
for Michael Marra

'First the phonecall'
as the man said – and he sure said a mouthful –
to that 'which comes first, words or music?' question.
Who knows? Except: for every good one
there are ten in the trash, songs you slaved over
that just won't sing, in which no lover ever
will hear some wisecrack twist itself to tell
his unique heartbreak (so sore, so personal) so well
he can't stop humming it. The simplest three-chord melody might
        have legs
once it's got the lyric, not tunesmith's ham-and-eggs.
Each catchphrase, colloquialism, each cliché
each snatch of overheard-on-the-subway or street can say
so much, so much when rhymed right, when phrased just-so to fit
its own tune that was born for it.

A Manhattan night in twenty-nine or thirty.
It's late, you're reading Herrick. Just back from a party,
your brother calls out 'Hey let's work!' You watch him shuck
his jacket, loose his black tie and grab your book.
'Gather ye rosebuds' he says, and slams it shut. He's right.
Hard against the deadline and at night –
shoes off, moon up (just daring you), piano open –
that's when you two can make it happen.
The tune that smells like an onion? Play it very
slow, then *the one that sounds like the Staten Island Ferry*
till you hear the words – brother, they're already there
under the siren and the train and the cab horn blare
of his jazz of endless possibilities that will only fit
its own fine-tuned lyric that is born for it.

THE BEEKEEPER
for Carol Ann Duffy

Happy as haystacks are my quiet hives
from this distance and
through the bevel of this window's glass.
This is the place I robe myself
in net and hat and gloves.
This is my vestibule,
crocked like a dairy, full
of the sexual smell of bees.

Bees that fizzle out singly
like smoke rising from one cigarette
then straighten up and fly right
hauled
by olfactory magnets
while, loaded, laden,
their fellow workers make a beeline home.

This is the business
and I mind the time the old man,
showing me my first stuffed queen, the
tawny intricate purpose moving on the quiet comb,
made me initiate of this gold, this goodness.
He taught me the riddle of Samson –
Out of the strong came forth sweetness –
the honeycomb in the lion's carcase.

Out of the eater comes something to eat
Out of the strong comes something sweet.

I flip my net back
and go bare-armed on and out to them
wishing only to trust my own good husbandry
and do nothing

nothing but feel them
crawl and trawl the follicles, stamens
and pistils of my unpollened arms.

THE NEW-MARRIED MINER

My shift is over that was night time all day long.
My love, it's lowsan time. Alone among
these dog-tired colliers my drouth's for home.
Bank up the fire with small coal till I come
and before tomorrow I'll not think again
how sore and small the space I have to hunker in
or how huge and hard but true it pulls all day
as at the pithead, black against the sky,
the big wheel turns. Now my bike's
coggling front wheel clicks and squeaks,
my cold bones ache as hard for home I pedal
still blacked up like a darky minstrel.

My long path home is starved of light
so I must do without.
No moon tonight, so round and white –
its Davy Lamp's gone out.
Frost edges every blackened leaf,
black snot-flowers on my handkerchief.

Heat my bath scalding
and, bonny lass, I'll make
the white lace of the lather black.
Squeeze the hot soapy flannel
at the nape of my neck
and scribble long white chalkmarks down my back.
Put the dark fire to the poker
till the hot flames burst in flower.
Stretch out the towel and I'll stand up.
Hold and fold me
rub and scrub me as hard as you can
till in your white warm arms I'll end up
a pink and naked man, my love
               your pink and naked man.

THE BAKER

I am as lucky for a funeral
as a sweep is at a wedding
when with his red eyes, furred brush and burnt smell
he blesses bridal lace with his soil and smirching.

Thus do my work-night whites,
the cracks on my dusted boots,
my overall trousers of flour-stiffened linen
handsel your black ties and pressed mourning suits

although I am not by your side, nor
does any one photograph my – or that rawest – absence.
Dawn delivery to this hotel had me
shoulder those boards of my generous dozens

as all week neighbours came with bakestuffs
up the saddest path to your door
wanting to bring something sweet and light
to where nothing can be so any more.

And now I sleep on sacks washed soft
while you – your time at the cold grave over,
or after that stare at the core of the terrible oven –
take tea and funeral cakes together.

Let sober girls in black and white replenish plates
and freshen up the cooling cups with warm
as if tomorrow like live yeast could rise and prove.
I say: such crumbs do no harm.

In nights while I will work and you will grieve
weak tea, sudden hunger for the heel of a new loaf,
white dawn and the surprise of appetite

will have you tear a lump of goodness off.

Sooner, later a new season's wind will lift –
though it may be many daily loaves from this dark hour
till you let go, fling, and feel the ashes sift
around your footsteps like spilt flour.

K I D S P O E M / B A I R N S A N G

it wis January
and a gey dreich day
the first day Ah went to the school
so ma mum happed me up in ma
good navy-blue napp coat wi the rid tartan hood
birled a scarf aroon ma neck
pu'ed oan ma pixie an ma pawkies
it wis that bitter
said: *noo ye'll no starve*
gie'd me a wee kiss and a kid-oan skelp oan the bum
and sent me aff across the playground
tae the place Ah'd learn to say
it was January
and a really dismal day
the first day I went to school
so my mother wrapped me up in my
best navy-blue top coat with the red tartan hood,
twirled a scarf around my neck,
pulled on my bobble-hat and mittens
it was so bitterly cold
said: *now you won't freeze to death*
gave me a little kiss and a pretend slap on the bottom
and sent me off across the playground
to the place I'd learn to forget to say
it wis January
and a gey dreich day
the first day Ah went to the school
so ma mum happed me up in ma
good navy-blue napp coat wi the rid tartan hood,

birled a scarf aroon ma neck,
pu'ed oan ma pixie an' ma pawkies
it wis that bitter.

Oh saying it was one thing
but when it came to writing it
in black and white
the way it had to be said
was as if you were posh, grown-up, male, English and dead.

LITTLE WOMEN

for Carol Ann Duffy and Jackie Kay

When Oona Cody left me
for that new girl Helen Derry
initially
I had everybody's fullest sympathy –
which entirely failed to comfort me.
That Helen Derry, yon one,
her with the wee fur cuffs on her bootees, the
knife edges on her accordion pleats which,
when she birled to swing them
in a quick scart along the peever beds
or bent to touch her toes, showed
a quick flash of her scut
in pants embroidered with the days of the week.
Rumour was she'd plain refused once to come to school
with Thursday on on a Monday and ever since –
oh, she was a hard case that Helen Derry –
her mother had learned her lesson, taken
a tumble to herself, got a grip and shaped up
good and proper.

My mother was predictable.
If that was the kind of friend Oona was, well,
she was no friend of mine, good riddance,
she was somebody anybody,
anybody with a bit of sense,
would be glad to see the back of.
Which was, wasn't it, just what a mother *would* say?
And everybody in the class said the novelty would wear off.
'Bide your time' and 'She'll come running back'
these seemed to be the bromides of conventional wisdom.
And Helen Derry, as for her, she could
get back to where they called Levoy 'Bendulum'
(Bendulum!)

and Dutch ropes 'French' and she could just
take her wee blue bottle of Evening-in-bloody-Paris
back with her, coming here breaking up the
true marriage of a best friendship
with her face like the back of a bus
and her bahookey like the side of a house
and the wings on the famous specs you couldn't get on the N.H.S.
and the 'auntie an airhostess'
and the wee lucky birthstone pierced earrings, the monster.

But I knew everybody knew what I knew.
There was something wrong with what I'd had with Oona.
Although the sanctity of our togetherness had
seemed unbroken
and her content – I'd thought – to swap scraps
with no thought of anyone else or anything 'missing' –
us able to run the gauntlet of a three-legged race
in perfect step together
with hardly a knot in the hanky that yoked us together.
Now I was bad luck, bad luck altogether.
No wonder all the other couples avoided me,
frantically spooling themselves into each other tightly
with loving lassoos of the French knitting that ravelled endlessly
from the wee dolly-things that were all the craze
and they worried at like rosaries.
'There but for the grace of God' and
'Please, please let it never happen to me, so help me'
seemed to be the size of it
as they jumped double bumps together,
arms down each other's coatsleeves, and chewed each other's
used bubble gum for luck and love.
What the magazines said was that this was a chance,
a chance to be truly honest with yourself
and see where you had gone wrong, or slipped up,
or let yourself go, or taken things for granted,
been lax about 'communicating' – for how many

of us could say we really took the time to talk or listen?
The magazines reminded that revenge
was a dish better eaten cold (and then you'd see it was only
good taste to leave it).

For Oona Cody's birthday – the first anniversary
since she'd left me – I bought her a copy of
Louisa May Alcott's two best-loved children's classics,
Yes, *Little Women*,
Little Women and *Good Wives* in a compendium edition
with a green marbled cover and one frontispiece,
a great book
I knew Oona – my Oona – would definitely love.
She was sitting under the pegs at playtime,
under the pegs with Helen Derry,
the both of them engrossed – or acting-it engrossed,
for God-knows-whose benefit though, so
(with hindsight) I'll concede it likely they *were* in
a mutual bona-fide brown study – engrossed
in a wee free-pamphlet entitled 'Growing Up'.
I clocked the cover (two doves and a butterfly
above the – open – gates of womanhood
with the pastel-coloured coloured-in country beyond).
And Oona Cody had the grace to blush
when I dropped the present – all wrapped up –
like a reproach in her lap.
I held my breath till lunchtime, when –
Helen Derry stood against the railings, watching –
Oona Cody marched up to me and said
she didn't want a birthday present,
not from me, and anyway Helen had already read it.
'She says it's pure morbid, the wee sister dies
and the boy-next-door marries the wrong one,
the eejit that talks French and sleeps with
a clothespeg on her neb to improve her profile into aquiline
and thinks of nobody but herself and flaming art.'

So I had to go home with it,
home to face my mother's scorn,
to stick it up on the shelf beside the identical one I had already
knowing I'd never have the neck to take it back and swap it
for *What Katy Did* & *What Katy Did Next*
but was stuck with it –
'*Christmas won't be Christmas without any presents,' grumbled Jo,
lying on the rug.*'

THE METAL RAW

was what we used to call
what must've really been the *un*metalled road or row,
a no-cars scratch across two farmers' tracts
between ours, with its brand-new scheme,
and the next
ex-mining village.

When I was four, or five or six or so, I thought
it meant the colour, though. *Metal raw*
was crude red (*rid*) gravel that you'd
better not brake your bike on and that surfaced
just the first hundred yards or so
then patched the worst of the ruts
on the dirt and mud and clinker of the rest of it. Rust
on corrugated iron, that was *metal* and *raw*, both.
A real remnant of *The Iron Curtain* for all I knew,
torn and gouged with nail holes along edges
that you'd to *watch they wouldnae rip the hand off you.*

Sheets of this stuff crumbled to red dust along the Metal Raw
among the black cold fires and rags and bits of brick
around the place the tinkers still camped
a week or two each spring
with their piebald ponies.
Always some story
among us weans around the scheme or at the swings
about somebody's big cousin creeping close enough
to kick the boiling billycan over, about a shaken fist,
cursing and swearing and how far, on the light nights,
that big man with the stick had hunted him.

I was wee enough then,
on a Sunday walk along the Metal Raw
with Mum and Dad in my good coat,

for the tinks' big black dog that *wouldnae do me any harm*
to knock me flying in the mulchy ditch among
flag iris and the reeds I called *bullrushes*
and that might have harboured Baby Moses
and not one bit surprised me.
See, I am talking of the time when I mixed up
Old Meg she was a gipsy
and that old woman up the Metal Raw
smoking a pipe outside a tilting lean-to of tarred and
patched tarpaulin stretched on hawthorn.

And this was the nineteen fifties.
We slept *under a mushroom cloud*,
feared *Khrushchev and Bulganin*, men in Cossack hats
in blizzards of interference on the tiny grey T.V. screens
of *the Cold War*.

This was the time when our mothers down the New Houses
stood on *Red Cardinal* doorsteps
far too scared not to buy the tinkers' pegs and prophesies.

LANARKSHIRE GIRLS

Coming into Glasgow
in our red bus through those green fields. And
summer annoyed us thrusting
leafy branches through the upstairs windows.
Like a boy with a stick through railings,
rattling us. We bent whole treetops
squeezing through and they rained down twigs, broken
bits of foliage, old blossom on the roof,
chucked hard wee balls of unripe fruit,
drumming us out of the country.

Then it was
shabby schemes, gospel halls, chapels, Orange halls,
doctors' surgeries, the crematorium, the zoo,
gap sites where August already frittered the stuffing out of
unpurpling fireweed and splintering thistles
till the blank blue sky was dot-dot-dotted
with whiskery asterisks.

Soon the coherent cliffs of Tollcross,
the many mansions of those lovely red and
blackened tenements. Our country bus sped
past the city stops, the women in their
slippers at the doors of dairies,
the proud pubs on every corner, accelerated
along the glamorous Gallowgate, juddered by
Reeta's gallus fashions and the
gorgeous dragons of Terry Tattoo Artist, till it
spilled us out, fourteen years old, dreaming ourselves up,
with holiday money burning a hole in our pockets
at the corner of Jamaica Street.

YOUR AUNTIES

for Elizabeth Miller

your auntie was
famous for being an air hostess or
famous for being a nurse
famous for being a bloody good sport
famous for being a Pain in the Erse
famous for being able to take a joke or
famous for Quite the Reverse.

famous for the office sweepstake and spectacular wins
your Auntie was
famous for her perra stoatin pins
famous for her big blue eyes
famous for her brass neck
famous for her mince pies
her harangues, her meringues, her am-I-right-or-am-I-wrangs?
famous for her talent contest
famous for Always Doing her Best
famous for For-Christssake-Wullie-will-you-give-it-a-rest?

famous for her bra
famous for her good bones
famous for her tattie scones
famous for her foxtrot
famous for her scarlet lipstick
famous for her scarlet fever
famous for Always Getting Up at Weddings and
                    Singing The Twelfth of Never.
famous for *turning*
famous for being a poppet
famous for being a Nippy Sweetie
famous for Always Being Im*ma*culate
or
famous for being a bloody mess

famous for the specs you couldn't get on the N.H.S.
famous for Signing the Pledge at the Bandy Hope
famous for her famous *esperegus* soup.

famous for being as daft as a brush
famous for fast thinking
famous for . . . What-do-you-think?
famous for her driving
famous for her drinking
famous for famously driving your Uncle Freddie to drink.

famous for the Famous Grouse
famous for her bought house
famous for her High Ideals
famous for her peerie heels
famous for her natural curls
famous for her Toni
famous for her fake tan
famous for her Wee Man
famous for her canary
famous for being the salt of the Earth
famous for being phoney
famous for being *gen*uine
famous for being a poser
famous for being a Literary Creation like Aunt Julia
the Auntie of Mario Vargas Llosa
famous for her Giaconda Smile
famous for making scenes like a Dickensian Aunt
or a Wodehouse Aunt, a Dylan Thomas
or a Graham Greene's . . .
famous for being Norman MacCaig's Gaelic Aunt Julia
in her black box bed
or Edwin Morgan's Aunt Myra
at a tea dance in the twenties with a new tune in her head or
famous for being one of Alan Bennett's Bradford Aunties

who were

famous for I-take-as-I-find and
always-speaking-me-mind and
not-being-taken-in-by-t'-toffs
famous for being Charlie's Aunt
or Roger McGough's . . .

A very well known phrase or saying
meaning you are
welcome to whatever you want is:

Eat up – you're at your Auntie's!

CLOTHES

for Helen Simpson

There are dresses – good dresses,
dresses you always loved –
that are suddenly so clean gone
they never become a duster or
leave so much as a square of themselves
rubbing around decades later in the ragbag.
This was what I learned listening
to my mother and my aunts
when on one of the good days in the long summer holidays
they sat out on backdoor steps
or – skirts spread out – on a tartan rug
on the back green under the white sheets
hung high. 'What *happened*
to that wee dress?' one of my aunts
would ask my mother or she'd ask them
coming out of one of the fridgeless kitchenettes
of the fifties with a jug of Boston cream
saying: 'Johnnie aye liked me in that costume . . .'

Maybe it was my grandmother saying:
'That was a good coat that'
with all the reverence and gravity
remembrance of such a garment
was rightly due. You knew how true it was
she liked *good things*. When someone said:
'That was something I always felt right in . . .'
what you heard was the real regret, the yearning.

If something could be explained away
as having been worn till it was well and truly *done*
this would dismiss it from discussion.
But the mystery of that *wonderful swagger-coat* –
a *great* coat – left on a train in the nineteen thirties

that *disappeared before it was gone back for*
only minutes later
was enough to make it mythical to me
as Joseph's Coat of Many Colours,
as the one dream dress every one of them had danced in
and no one was sure who it actually belonged to or
whatever happened . . .
You learned that everything was in the detail,
that their mouths made rosebuds
to recall *rows of toty-wee covered buttons.*
Their knowledgeable eyes narrowed at *darts*
or *edge-to-edge, bugle-beading, Peter Pan collar,*
gleamed when they as much as said *sateen.*
Something had never been 'blue' but
saxe or *duck-egg* or 'a shade somewhere
between *peacock* and a *light royal*
almost an *electric blue* – but no as gaudy' . . .
Talk was of *barathea, grosgrain, watered taffeta*
organza, covered coating.
When it came to this stuff *stuff*
every one of them was her mother's daughter.
I'd say every sister had three sisters
who were women after their own hearts

if I didn't remember my youngest aunt, the looker,
the one who later divorced and remarried,
the one with the perfect eyebrows,
the one who never had a bad perm or a tint that
went metallic, harsh, who never had fireside tartan
or visible veins measling her legs in their glassy nylons –
smoothing down the glazed cotton over net
splashed with huge impossible blue roses,
admiring the *this-year* almond toes
of her gorgeous gunmetal shoes
and saying nothing

while her mother and her sisters argued enjoyably
over a past no one could quite agree the colour of
and that might or might not have been
                sprigged with tiny flowers.

SOCIAL HISTORY

My mother never
had sex with anyone else
except my father. A week before
her three-day leave to get married
my mother was examined by the Army Doctor
and pronounced *virgo intacta*
twenty-four years old and virgo intacta
an unusual thing in the ATS
an unusual thing in wartime
if you believe even half of what you read
in the social history books.
And the joke was I wasn't even sure
your dad was going to make it. Rumour was
they were going to cancel all leave prior to D-Day
so it was touch and go till the last minute . . .

The sex my mother could've had
but didn't
sounded fantastic. Clever Jewish boys
from the East End of London
whirled her round the dance floors
niftily slow foxtrotting her into corners
telling her the khaki matched her eyes.
A soldier in a darkened carriage on a slow train
wept on her shoulder when he told her
that he'd lost his brother in North Africa.
Two naval ratings on Margate pier
slipped a string of cultured pearls in her pocket
said: 'Miss, we just found these on the beach
and you are so pretty we thought you ought to have them.'
She had a very close and very tender
friendship with a lovely, lovely gentle N.C.O.
from the North of England who told her she was
the image of his girlfriend. An Italian

prisoner of war sketched her portrait and
her sister who had her eye on him
was quite put out.
She didn't care for Yanks but that didn't
stop them trying. A Free Frenchman
fell in love with her. A Polish Airforceman
proposed. Any Scotsmen she met
down there had lovely educated accents
and tended to be Top Brass.
She mixed with folk from All Over.
Which was the beauty of the services
and the best of the party that was wartime,
while the buzzbombs overhead didn't quite
cut out.
She was quite capable of downing her half of bitter
and rolling out the barrel with all the other girls
without ending up squiffy up against the wall
afterwards with her knickers down, unlike some.
When they all rolled back to barracks late,
swinging their lisle-stockinged legs
from the tailgate of a lorry singing Apple Blossom Time,
Military Policemen turned a blind eye
in exchange for nothing more than a smile.
Officers messed around with her in the blackout,
but then my mother told them
she was engaged to be married to my father
and they acted like the officers and gentle-
men they were and backed off sharpish, so
my mother never
had sex with anyone else
except my father, which was a source
of pride to her, being of her generation
as it would have been a source
of shame to me, being of mine.

AFTER THE WAR

for Susanne Ehrhardt

After the war
was the dull country I was born in.
The night of Stafford Cripps's budget
My dad inhaled the blue haze of one last Capstan
then packed it in.
You were just months old . . .
The Berlin airlift.
ATS and REME badges
rattled in our button box.

Were they surprised that everything was different now?
Did it cheese them off that it was just the same
stuck in one room upstairs at my grandma's
jammed against the bars of my cot
with one mended featherstitch jumper drying
among the nappies on the winterdykes,
the puffed and married maroon counterpane
reflected in the swinging mirror of the wardrobe.
Radio plays. Them loving one another
biting pillows
in the dark while I was sleeping.
All the unmarried uncles were restless,
champing at the bit
for New Zealand, The Black Country, Corby.
My aunties saved up for the New Look.

By International Refugee Year
we had a square green lawn and twelve-inch telly.

SORTING THROUGH

The moment she died, my mother's dance dresses
turned from the colours they really were
to the colours I imagine them to be.
I can feel the weight of bumptoed silver shoes
swinging from their anklestraps as she swaggers
up the path towards *her* dad, light-headed
from airman's kisses. Here, at what I'll have to learn
to call *my father's house*, yes every
ragbag scrap of duster prints her even more vivid
than an Ilford snapshot on some seafront
in a white cardigan and that exact frock.
Old lipsticks. Liquid stockings.
Labels like Harella, Gor-ray, Berkertex.
As I manhandle whole outfits into binbags for Oxfam
every mote in my eye is a utility mark
and this is useful:
the sadness of dispossessed dresses,
the decency of good coats round-shouldered
in the darkness of wardrobes,
the gravitas of lapels,
the invisible danders of skin fizzing off from them
like all that life that will not neatly end.

1953

All the dads, like you, that spring
had put the effort in.
Stepped on it with brand-new spades
to slice and turn
clay-heavy wet yellow earth
to clods that stank of clay
and were well marbled
with worms and rubble.
You set paths straight
with slabs it took two men to lift.
Tipped barrowloads of topsoil. Riddled.
Sowed grass seed from illustrated packets
that showed tall flowers, long English lawns
striped green like marrows. Then
stretched over paper bowties on strings
to frighten birds.
So gardens happened
where the earth had been one raw wound.

And behind whitened windows
the mums were stippling walls
or treadling Singers as they
ran rivers of curtain material
through the eye of a needle and out again,
fit to hang by Coronation Day.
This was in rooms
that had emptinesses, possibilities,
still smelled of shaved wood
and drying plaster.

In no time at all
in a neat estate a long time later
I will watch in a dawn
through a crack in drawn curtains

this lawn, the late September borders,
mature roses
and the undertaker coming up the path
carrying a pint of milk.

III

VIEW OF SCOTLAND/LOVE POEM

Down on her hands and knees
at ten at night on Hogmanay,
my mother still giving it elbowgrease
jiffywaxing the vinolay. (This is too
ordinary to be nostalgia.) On the kitchen table
a newly opened tin of sockeye salmon.
Though we do not expect anyone,
the slab of black bun,
petticoat-tails fanned out
on bone china.
Last year it was very quiet ...

Mum's got her rollers in with waveset
and her well-pressed good dress
slack across the candlewick upstairs.
Nearly half-ten already and her not shifted!
If we're to even hope to prosper
this midnight must find us
how we would like to be.
A new view of Scotland
with a dangling calendar
is propped under last year's,
ready to take its place.

Darling, it's thirty years since
anybody was able to trick me,
December thirty first, into
looking into a mirror to see a lassie
wi' as minny heids as days in the year –

and two already since,
familiar strangers at a party,
we did not know that we were
the happiness we wished each other
when the Bells went, did we?

All over the city
off-licences pull down their shutters,
people make for where they want to be
to bring the new year in.
In highrises and tenements
sunburst clocks tick
on dusted mantelshelves.
Everyone puts on their best spread of plenty
(for to even hope to prosper
this midnight must find us
how we would like to be).
So there's a bottle of sickly liqueur
among the booze in the alcove,
golden crusts on steak pies
like quilts on a double bed.

And this is where we live.
There is no time like
the present for a kiss.

NECKTIES

Paisleys squirm with spermatozoa.
All yang, no yin. Liberties are peacocks.
Old school types still hide behind their prison bars.
Red braces, jacquards, watermarked brocades
are the most fun a chap can have
in a sober suit.

You know about knots,
could tie, I bet, a bowtie properly
in the dark with your eyes shut, but
we've a diagram hung up
beside the mirror in our bedroom.
Left over right, et cetera . . .
The half or double Windsor,
even that extra fancy one it takes
an extra long tie to pull off successfully.
You know the times a simple schoolboy four-in-hand
will be what's wanted.

I didn't used to be married.
Once neckties were coiled occasional serpents
on the dressing-table by my bed
beside the car-keys and the teetering
temporary leaning towers of change.
They were dangerous nooses on the backs of chairs
or funny fishes in the debris on the floor.
I should have known better.

Picture me away from you
cruising the high streets
under the watchful eyes of shop boys
fingering their limp silks
wondering what would please you.

Watch out, someday I'll bring you back a naked lady,
a painted kipper, maybe a bootlace
dangling from a silver dollar
and matching collar points.
You could get away with anything
you're that good-looking.
Did you like that screenprinted slimjim from Covent Garden?

Once I got a beauty in a Cancer Shop
and a sort of forties effort in Oxfam for a song.
Not bad for one dull town.
The dead man's gravy stain wasn't the size of sixpence
and you can hide it behind your crocodile tie pin.

A NIGHT IN

Darling, tonight I want to celebrate
not your birthday, no, nor mine.
It's not the anniversary of when we met,
first went to bed or got married, and the wine
is supermarket plonk. I'm just about to grate
rat-trap cheddar on the veggie bake that'll do us fine.

But it's far from the feast that – knowing you'll be soon, and
suddenly so glad to just be me and here,
now, in our bright kitchen – I wish I'd stopped and gone
and shopped for, planned and savoured earlier.
Come home! It's been a long day. Now the perfect moon
through our high windows rises round and clear.

IV

EPITHALAMIUM

for Joe and Annie Thomson

For Marriage, love and love alone's the argument.
Sweet ceremony, then hand-in-hand we go
Taking to our changed, still dangerous days, our complement.
We think we know ourselves, but all we know
Is: love surprises us. It's like when sunlight flings
A sudden shaft that lights up glamourous the rain
Across a Glasgow street – or when Botanic spring's
First crisp, dry breath turns February air champagne.

Delight's infectious – your quotidian friends
Put on, with gladrag finery today, your joy,
Renew in themselves the right true ends
They won't let old griefs, old lives destroy.
When at our lover's feet our opened selves we've laid
We find ourselves, and all the world, remade.

THE BRIDE

I am the absolute spit of Elsa Lanchester.
A ringer for her, honestly,
down to the zigzag of lightning in my frightwig
and it's funny no one, me in-
cluded, ever noticed the resemblance before
because
this fine morning
jolted awake by a crash in the kitchen
the smell of burning
and the corncrake domesticity of dawnchorus
toast getting scraped, suddenly
there's the me in the mirror staring back at me
and me less than amazed at me all marcelled
like Elsa Lanchester.
Well, it's apt enough,
this is my last morning as a
single girl.

Despite your ex-wife's incendiary good wishes,
there's the new frock I've been dieting into
for more than a fortnight
quite intact
over the back of the chair.
And because last night was my last night,
last night I left you,
left you to your own devices under the double duvet
and went home to home-home
to sleep my last night in my own
single bed.
I'd love to say I've my own
old toys around me, et cetera and the same old old-
gold counterpane, but is it likely?
Is it likely what with the old dear's passion
for continuous redecoration?

There's not so much as a Sunday school prize
not long gone to Oxfam –
just one wall-eyed
teddybear some rugby player gave me for my twenty-first
and an acrylic still life with aubergine
(which for one moment I consider asking for –
except where could we hang it?)
to take home to our home, our
old home which today's nuptials must make
our new home,
take home to remind myself of what I can't remember
which is what the hell the girl who did that picture
and was as far as I can remember
painting-daft
has to do with me,
the me with the Lanchester look.

Breakfast.
Breakfast on a tray and like a
condemned man I
can have anyting I want for
breakfast, but
before I can lop the top off my boiled egg,
before I can say soldiers far less
dunk them, the place is
bristling with sisters
stripping me and unzipping me
and down the hall the bathroom taps are pounding
Niagara and bubbles.
'Bucks Fizz three fingers cheers kiddo cheerio'
this is Ellen
the older one
the matron of honour
clashing glasses knocking it back
in her slip and stocking soles
plugging in her Carmens

drenching herself in the Duty Free Diorissimo
Dave brought back from that refresher course in
Brussels with his secretary
unpacking Mothercare plastic carriers
of maximum security sanitary protection from
her Antler overnight case because
she never knows the minute
with that new coil she had fitting after Timothy.
And Susan
our Susan
sixteen, sly eyes and skinny as a wand
she's always fancied you,
ecru and peach, apple green satin she'll
take all the eyes even though it's meant to be
My Day,
the bizzum's in kinks over the under-
crotch buttons of my camiknickers and I'm
to touch nothing till that
Hazel comes to comb out my hair.
Mother is being very mother-
of-the-bride, rushing round squeezing
Euthymol-pink shrimp-flavoured creamcheese
on platters of crackers bigger than millwheels
and though her daughters all agree
a donkey brown two-piece is somewhat
less than festive
at least we're all thankful she's not
drawing squinty seams up the back of her legs
with eyebrow pencil
in memory of her wedding in
nineteen forty-three.

And here's the taxi
and I stretch up my arms
like one beseeching heaven
like one embracing fate

and four sets of hands help me into my dress
my dress I don't want to wear
my dress that after the whole kerfuffle
is really nothing special
my dress that, should you jilt me
leave me in the lurch at the altar of the registry office
tilting my
fragile psyche
for ever permanently agley,
the dress I'll have to wear for ever
till I'm dafter than Miss Havisham
in mourning for my life until it rots under the oxters.
I should have
chosen really carefully.

And then with Dad in the taxi
and I know
it's going to crash because there's got to be
something
going to stop me from ruining my life like this
but no,
no Dad winks and one swig
from his hipflask and we're bowling
gaily down the aisle towards you,
you and the best man I've been
knocking off for yonks
with his grin
and the ring
and his pockets
bulging obscenely with apocryphal telegrams.

Because we have opted for a
Quiet Wedding
and a civil sort of civil ceremony
the front four pews are choc-a-block with
all our old lovers

who (since we've taken
so long to tie the knot) have all been
married to each other, separated, been
divorced so long
they're on really friendly terms again and
surely someone,
someone will declare some
just impediment to stop this whole ridiculous
charade?
I make my vows
but all the time I'm screaming
'No No No' I
hear a voice
a voice I'm sure I recognize to be my own voice
loud as you like 'I do'.

Despite
the unfortunate business at the
Reception and the
manageress's Jack Russell
depositing that dead rat right at my satin slippers
under the top table while
(animal lovers to a man) the company
applauded laughed and cheered –
despite
the fact that when we came to cut the cake
it collapsed
like a prizewinning office block
in a spectacular shambles of silver
cardboard Ionic columns and white
plasterboard icing sugar we got
into the going away car while the going
was good and now,
now here we are
alone at last
in the plumbed-in-twin-

bedded room of this hotel
where we told the man we'd booked a double
but he smiled shrugged said
he'd no record of that and this was all they had
so take it or leave it.
So we did.

We unpack
our paperbacks. We
scorn such sentiments such institutionalizing as
making love on this our wedding night
and it's only
after (sudden lust
having picked us up by the scruff of the neck and
chucked us into
that familiar whirlpool) and
practised and perfect
we judder totally together
into amazed and wide-eyed calm and
I lie beside you
utterly content that I know for sure
that this is never
ever going to
work.

THE REDNECK

The day I got married I was like a rake.
Six months on the popcorn diet. Starving
but I wouldn't give the girls at work the satisfaction.
All so as I could swan down the aisle in my Scarlett O'Hara
towards that pig with a knife stuck down his sock.
Kilt suited him, but. Unlike ma da.
A toss-up between the Ancient Buchanan
and the Hunting MacIntyre.
I wanted tartan yes but no too roary.
State I was in everything had to be just so.
I had my mammy roasted in a pinwheel hat.
Ended up whole thing was nothing but a blur
and him shouting 'Perfect Working Order'
every two minutes mooning his mates
and flashing the photographer with his
Lion Rampant boxer shorts. A right red neck.

During my marriage I ballooned.
None of a family thank God.
Bad enough splitting up without the complications.

THE BRIDEGROOM

is a necessary
accessory –
if often irrelevant
a bit of a white elephant
after the event.

He should be tall, but not *too* tall – the ideal's
tall enough to top but not
tower over her in her highest high heels.
He should, at the risk of being banal,
have quite a pleasant personal-
ity, be well-built
in morning suit and top hat (or tuxedo . . . or kilt)
whichever
but he'll never, however
nice his smile
or perfect the profile
next to her in the getaway car
be more than a penny stick of licorice
to her sixpence worth of candyfloss
– the bride's the star!

He's of frankly secondary importance to the dress.
Not optional but an extra
nevertheless.

Yup, the role of bridegroom as they scatter
the confetti's
a bit of a bit part – but *husband*, don't forget, is
ha! another matter.

V

TWO POEMS ON CHARACTERS SUGGESTED BY BRAM STOKER'S *DRACULA*

1. LUCY'S DIARY

1.
When the big car came for me
I could have sworn I still smelled
my dad's cigar as I leaned back among the leather.
When Jim and the porter sweated to heave
my locked trunk into the back I shrugged
that this was my last time for leaving.
My scorn was all for those
sentimental girls who pressed
keepsake handkerchiefs and cameos and cachou-
boxes into each other's hands and wept and kissed.
I did not look back as we drove off.

Near Birmingham,
red dust, the smoke from my father's factories.
The sunset extra beautiful because polluted.
Dark and a thin, thin moon
by the time we reached seven, the Crescent,
Whitby. Sitting pretty on its cleft cliff.

2.
Heartwood is gloomy.
Mama and I quarrel, constantly.

She says I vex her toying with my fork
but imagine if something on your plate
had been a bird once,
well I can't
eat that!
I'll not pick at so much as one feather of flesh,
never. My mother!

Mourning is only a hair brooch
and a heavy dress she will put on.

3.
Yesterday
the gardener's big lad
gave me a peach from the greenhouse.
Unthinking, I bit and sucked
then suddenly flung it from me
in a real rage at its beauty.
Something in its furred blush hurt me,
stuck in my throat
like a lump and made me spill,
deliberately,
clouded paint-water all over my watercolour
I'd worked on all morning, spoiling it.

4.
I walk and walk and walk.
Florrie says that dog
doesn't know it's born now I'm back.
I wish I were as thin and clean
as that tinkerish boy I caught out today
scudding back with a daft grin –
he must've been all of ten –

from whitecap waves to squirm
into his dirty clothes again.

I'd like to swim far out, not drown.

5.
I don't like
the way I look.
I will freckle far too easily, my hair
just won't do the right thing.
When Quincey Morris calls me mighty pretty
it only makes me hate him.

I tilt at
the big, big oval mirror in its mahogany.
This gross flesh I will confine
in the whalebone of my very own
hunger. All term
I would not bleed, not
for Matron, Mama, Mademoiselle,
nor my sister Mina.

6.
Despite myself,
the sea air is giving me an appetite.

2. RENFIELD'S NURSE

When I go in to him
I never know what to expect.
I move in antiseptic corridors.
I come bearing a bedpan like a begging bowl.
I bring hot water, carbolic, huckaback.

I bring a hypodermic, a bowl
of brown stew I've saved for him special,
or three dicey horse pills
rattling like chance in a plastic cup.

Times
he'll be nice as ninepence
sitting up smiling
that pink and bland you'd
swear he'd all his marbles.
Lucid as the next man.

Others
when he doesn't know me from Adam –
though he's always got a glad eye for the girls.
I blame the uniform.

Sometimes
he cowers in his own dirt in the corner
whimpering
Doctor don't you hurt me Doctor.
I say it's just the nurse
I say come on you know it's only me.

He looks up at me
with them dog eyes and says
you the nice one or the nasty 'cause I never
know what to expect?

My hands are gentle.
My starched apron cracks
like a whip hand.

VI

FIVE BERLIN POEMS

5TH APRIL 1990
for Edwin Morgan on his 70th birthday

Today I got back from Berlin and the broken Wall.
With bits of it.
Smithereens of history, the brittle confetti
of chiselled-off graffiti,
trickle on to the brave blue dogeared cover
of my signed copy of *Sonnets from Scotland*
that I had with me and have just unpacked.
It hasn't travelled well, but crumbled,
this souvenir I brought for Fünfzig Pfennige
picked out from the brightest chips,
from the priciest slabs with names
or obscenities half intact – all on offer
from that grinning gap-toothed Kreuzberg
Gastarbeiter kid who really thought
he had it made.
Well, he saw me coming all right –
another dumbcluck tourist
taking the slow curve of the Wall
towards Mariannenplatz, gawping at
the Bethanien-House artists mending
still-serviceable slogans on what was left standing.
This was a facelift the
chinking chisels of stonepeckers would
only worry at in turn and yet
they painted, and lovingly,

as if these fluorescents and enamels
would last one thousand years
and make good sense.

Every night I spent at Wannsee
at the Writers' House by the Lake,
Morgan's poems whirled me from space
to the bedrock of my own small
and multitudinous country, swung me
through centuries, ages, shifting geologies
till I was dizzy and dreamed
I was in the sands of the desert and the dead
as the poets lived it, just before my time,
then I was following Gerard Manley Hopkins
in priestly black up North Woodside Road
like a taunting Irish boy till I was suddenly,
stone cold sober, contemplating De Quincey
out of his mind in Rottenrow.

And all there was was
the symmetry of these turning pages,
fourteen lines mirroring fourteen lines,
the small circle of light
from the Bauhaus lamp on my borrowed desk
and the sough of trees in the Grunewald.
And outside there was Berlin.
The moneychangers at Zoostation
fanning out fistfuls of Ostmarks,
little lozenges of polystyrene, drifts and
spills from the packaging of dragged
video recorders and ghettoblasters,
blown white as hailstones and as light as popcorn
about their feet.

There was the wasted acreage of the Polish market
beside the National Gallery where

the Ein' Mark, Ein' Mark, Ein' Mark
everything cost was so slow coming in
some of these sellers-in-hell bought
bottles of berry vodka from fellow blackmarketeers
with all they'd made and more, gave up,
got too blitzed to even pretend
to peddle bits of tractor, tools, laces,
mushrooms from polluted fields
bashed tins filched from hungry Warsaw,
bumpy Eastern European school shoes
to the haggling Turkish families from
the U-bahn's Istanbul Express.

And now I'm home
with three painted Polish Easter eggs,
Hungarian opera duets, Romanian symphonies,
an uncopyrighted East German Mickey Mouse
painted the wrong colours,
funny-tasting chocolate
and the Rolling Stones 'in ctepeo'
Made in Bulgaria *Made in the Shade*.
And bits of the wall that are almost powder.
I think who could make sense of it?
Morgan could, yes Eddie could, he would.
And that makes me want to try.

AQUARIUM 1

in the fin-
de-siècle gloom
of the berlin aquarium
what little what thick
light we move through (so
slowly) is
underwater green.

lugubrious big fishes
in cross sections of small ponds
bump blunt noses
against their world's end.
there are razorbills, swords, pig snouts, fronds,
metallics, micas, twists of tiffany glass –
impossible in this changed air to say
what's animal, or vegetable, or mineral.
louvred shoals flicker open shut off on are gone.
one's a
tilted tin box
articulated awkwardly,
the next is a sinuous slip-of-a-thing
swivelling through tattered café curtains of bladderwrack
with a torchsinger's pout
to a bug-eyed audience of
little fish who roll their eyes as if to say
get this
and gasp with just-too-regular-
to-not-be-phoney
openmouthed surprise.
things pulse
like hearts and lungs
in hard-to-look-at
medical programmes on your home aquarium
and anemones bloom and close
in fast photography through
day night day night day night day
five un-shrivelling seasons every minute.
here are the lurid tentacles
of amazing latex nineteen-fifties'
Woolworths' swimming caps.
there is a real
ripper's peasouper
encased in a green glass box

and in it
one obscene frill ripples.

and this, this
is neon graffiti
writing itself, wiping itself
on a wall of water.

AQUARIUM 2

everything
looks more alive
than a crocodile
even the
slimy reptilian turds
of the crocodiles
more likely to slither
or the lumps of terrible meat
nacreous with the iridescent
sickness of the pearl on their
cruel red stumps rejoin and walk
than this shrivelled elbow or
these claws engage not a
splash or even a bubble in this
dire stink you cannot breathe in.

but the ragged long mouths
of the crocodiles and their various
species and snouts
are as indistinguishable and divers
as the sleeping hatreds of europe
and you cannot tell what crocodiles
are made of any more than the
sleeping hatreds of europe
(whether bark or hide or barnacled stone

ancient and primeval and awful)
but these sleeping monuments
are alive and dangerous
as the sleeping hatreds of europe.

THREE VISITS

one was eighty seven and hugging john and jane
at tegel then in his big beatup munich car to tadeusz's
open house on schlesische strasse slam bang against the
hard fact of the wall and schlesische tor the end of the line
for gastarbeiters tadeusz's place and the coffeepot that
never emptied kreuzberg kids in and out the trickle of the
wheels of rolf's bike as as he brought it in undoing cycle clips
and reaching for a beer and berlin lou reed's berlin belting
out big speakers in berlin by the wall you were five foot
ten inches tall it was very nice candlelight and dubonnet
on ice but it was extra ouzo all round for us at the greek
across the road where any friend of tadeusz was a friend
of the boss and tom and I slept
back in my artschool days it seemed in a borrowed
flat next door where old beaded dresses hung across
the wall in a tangle of bedclothes on the floor newbuild
newbuild newbuild with tom and john and jim arguing
architecture architecture architecture and it was
berlin 750 jahre and the biggest bigdipper in europe
checkpoint charlie where tom was stopped two hours for
carrying in mcniven's tape he wanted us to post in the east
to his musician friend boiled cabbage and you must hang up
coats in the cloakroom in the palace of culture and queue
to go up the fernsehturm to see the whole divided city
spread out below ugly ugly alexanderplatz and die
dreigroschenoper at the berliner ensemble which felt
exactly like the citz death and destruction in detroit
at the schaubühne which didn't and walls came up

enclosed us queenie lying on the floor four hours long
the play and her belly huge two weeks before louisa we stayed
up all night dancing and took the plane home reeling drunk.
two was george wylie a bird is not a stone a christmas
schoolkids' sculpture project at the wall schmuck and trees
glühwein and sugared cookies in the cold cold glittering
square around gedächtniskirche ka de we brandied fruits
like jewels jewels like brandied fruits frozen wannsee
to friedrichstrasse and duty free whisky to take to the
east berlin poetry reading in the pottery where the wheel
turned and the poets were illegal and it was nearly the
darkest day of the year the first snow of winter
nineteen eighty-eight.

three was after the wall was opened
and one single city amazed
and bursting at the seams in nineteen ninety

ALMOST-CHRISTMAS, THE WRITERS' HOUSE

Morgan, master of the Instamatic Poem,
has flung open the glass door
– three storeys up –
of this high guest suite, and,
his own camera cocked and ready,
flashgun primed,
is muttering 'Mag-ritte, Mag-grrritte'
with a mock-burr and much glee.
About to freeze-frame the scene before him.

Untouched by even a spring of birdclaw,
perfect behind wrought-iron battlements,
twenty or thirty feet of
snowy rooftop
sports a chair and round terrazzo-table

tipsily iced with an inches-deep drift.
Directly opposite
behind another rooftop door
which mirrors this,
lit up by slicing beams of anglepoise
but quite, quite empty this late at night
is the beautiful Bauhaus calm
of the office of the director of the
Literarisches Colloquium.

Behind Morgan,
Withers, Mulrine, McNaughtan, Lochhead,
well-clad, scarved and booted
stamp and laugh
(impatient for Gulaschsuppe and Berliner Weisse
at the restaurant by Wannsee S. Bahnhof)
then breathe, stilled
as his shutter falls, stopped
by this one moment's
crystalline unbroken vision
of the dreaming order in the
purring electric heart of the house of our hosts.

VII

GOOD WOOD

hardwood
softwood.
sapwood
heartwood.
firewood
dyestuffs coal and amber.
bowls broom handles platters textile rollers
maple sycamore wild cherry gean.
Paper pulp brushbacks besom heads horse jumps
birch.
alder clogs a certain special charcoal
used in the manufacture of gunpowder.
spindles dogwood skewers.
cricket bats fine willow charcoal for artists' use.
hornbeam ox-yokes
mallets cogs and butchers' chopping blocks.
walnut gunstocks
tableware veneered interiors.
poplar and aspen woodwool
chip baskets matchsticks and matchboxes.
chestnut hop poles posts and stakes.
blackthorn walking sticks
(the traditional shillelagh).
wattle wattle hurdles
peasticks beanrods heathering hazel-withes and hoops.
ash tennis
racquets billiard cues and hockey sticks.
holly for turnery inlaid work and marquetry.
larch planking.

linden hat blocks and piano keys.
grand fir noble fir douglas fir spruce cypress pine
pitprops paperpulp packing cases
roofing flooring railway sleepers and telegraph poles.
bathtime fragrances of cedarwood and sandalwood.
oak tanning pigmast panelling
and scottish fishing craft.
elmwood coffins in damp earth might warp won't split.

PAPERMAKER

for Jacki Parry at Gallowgate Studios

Rags and flowers perhaps.
What goes into the mulch of memory
is what does not always
grow on trees.

Linen, worn cotton, tattered silk are proper
for the making of fine new paper.
It must have a history
the grind of this hollander
can macerate to what is truly permanent.
Then what pulps, what fluffs of fibres!
Nothing but pure water will gloriously
plump and floss.

What do you love most of all?
Is it the gathering and beating of the fibres?
Or feeling Japanese to be in the morning marshes
gathering cattail-reeds for papermaking,
begging banana-leaf at the botanics,
hanging sheaves of marrams and marshgrasses
from your ceiling like good-cook's herbs
in a giant's kitchen –
singing 'oh I am like the barley
bags of silk'?

The long hairs of inner bark,
the essentials of feather, seed, leaf, grass,
are not like
the industrial slurry of woodpulp and linters
(this too you love:
bleached, maybe?
or dyed brilliantly).

Is it best to be more than elbow deep
in the swirled mucilage of the vat
agitating to perfect suspension
every last particle
before you panhandle with your mould and deckle?
Or is it, a minute later,
to know again your own surprising strength
when you, only just, win out against
the dreadful, draining suck
of ton weight water pouring from the mould?
You smile to yourself
satisfied to see a substance
obeying its own laws, cleaving to itself,
every fat fibre loving fibre
when you flip it, single, coherent
brand new on the blanket.
It is like a snowfall,
the first thinnest layer,
almost enough for just one snowball.

What will you make of it?
Rainmaker,
seabeach in a box,
pages from a diary,
wordless books?

Pails of dense dyes, bowls of pulp.
In the big sink continuous water drips.
Stirred up, the vat reeks of flax dams.
Unshelved
the new Japanese books concertina open
still smelling of kozo, mistumata, gampi.

A WEE MULTITUDE OF QUESTIONS
FOR GEORGE WYLIE
On his 75th birthday

Who is the man
'it pleases as much to doubt
as to be certain'?

Whose faith
is in the questioned faith?

Which Great Scot
(pronouncedly Scottish) pronounces
Scul?ture
most Scotchly with a question mark and a
glottal stop?

Who puts a question mark at the centre of everything?

Who lives unbowed under the slant of Scottish weather,
loves the white light of stones,
walks on wiry grass
and, feeling the electric earth beneath him,
turns his wide gaze to the open sea?

Who was the young sailor
who walked in a place of ash and char, fused glass, bone?
Who saw that, aye, rocks *do* melt wi' the sun
and let pulverised granite run through his fingers
like *the Sands of Time shall Run*?
(The name of the place was
Hiroshima
and in the middle of the word
was the hugest question mark.)

Who will surely
interpret for us the monograms of the stars?

Who is the man
whose name belies his nature?
(for 'wily' he is not; there is
craft in it, and art, but no guile. He is true
and straight, his strategy is honesty, and to ask –
in all innocence
in all experience –
the simplest, starkest, startling
questions.)

Who makes biting satire out of mild steel?

Who wishes to avoid Incorrect Assumptions leading to
False Conclusions? Wants us to question mark,
yen, buck, pound?

Who in *A Day Down A Goldmine* asked us to resist
the Golden Fleece, the Big 'I-con'
that would swizz us all to sell our souls?

Whose
Berlin Burd
faced an absurd
obstacle?
(Which the bird keeked over
and The Wall keeled over.)

Who, one Christmas, made
gorgeous guano-free robins
cheep in George Street, Edinburgh,
more multitudinous
than were starlings once in Glasgow's George Square?

Which George is the Captain of *The Question Mark*
and Daphne his first mate?

Whose Jubilee
was happily misspelled *Jubliee* on page thirty-five
of his lovely, jubbly, jubilee catalogue?

Who decided a locomotive might descend a staircase
and a tramcar might have wings?

Who made the out-of-order
Standing Stones walk?
Who made Holyrood into almost Hollywood
for the Festival Fringe?

Whose spires inspire us,
unquestionably celebrate?

What the devil was the de'il
wha danced away wi the exciseman?
(Art did! Art is the very devil that danced
awa wi the exciseman.)

Who is the Mad Professor up all night in the attic
inventing *The Great British Slap and Tickle Machine*?
Who is our ain
National Genius, wir true Caledonian McBrain?

Who speculates about what is
below the surface, douses, divines?
Whose rod is not a Y
but a why? Whittled to a ?
(His *by hook*, *by crook* he advances with, slowly
over rough ground in his good grasp)
his shepherd's crook;
his boat hook

hauling us aboard – hang on to your sou-westers,
shipmates, it'll likely be a bumpy ride.

In the dark spaces of our heads
divers, multitudinous, unmarked, the questions float
above a straw locomotive and a paper boat.

WARPAINT AND WOMANFLESH
for Lys Hansen, painter

because the flesh can be
tortured
because the flesh can be
raped
because the flesh can be
mutilated
because the flesh can be
burned
because the flesh can be
scorned
because the flesh can be
corsetted within the skin
because the rage can be
held in
the flesh must be painted.

because the skin can be
displayed
because the skin can be
flayed
because the skin can be bruised used abused
gorgeously gored gilded
pierced grafted grazed greased
split slit skelped scuffed stretched scratched scored stroked
caked with make-up
tanned tattooed tabooed
because the skin
can be the tip of the iceberg
because
the skin
can be the bag with all the boiling blood and bones within
the skin must be painted.

because the lip can be
any of your and all of your
old lip
because the lip is tender
because the lip can slip
because the lip can kiss and tell
because the lip can frame the mouth that is the mouth of hell
because the lip can be
lipsticked slicked smeared larded lauded glossed bossed
                                            breached
because the lip can be zipped
the lip must be painted.

because of the white of the eye
because of the white lie
because of the truth of the colour of fire
because of the iris of desire
because
the limb can be akimbo
the limb can be dismembered
because the love can be remembered
because the lady can be sawn in half
because the lady can bellylaugh
because the lady's got guts
because the lady's not for turning
because of the good times
because of the war crimes
because of the iron maiden
because of the presidential wink
because of everything except the kitchen sink
Lys Hansen must be always painting.

THE JOURNEYMAN PAUL CÉZANNE ON
MONT SAINTE VICTOIRE

for James Runcie

What do I paint when I paint the blue
vase, the hanged man's house,
the still life of Hortense's hands
arranged on the still life of her lap,
domestic arabesques
of the red armchair, petrified drapery,
this mountain?
I paint
the blue in the blue
the red in the blue,
the violet in the gold,
this mountain.
The cylinder, the cone, the sphere,
this mountain.
In the light of perfect logic
this mountain built of paint more permanent than stone:
constructed.

An apple, an orange, a ball, a head –
every day this mountain.
When that critic called me 'a carpenter
with paint', he did not insult
this journeyman!
Colour can move, can make, mountains.

VIII

YEAR 2K EMAIL EPISTLE TO CAROL ANN DUFFY
Sister-poet & Friend of my Youth

Duffy, *I'm fifty-two* – how come?
I'm a wife. You're over forty and a mum.
Clichés like *tempus fugit, yeah it's going some*
Fall from our lips.
– While into each new moment, day, millennium
Your Ella skips.

Ella skips. Time marches on. We're history
By two thousand and something or other, A.D.
If *forward though we canna see*
We guess and fear,
We'll live as though we don't, OK? From me –
Happy New Year.

BLACK AND WHITE ALLSORTS
for Jackie Kay

a liquorice bootlace
a cultured pearl necklace
a little black dress
lux flakes, snowflakes
sno-pake, Tipp-Ex
a black bra
a zebra, an op-art umbrella
ebony, ivory, black Sobranie, a skunk
a black eye, a white feather, a pool of printers ink

a brand-new *broderie anglais* bikini
pasta al nero di seppia (squid ink linguini)
one single earring of jingling jet
and, like a big black sugar-cube, a perfect *briquette*
black suede boots just out of the box
and, to go with your good black patent shoes, pet,
new white socks

coconut, caviar, a wee pet lamb
a jar of home-made blackcurrant jam
spilt salt, wet tar, black ointment, The Broons
a box of Black Magic and an old black-and-white
on a Sunday afternoon
a white dove
a long black glove
a scoosh of mousse, the full moon
a soot crust, a snowball, a Lee's macaroon
a meringue, mascara,
a dollop of Nivea
talc on black lino
the (shuttered) dark
a dropped domino

a white angora bolero
two daft dalmations in the snow
in Kelvingro-
ve park

HELL FOR POETS

It's Hell for the poet arriving for the gig
Off the five thirty-three to meet the organiser
Who claps her in a car that reeks enough of dog to make her gag,
Tells her he's *looked at her work* but he was none the wiser.
Call him old fashioned, but in the 'little mag
He edits for his sins' stuff *rhymes* – oh, he's no sympathiser
With this modern stuff! Is it *prose*? What is it?
Perhaps the poet can enlighten him this visit?

– For which his lady-wife's made up a futon hard as boulders
In the boxroom. 'So much *friendlier* than an hotel!'
Will anyone turn up tonight? Shrug of his shoulders.
'Even for *McGough* or *Carol Ann Duffy* tickets have not been
                                                    going well.
Meanwhile: here's *his* stuff.' Each ode encased in plastic in
                                                    three folders.
'Publishable?' Perhaps she'll advise him where to sell
Over a bottle of home-made later? Oh shit. She can tell
This is going to be The Gig from Hell . . .

But it's real hell for *real* poets when love goes right
When the war is over and the blood, the mud, the Muse depart
Requited love, gratified desire 'write white'
And suffering's the sweetest source for the profoundest art.
Blue skies, eternal bliss, bland *putti* – Heaven might
Not be the be all and end all . . . ? For a start
Hell itself's pure inspiration to the creatively driven.
Hell was (f'rinstance) Dante's idea of Hog Heaven.
Hell's best! Virgil knew it too before him. Heigh ho!
Man calls himself a poet? St Peter'll bounce him.
(Unless he's maybe Milton – it's Who You Know.)
Could end up in Hell with Burns? (Hear his rolling r's announce him).

Could end up with Villon, Verlaine, the Rabelaisian Rimbaud,
With Don Juan, *Don Whan* – however you pronounce him –
Bunked up with Byron, still so mad, so bad, and so delic-
iously dangerous to know? Not a snowball's chance, but oh, *I wish.*

ALMOST MISS SCOTLAND

The night I
almost became Miss Scotland,
I caused a big stramash
when I sashayed on in my harristweed heathermix onepiece
and my 'Miss Garthamlock' sash.

I wis six-fit-six, I wis slinky
(yet nae skinnymalinky)
my waist was nipped in wi elastic,
my powder and panstick were three inches thick,
nails? Long, blood-rid and plastic.
so my big smile'd come across, I'd larded oan lipgloss
and my false eyelashes were mink
with a sky-blue crescent that was pure iridescent
when I lowered my eyelids to blink.

Well, I wiggled tapselteerie, my heels were that peerie
while a kinna Jimmy Shandish band
played 'Flower of Scotland' –
but it aw got droont oot wi wolf whistles –
and that's no countin 'For These Are My Mountains'
– see I'd tits like nuclear missiles.

Then this familiar-lukkin felly
I'd seen a loat oan the telly
interviewed me aboot my hobbies –
I says: Macrame, origami,
being nice tae my mammy –
(basically I tellt him a loat o jobbies).
I was givin it that
aboot my ambition to chat
to handicapped and starvin children from other nations

– how I was certain I'd find
travel wid broaden my mind
as I fulfilled my Miss Scotland obligations.

Well, I wis in Seventh Heaven
to be in the Final Seven –
but as the Judges retired
to do what was required
and pick the furst, second and thurd
well, the waiting was murder and it suddenly occurred
there was something *absurd*
aboot the hale position
of being in competition
wi other burds like masel
who I should of kennt very well
were ma sisters (at least under the skin)
yet fur this dubious prize I'd have scratched oot their eyes
and hoped they'd git plooks, so I'd win!
Aye, there wis somethin ridic'lous
aboot sookin in wi thae prickless
wonders o judges, their winks and their nudges.
Wan wee baldy comedian bloke
whose jokes were a joke,
wan heuchter-choochter singer who wis a dead ringer
for a cross between a pig in a tartan poke
and a constipated bubblyjock,
plus wan well-known soak –
a member of our Sporting Fraternity
who was guaranteed his place in Eternity
as a well-pickled former member of the Scotland Squad.
And the likes of them were Acting God,
being Real Men,
scoring *us* on a scale of one to ten –
they'd compare and contrast, and then at last
they'd deign to pronounce
and reverse-order-announce it.

Then I wid simper, look sweet, an
I'd burst oot greetin
gasp 'Who me' – the usual story –
they'd plonk me down, stick on the Miss Scotland crown
to crown my crowning glory.

How would *thae guys* like to be a prize –
a cake everybody wanted a slice of –
have every leering schoolgirl consider them a pearl
everybody kennt the price of?
How would *they* like their mums to say that their bums
had always attracted the Ladies' Glances,
and nothing wrang wi it, they'd aye gone alang wi it
and encouraged them to take their chances?
And they were Good Boys, their Mum's Pride & Joys,
saving it for their Future Wives?
And despite their fame they still steyed at hame
and lived real clean-living lives?

In a blinding flash I saw the hale thing was trash
– I just Saw Rid
and here's whit I did:

– Now I'd love to report that I was the sort
to speak out and convince the other lassies
pick bones wi aw the chaperones
and singlehandedly convert the masses
till in a bacchanalian Revenge of the Barbie Dolls
crying 'All for One and One for All!'
we'd advance on the stage, full of bloodlust and rage –
but, I cannot tell a lie, the truth is that I
just stuck on my headsquerr and snuck away oot o therr –
I know I did right, it wisnae contrary –
and I let my oaxters grow back in
really rid and thick and hairy.

Because the theory of feminism's aw very well
but yiv got tae see it fur yirsel
every individual hus tae realise
her hale fortune isnae in men's eyes,
say enough is enough
away and get stuffed.

IN THE BEGINNING

There was this man alone
in a beautiful garden.
Stark bollock naked
(scuse my French, beg your pardon).

He was, yes, the original Nature's Gentleman.
He was in tune, at one, with nature
and the lion lay down with the lamb,
each peaceable creature
knew its place in the Order of Things.
(Hey, if God had meant men to be angels
he'd have given them wings).

The climate was brilliant
the weather was sunny
the whole land flowed with
milk and honey
soothing fragrant grasses
waved verdant in the breeze
breadfruit baked itself in the sun
and fell out of the trees
where, by the way, songbirds were singing
with bees for a backing
– oh a right bed of roses!
But there was . . . Something Lacking

he couldny put his finger on it,
he was in a right tizz.
But, the Lord Our God being a Male God,
he knew exactly whit it wis . . .

A slave.

And soon she was worn to a frazzle
waiting on His Nibs
ironing his figleaves
barbecuing his ribs

while home came the hunter
with the bacon for the table
she was stuck raising Cain
and breastfeeding Abel.

Him: the Big Breid-winner
her: a Machine for Breedin
barescud and pregnant?
Some Garden of Eden!

The sort of sexist division of labour
that went out with the Ark –
i.e. the nuclear family –
bugger that for a lark.

So they were both ripe for revolting
when that slimy serpent came
but – would you Adam and Eve it? –
She got the blame.

Oh Eve took the rap
Eve got framed
Eve was the fall-girl
she got the blame.

THE BALLAD OF MARY SHELLEY'S CREATURE

The man who made him – the real monster –
was the man called Frankenstein.
He said I'll try it by science not sorcery
till the Secret of Life is mine.

So Frankenstein to college went
abandoned alchemy,
found himself a famous Professor
of Natural Philosophy.

Long, long in the laboratory,
and at the dissecting table
he'll find the Mystery that is Man
if anyone is able.

And deep deep in the dustiest books
from off the highest shelves –
he's made a pledge to wrest knowledge
where no man safely delves.

And late, late in the charnel house
where pale cadavers grin
he's unwound the worms that feed on the flesh
when Death shall let them in.

Among pockmarked victims of the plague
and cut-up casualties of war
dead for weeks, or with the flush still in their cheeks,
he's mined for precious ore.

He's tinkered with the mechanics of muscles,
tightened sinews in between.
he might, who knew the machine that was Man,
make a man of a machine?

but he couldn't cultivate a homunculus
or jerk him with the galvanist's jolt
till the simple secret struck him
clean as a lightning bolt.

Thus Frankenstein has stolen the spark
that makes all the living draw breath –
he knows that who can once create Life
soon may triumph over Death.

He clinks his glass against a test tube,
toasts the Triumph of the Will
and the bloodiest stash of his most ghoulish cache
is grist to his ghastly mill.

And long, long, in the laboratory
as late as he is able
with a hellish dolly-rag of a charnel-house bag
stretched out on the table.

His brow is of the abattoir,
the jawbone of an ox,
limb by limb he's constructed him –
ten-foot-two in his socks.

He's threading up his backbone beads
stitches his hide with a pleat and a tuck
from discarded spare parts of the surgeon's dark arts
makes him arms like a fork-lift truck

he has a bolt in his neck and a zip in his cheek
and a ripped-off shroud for a quilt –
nature's assembly line may be all very fine
but this is custom-built,

and correct to every last living detail,
oiled in every working part.
He has a clockwork brain resistant to pain
but a resurrected human heart.

Frankenstein smiles down on his creature,
feels himself to be without blame.

He's going to pull that lever and nothing
will ever be the same.

LADY OF SHALOTT

Fifteen or younger
she moons in the mirror.
Penny for your thoughts,
Lady of Shalott.
In her bedroom tower
with mother and father
watching T.V. downstairs,
she moons in the mirror
and swears she will never
lead a bloody boring life like theirs.

Maybe you'll find true romance
at the youth club dance,
Lady of Shalott.

She paints her nails scarlet,
she moons in the mirror.
Ingénue or harlot?
The mirror is misted,
every mirror image twisted –
like real life but larger.
That kid-glove dream love
a knight on a charger.
Sure,
you can lure
him, keep him enslaved,
buy him Christmas aftershave.

She moons in the mirror
asks it to tell her
she's every bit as pretty as the other
gadfly girls.

Yes, you'll tangle him in your curls,
my Lady of Shalott.

Maybe tonight's the night for
true romance.
And you'll find him at the youth club dance,
Lady of Shalott.

But alas
no handsome prince to dare
ask Rapunzel to let down her hair.
Her confidence cracked from side to side,
by twelve o'clock her tattered pride
is all Cinders stands in.
You're the wallflower the fellows all forgot,
Lady of Shalott.
Oh, how she wishes she could pass
like Alice through the looking glass.
You're waiting to be wanted,
my fairy-tale haunted,
Lady of Shalott.

Silver dance shoes in her pocket,
no one's photo in her locket,
home along through the night.
On either side suburban gardens lie,
bungalows and
bedded boxed-in couples high and dry.

But you're
lovely in the lamplight,
my Lady of Shalott.

ADVICE TO OLD LOVERS

How to be the perfect Old Love. The etiquette?
Well, smile at her a smile that hints at gentle but infinite regret
(when you bump into her, years later, at, say, one-of-the-old
                              crowd's 'Big Four O')
project a certain sense of 'if-you'd-known-then-what-now
                              you-know . . .'
suggest (wordlessly) that once upon a time you were a lucky
                              so-and-so,
then, when she loved you better than she should of
and you were so mad about her that it was for the good of
both of you, that you split, but – once, oh yes, you could of.

That should go down well. Well, you know women
do dance with her by all means. To – e.g. – 'Still Crazy
After All These Years' by Paul Simon and she'll be swimming,
I guarantee it, in sentiment, nostalgia and hazy
but potent memories of how, together, you were terrific.
Please, though, have the manners to refrain from anything
                              too tastelessly *specific*,
do steer clear of anything that might embarrass
on your little light-and-laughing sorties down Memory Lane.
Don't remind her of that night on the hearthrug after *Last
                              Tango in Paris*
well, nobody wants to go raking all *that* up again.
No apologies. No post-mortems. As Billie Holliday will have
                              it: Don't Explain.

No 'I-didn't-mean-to-hurt-yous'. Nothing worse.
If you broke her heart have the grace to imply that, the way
                              you remember it, it was quite the reverse.
Some subtler variation on 'We-were-My-God-*wild*-together
                              but-quite-incompatible,
you-drove-me-mad-it-was-impossible!'

That's the line to take. It flatters both,
is more morale-boosting all round than the truth.

And gentle ego-stroking's what it's for. You might just mention
her Bloke and Your Wife are getting a touch jealous of the
attention
you are paying each other, but what the hell –
you always loved each other not wisely but too well.

Don't tell her current Younger Man that she was brilliant at
the Twist.
Do be married to someone who has an even worse record than
her as a Weight Watchers recidivist.
But, please, be ageing well yourself. Not sad, seedy or pissed
or boring, or balding, or wearing a nylon shirt.
To find an Old Love ludicrous, that's what would hurt!
Well, nobody likes to think they misspent their misspent youth
with someone they can't-see-what-they-once-saw-in-and-
that's-the-truth.
The last thing she wants is to see her current love laughing up
his sleeve –
(*'That's* the guy you tried to slit your wrists over? I find that
hard to believe!
You were six months on Valium? It almost did you in?
That's the guy who really *made the coloured lights spin?'*)
No: if your Brief Re-encounter is to be entirely mutually
delightful and not at all stressful
you ought, really, ideally, to be almost (but not quite) as handsome
and successful
as the man in her life now, if this can be arranged.

and – if you ever loved her – *tell her she hasn't changed.*

SEXUAL ETIQUETTE

Sexual etiquette,
sexual etiquette,
how to get more of it
and get more out of what you get.

I wonder if you realize
how across this once-proud nation
night-in night-out
there's thousands of women on the receiving end
of premature ejaculation.

See, there's women knowing what they want
but being too shy to mention
so that what ought to be
a fountain of joy
is more of a bone of contention.

Sexual etiquette,
sexual etiquette,
how to get more of it
and get more out of what you get.

How to ask – very nicely –
yet sufficiently precisely.

If your husband tends to kiss you
as if you were his auntie,
if he thinks that a clitoris
is a flowering potted plant, he

really *needs* sexual etiquette,
Sexual etiquette –
how to (a) get more of it
and (b) get more out of what you get.

If he's rolled over and snoring while you're
screaming, 'Not yet!'
if it's a romantic anniversary but he tends to forget,
if he treats you like you're
a refugee from *Auf Wiedersehen Pet*,

He needs sexual etiquette,
sexual etiquette.

MY WAY

I only did it for a laugh
I did it because I'm a fool for love
I did it because push had come to shove
I did it because – my age – I've got nothing to prove

But I did it
I did it
I did it
Yes I did

I did it to settle an argument with a friend
I did it to drive our Hazel round the bend
I did it to get one over on our kid
I did it to nip it in the bud
I did it that way because I couldn't stand the sight of blood

But I did it
I did it
I did it
Yes I did

I did it to bury the hatchet and get a night's sleep
I did it to get out before I was in too deep
I did it to piss on his chips and put his gas at a peep

But I did it
I did it
I did it –
Mea absolutely culpa, me!

I did it to go out in a blaze of glory
I did it to make them listen to my side of the story
I only did it to get attention
I did it to get an honourable mention
I did it to put an end to it all
I did it for . . . no reason at all

But I did it
I did it
I did it
Yes I did

FUGITIVE COLOURS

(2016)

I. LOVE & GRIEF,

ELEGIES & PROMISES

FAVOURITE PLACE

We would be snaking up Loch Lomond, the
road narrow and winding after the turn at Tarbet,
and we'd be bending branches as we slid
through the green and dripping overhang of the trees.
All the bickering over the packing, and the – as usual –
much, much later-than-we'd-meant-to-be-leaving,
all that falling from us,
our moods lifting, lightening, becoming our good mood
the more miles we put
between our freed-and-weekend selves and Glasgow.

Driving in the dark meant: slot in another CD
without even looking at what it is,
just any old silver disc from the zippered case
that, when you reminded me, I'd have quickly stuffed
far too full and randomly, then jammed it,
last minute, into the top of my rucksack.
Golden oldies, yours or mine, whose favourite?
Anyway, the music would spool us through Tyndrum,
past the shut Real Food Café where other days we like to stop,
and over moonscape Rannoch Moor to the
moonlit majesty of Glencoe,
over the bridge at Ballachulish, past Corran
with the ferry stilled and the loch like glass;
we'd be wriggling along Loch Linnhe then straighten up
past the long strip of darkened lochside big hotels and their
Vacancies or *No Vacancies* signs

to 30 mph Fort William –
Full-Of-Rain-Town-With-Its-Limitless-Litres-In-A-Mist! –
we'd shout it out and we'd be honouring a
long-ago and someone else's
family pass-the-time
car-journey game we never even played, but Michael,
proud of his teenage wordsmith son,
once told us about – and it has stuck.
We'd be speeding up now, taking the bend's wide sweep as
we bypass the sleeping town, making for
the second-last turn-off: *Mallaig and The Road To the Isles*.
And you'd say,
'Last thirty miles, Lizzie, we'll be there by midnight.'

The always longest fifteen miles from Glenfinnan to Lochailort
and a wee cheer at the last turn,
down past the big house and the fish farm,
beyond the lay-by – full of travellers' ramshackle vans
now the yellow's on the broom again –
our eyes peeled now for the white-painted stone so we'll not miss
the overgrown entrance to the field of caravans.

There would be that sigh of
always-glad-to-see our old van still standing,
opening the door, the sniffing – no dampness, no mice . . .
I'd be unloading the first cool-bags of food,
while you'd be round the van's side, down in the mud
turning the stopcock for the water,
fixing the gas – and soon,
breathing a big sigh, laughing in relief at
how that huge stag
that had suddenly filled the windscreen a mile back
stopping our hearts as – ho! – we'd shouted our alarm –
had somehow astonishly leapt free, was gone,
and no harm done,
we'd be lighting candles, pouring a dram,

drinking the first cup of tea
from the old black and white teapot.

And tonight the sky would be huge with stars.
Tomorrow there would be the distant islands
cut out of sugar paper, or else cloud, the rain in great veils
coming in across the water, the earliest tenderest
feathering of green on the trees, mibbe autumn
laying bare the birches stark white.
There would be blood-red rowan berries, that bold robin
eating from my plate again, or – for a week or two in May –
the elusive, insistent cuckoo,
or else the slow untidy flapping of the flight of the heron,
the oil-black cormorant's disappear-and-dive,
shifts of sun, double or even treble rainbows.
The waterfall would be a wide white plume or a
thin silver trickle, depending . . .
There would be bracken's early unfurling or
late summer's heather pinking and purpling over, there'd be a
plague of hairy caterpillars and the last drunken bees.
Mibbe you'd nudge me, and, hushed,
again we'd watch that otter swim to shore
on New Year's Day with a big fish in its mouth, emerge
so near us on the flat rocks we
wouldn't dare to breathe as we'd watch it,
unconcerned, oblivious,
make a meal of eating it before our eyes.
Or it would be a late Easter this year and,
everywhere along the roadside,
the chrome-yellow straight-out-of-the-tube-and-
laid-on-with-a palette-knife brashness,
the amazing coconut smell of the gorse.

But tonight you are three months dead
and I must pull down the bed and lie in it alone.
Tomorrow, and every day in this place

these words of Sorley MacLean's will echo through me:
The world is still beautiful, though you are not in it.
And this will not be a consolation
but a further desolation.

PERSIMMONS
for Tom

You must've loved
those three globes of gorgeous orange
dense and glowing in our winter kitchen
enough
to put coloured pencil and biro to the
reddest page left in your rainbow sketchbook
and make this drawing of
three persimmons in that Chinese bowl.

The supermarket flagged them up as
this season's Sharon fruit
but we prefer persimmon (for
didn't it seem the rose of
their other name
would neither taste or sound as sweet,
would be a fruit of quite
another colour?)

Such strange fruit . . . we bit and ate,
enjoyed.
Before we did you drew them.
– *oh*, you'd say, *so what?*
(drawing, to you, is as everyday as apples)
but I know
they'd have come and gone like Christmas
if you'd not put them down
and made them worth more than the paper
they're inscribed on – see
those deft soft strokes of
aquamarine and white that
make our tabletop lie flat, the fruits
plump out real and round and
perfectly persimmon-coloured

upon their lilac shadows in the bowl's deep –
still life
still life, sweetheart,
in what's already eaten and done with.

Now, looking, I can taste again.

A HANDSELLING, 2006

1. TWENTY-ONE-YEAR-OLD

On our first night at Jura Lodge you say,
'here's a bottle of the Twenty-One-Year-Old,
hey Lizzie, let's taste . . . ' and we toast
– once we've managed to track two nip glasses down –
oh there they are of course, my deah,
on the decanter tray,
mayhap, in the Music Room!
I laugh, oh I have to, as you slosh us each
a generous inch or more of gold, yes
you gently clink your glass with mine
and we toast our good fortune and the holiday to come.

All holidays
are whole small lives lived somewhere else
and all lives consist, in part, of habits
but we don't yet know this will be
one of the habits of this holiday –
on the long
light
nights of July
to sit astride that pair of purple velvet stools in the big
bay window of the Music Room looking out to the bay
with our
big brand-new sketch books balanced before us and
something more than twenty-one-years-old and easy-listening
playing – like old Van Morrison
predicting it's a *marvellous night for a moondance*
or Dylan groaning *out tangled up in blue*
as I scrabble for that and every other colour, for
on the little gaming table between us
a jumble of oil pastels and coloured Conté crayon
is rolling around our rested whisky glasses –

occasionally savoured and sipped from, but never refilled –
as busily, fluently, more or less silently,
we sketch and scratch away and scribble
not stopping till – late – all the last of the light is gone
and we can't see
either what we're drawing or the marks we've made.

It'll be tomorrow
before I can enjoy the garish glad-handed sweep
you've made of a bit of the bay and pier and shrug
to see how hopeless was my
daft task of putting down the ever-changing sky
with its bands and streaks and shifting clouds
and almost every colour
except
sky blue.
But in spite of what
– on paper – neither of us captured
neither of us I'd bet
has ever been happier or easier with a crayon in our hands
since we were five years old –
nor less self-critical about the outcome, so
we can look at the nothing much we've caught
(*happiness writes white* said Philip Larkin) and
remember last night's peace
and us watching the always eventful nothing happening
as the light spilled from the poolroom of the hotel
and the players' movements went like fiddlers' elbows,
remember how now and then one person,
sometimes joined by another, then another
might linger by the back door with a smoke
and how – till it got too dark –
you could see the laughter you were far too far away to hear.

2. SOME THINGS I COVET IN JURA LODGE

(even though my Tom finds them just a wee bit too much)

that fearsomely fantastical
armchair upstairs made entirely of antlers and deerhide like
    something out of Cocteau's *La Belle et la Bête*
the tinpot suit of armour
the little green chipped 1940s kitchen chairs
the lobster creel for a lampshade
the pink teacup the typewriter the old black phone
the old scuffed leather sofa the red Paisley throw
the floral lining of the Edwardian cabin trunk in the Rose Room
the Mozart-printed cushions in the Music Room
that big mad portrait in the Portrait Room
of some little plumed Lord Fauntleroy riding on a goat!
the tall French mirror in the Portrait Room
the huge shell in the White Room
the bluebirds
on the glass fingerplate in the Bluebird Room
the tipsy wooden seagull
on the bedside table in the Bluebird Room
the Victorian ladies' hunting jacket
the American Folk Art hangers with the heart-shaped cut-outs
the tall window in the hall
on the blue wall
with the perfectly framed view of one of the Paps

3. CORNUCOPIA

Darling, it is your birthday.
This would be the twentieth we have woken up to together
– except last year you were in hospital
and I woke alone at home early in our empty wide bed
thinking of you a mile away in that
bleak narrow one with the hospital corners.

Today I woke first – the sun so bright it almost hurt
streaming in through that swathe of white linen at the window
and, picture of health, your head on the pillow
ablaze in its storm of grey curls I love.
Caught the sun, caught the sun, my love,
didn't you, yesterday
on our first full day on the Isle of Jura?

Was it late in the afternoon, exposed on that
clifftop walk we took from above the Ferry at Feolin past
Sailor's Grave towards Inver and the ruins of Cnocbreac?
Was it earlier in the deceptively dappled light
on the walk to Jura House Garden?
On the shore path at Ardfin, where the
fuschia flared and the flagrant rhododendrons blossomed
along the loud banks of the Abhainn Beag Burn?
Was it when we took our picnic of
oatcakes and cheese and apple and lay in the sun
against the rocks at Traigh Bhan, the White Beach,
where those five blonde, tall
teenage lads, down from the Big House, no doubt,
were splashing and shouting in the surf till they
ran out, shaking themselves like dogs, laughing,
then paused to pass a pleasant time of day with such
impeccable public-school good manners
it was almost parodic?
Was it when, alone again on the empty beach,
we squinted into the sun
and looked for Heather Island and the ruined castle, argued
whether in the distance
what we could see was Arran, Kintyre or Ireland
and you were trying to persuade me that
it might just be worth it to brave the water's cold?
Or did we catch too much sun later
in the blaze of the gardens,
among the astonishing arches, barbered slopes

and walled gardens of exuberant exotica?
Was it when I lingered in the shade of the sheds
selecting us each an artichoke for supper,
till, leaving the money in the trustbox,
I came out into the sun again to
see you with Peter Cool, the gardener,
who was showing you, cupped in his hand, that
perfect-looking house-martin that somehow could not fly?

No, I think we burned up
as we were drawing by the tea-tent,
you and I facing in different directions
and so engrossed in what we were doing
we didn't notice time passing or the sun beating down
or those so cheeky chaffinches sneaking under
the paper napkins to steal our lemon cake.
Yes, we must have spent an hour, more,
you with your big blue A3 sketchbook, I with my green.
Your choice (outward) was wild meadow, trees, sky, sea
mine, didn't know why, simply the tea-tent.
Was it that in my mind sang out the first line
of the sonnet *She is as in a field a silken tent*?
Was it the cool dark of its interior, taut ropes,
the festive arabesques of its tent-white roof
against the intricate sky?
The swipe of its bonny blue awning?

Was it my longing to
loop across the page with blue those scalloped edges
and dot the tall swathes of long grass and wildflower
with poppies, kingcups, dandelions and something blue?
I remember when it was time to pack up you said,
OK, a challenge, five minutes, we change sides
and draw the other person's view and, as it happened,
in five minutes
you caught more than I had in that whole hour.

Wake up, my twenty-years' love, and see
how many things can happen
today, for
that whisky we had a nip of last night had already
made it to its bourbon cask for ageing
when your Dionysus curls were black as grapes
and I buried my face in them on the
first
of the lovely,
finite
birthdays we'll have together.

Wake up, wake up
in this ridiculous room with
the huge shell bigger than a basin on the chest of drawers
for this is a house of many concetti
and here where we sleep
the motifs
are the coral and the scallop and the conch,
a mollusc multitude
of small shells that are cockles whorls and spirals
tiny dishes of mother-of-pearl and unicorn horns all
spilling from the ceiling's chandelier
like grapes from a cornucopia.
So wake up, won't you,
and enjoy being us
inside the shell of this morning here in the White Room?
In the bleached light the only colour
your old blue tee-shirt over the back of the basket chair
and the mottled, bottled shells
in those glass jars beside that great pile of blue-grey, slate-grey,
sea-washed pebbles
making a raised beach of the mantelpiece.

The big deep roll-top bath that stands in this bedroom
is the biggest and shiniest shell of all,

its inside so new it's nacreous.
Oh, I'm going to let the
Buck's Fizz we always have on birthday breakfasts
spill over
as I lie up to my neck in bubbles,
swigging it, be the
oldest, plumpest, homeliest, happiest,
most shameless Aphrodite on the half shell –
white curtains wide open
to the astonishing un-Scottish sun and the dazzling sea
and you, my love,
sprawled across the bed opposite
talking to me and opening your presents.

Word in your shell-like, sweetheart,
wake up!
With your birthday
a whole day
a holiday
before us.

4. NO EXCUSE, BUT HONESTLY

it's hard to draw
Jura's beauty –
foxgloves and fuchsia far too flashy for
just black and white
hard to write –
the mountains with their purple passages
the long curve of empty road
the wide swathe of empty moor
the too-blue-for-Scotland sky
this
intricacy of thistles
far too intent on being emblematic

5. LEGACY

Scribbled in my Jura notebook:

here the willow is called the sallow
today we saw an adder its
arrow markings & that slither-under
also a pair of eagles up near Three Arched Bridge
v. big! the first rose up from long grass with smthng in its talons

J
U
R
A

written so
long & thin up & down the lovely shape of it on tht old map
there are 2 brand-new crofthouses at Ardfernal and Knockrome
and Gwen the busdriver is v. happy (new
children for the school) thanx 2 Crfting Commission
Tarbert Inverlussa Lowlandman's Bay
Barnhill Orwell E. Blair TB motorbike 1984
Corrievrechan? (sp?)
Corryvreakan?
Corryvreckan (!)
Cauldron of Breakan (superstition) Devil's washing tub
Wow!!!! Corryvreckan really whirls well worth the
long shoogle in Landrover & the climb
loaded pleasure boats so far below
come out from Crinan to dare Corryvreckan
I wouldn't!
Corran Sands so wide and empty xcept fr
tht one wee boy in a red sunhat with hs spade
Corran Sands yes – Scotland! – swam (not cold!)
Shy red-haired lad at Friday Ceildh fantastc dancer (best)
6,500 deer 170 people (cull Autmn annual)
Craighouse Dstillry palmtrees hotel
Bay of Small Isles

Small Isles Bay
squat lobster tails delish – at the hotel (birthday dinner)
deer so many herds so close U can see
the velvet on their antlers calm as cattle cropping grass
wot abt those ducks! Mergansers? Eiders?
Came def. conversing – cos we heard them –
flock of 12 from out at sea somewhere in to pier
then simult. all dive –
under fr ages!
every 1 xcept 1 bck up with 1 pink fish in beak
distillery tour from Margaret (Islay orig.)
peat-reek barley smoky air
grist mash tun wort hopper
mill maltster 20 thousand litres of water
(Market Loch) maun yeast sugars
copper stills lantern or half-ball stills
feints 'low-wines' the foreshots and the tails
20 millings a wk
20 maltings
10 washbacks
not whsky unless oak cask in Scotland minimum 3 years
sherry butts Spain (oloroso)
Isle of Jura aged in Bourbon Casks
brought frm far America & charred inside
88 degrees 78% alcohol
Tom saw an otter up close & swimming
down by the ferry Sat. jst as we were leaving

In my sketchbook:

Monday: clouds, clouds, Tom (profile)
Tuesday: tea tent at Ardfin Gardens, quick calligraphic landscape
Wednesday: Camas an Staca – Standing Stone/ sheep/ Islay ferry
Thursday: nothing (Corryvreckan trip, Land Rover then long trek)
Friday: the wee boy in the red hat
UL72 the blue boat (best sketch yet though at the time felt

just wasn't working)
and last was from
the pier-end in black and white
Craighouse stretched out
underneath
the Paps

and
home with
in the winter
a nip
of Legacy to sip.

Note: during the extraordinarily fine July of 2006, my husband Tom and I had the great good fortune to be – as guests of a Scottish Book Trust writer-in-residence scheme – the very first people to sleep in the brand-new, bonny and baroque (just designed and redecorated 'by the Paris interior decorator Bambi Sloan', it said) Jura Lodge, where we spent five days and nights, handselling it.

LAVENDER'S BLUE

In memory of Adrian Mitchell

First of April, old friend,
best of friends
and you are three months dead.
Fool's Day and I wish you'd jump up and
shout *huntigowk!* and it
would turn out to be the cruellest joke.
But no, it's true – 2009, and you'd have none of it,
three months in and this whole bloody
turning world
has piled new atrocities and lies on old
– Gaza's latest hell happened
without you to sing the song
of simple *this is wrong*

You're gone
and, boy, we're going to miss you

So
I'm out in the new April sunshine of Sauchiehall Street
buying the best two books of nursery rhymes
for two brand-new babies – thinking of you
not dead
any more than the *other* Adrian
or Burns or Byron or Bix – yes,
there you go, chewing the fat with John Keats
walking Daisy the Dog of Peace
on Hampstead Heath

Boys and girls come out to play
the moon doth shine as bright as day –

now there's too little action,
too much talk:
when the bottle's open,
throw away the cork

your books ain't on my bookshelves,
but in my heart and on my kitchen table
and you tell me to just sing my own silly songs
as well as I am able.

THE OPTIMISTIC SOUND

In memory of Michael Marra

'I'd wheel my wheelbarrow up Kilimanjaro' – from the Michael Marra
song, 'If Dundee Was Africa'

'Make the optimistic sound' – from the Michael Marra song, 'Like Another
Rolling Stone'

Today
one of the hundreds of friends at your funeral
was just desperate to tell me the story of when he first met you,

'Michael just came on, sat down at the piano,
started singing and och! . . .
anyway, after he was finished and we were
standing together in the wings, well,
I was that over the moon I was
jist gittering on and on I was, about how
knocked out I was, and here onstage the orchestra
had started and he was quite entitled
to tell me to shut it, anybody else
would have just said *shut up!* – it was called for –
but no, he just puts his finger to his lip, says
ssh! so soft you could hardly hear him and one word, whispered:
listen.
That was Michael.'

This morning Marianne and James and I
drove past your house around the corner.
Drawn curtains, and
I thought of Peggy pressing her good black clothes, Alice
bringing her a strong hot cup of tea I hoped, Matthew
mibbe polishing everybody's shoes, and –
this was Marianne's good and right idea –

we went on to where you
went every day you were at home
to see the ospreys.

October's end and an empty nest.
That big bunchy structure of sticks and moss not
ramshackle in the least but
firm, safe as houses in the high winds,
not perched but planted,
strong and wild and grand as the absent birds themselves
on top of its high pylon, a nest
returned to every year for decades now,
a local secret easily visible from the long straight road
bordered in tall trees and this year's
extra braw show of bright autumn colour.
In a line of pylons striding across a flat plain field
in farmland in Angus, that one flat top
crowned by the ospreys' nest,
and, in the electric air,
all around the slow leaves falling.

Michael,
how proud you were – most years –
if you were home – to witness the young ones' maiden flight,
how determined this year not to miss it.

And there was silence, Michael.
Not even a whisper of rustling leaves,
the wind dropped and just one great leaf took an age
to come spiralling to the ground in
perfect silence.
Till suddenly a honking and a ragged vee of urgent birds,
wings beating in double time, forming and
reforming as they went their
flock-perfect travelling shape as best they could as

they crossed the wide sky above the ospreys' nest in no time
and I don't know if it was an optimistic sound or not
but anyway it was the sound of being alive, and they were making it.
Wild geese
coming back from their far cold wherever
to winter here
as if they were ospreys
and Angus was Africa.

WEDDING VOW: THE SIMPLEST, HARDEST AND THE TRUEST THING

a dialogue to speak

One: We live in love, so finally are come today
    (beyond the gladrags and the sweet bouquet
    beyond cake or ring or all this fuss)
    to this, the simplest and the truest thing for us.

Other: If you can say, my love – and hand on heart –
    I will love you until death do us part –

One: Hand on heart,
    I will love you till death do us part.

Other: Then look me in my eyes – and now!
    and here! – this kiss we kiss shall be our vow.

Written as part of a series of vows for weddings and partnerships, commissioned by Carol Ann Duffy for the Guardian on the occasion of the Royal Wedding, 29 April 2011.

ANNIVERSARIES

for Sophie Logan and Vas Piyasena on your wedding day

By the time, a year from now,
when the anniversary is 'paper'
you'll have been, I reckon, Vas and Sophie,
the best part of a dozen years together.

On your Wooden Wedding – isn't that five? –
wee Sonny will be a seasoned schoolboy already
and 'Mr & Mrs', those
lovely, ordinary words 'my wife', 'my husband'
long, long so habitual by then that –
even though you've long been
lovers, partners, are *parents* now and will be
each other's best friend forever –
are words that sound so new and strange,
words to be lump-in-the-throat proud of today.
After the grown-up, take-a-deep-breath, 'I do', 'I do'
what can you say?

'My wife', 'my husband', that's what!
And when, paper, cotton, linen – I forget the order –
roll around remember,
whether (ruby, silver) they seem to call for
flowers, something precious, or (wood, iron, steel)
a thing as plain prosaic as new utensils
they neither mark accurately the years together nor
can they begin to list what marriage is made of.

May that be dailiness – and delight in it,
sunsets sometimes, full moons,
music, moments, meals, long sleeps curled like spoons
together, your children, hard work, holidays,
home, laughter, friends and family,
love always.

A CAMBRIC SHIRT

for Gordon and Camrie Maclean (father and daughter)

Because the sound of his daughter's name
was as soft to him as the cloth it was,
in Scots, the auld word for – *camrie* – chambray,
a cambric shirt was what that day
he wore to her wedding.

                      And it was
the two of them alone knew the why of it.

Because he'd hap her up forever in the love
that, light in his heart, let her go to the good man
any father would be glad to see his lassie
married onto, this was atween them baith
one small secret hanselling: a cambric shirt

the shirt he'd have gien aff his back for her,
would still without the asking, *the coat so warm*
when the rivers freeze and the snowflakes storm
to keep her from the howling winds,
his plaidie to every angry airt
he'd shelter her
hap her weel-clad
in the cauld blast
in the cauld blast

his father-love
the camrie sark
withoot ony seam or needlewark.

11. THE LIGHT COMES BACK

IN THE MID-MIDWINTER

After John Donne's 'A Nocturnal on St Lucy's Day'

At midday on the year's midnight
into my mind came
I saw the new moon late yestreen
wi the auld moon in her airms
though, no,
there is no moon of course –
there's nothing very much of anything to speak of
in the sky except a gey dreich greyness
rain-laden over Glasgow and today
there is the very least of even this for us to get
but
the light comes back
the light always comes back
and this begins tomorrow with
however many minutes more of sun and serotonin.

Meanwhile
there will be the winter moon for us to love the longest,
fat in the frosty sky among the sharpest stars,
and lines of old songs we can't remember
why we know
or when first we heard them
will aye come back
once in a blue moon to us
unbidden

bless us with their long-travelled light.

AUTUMN WITH MAGPIE, POMEGRANATE

this morning
a cruel curve of black-patent beak,
a single terrifying eye
at my high window looking in –
the cocky, glossy bulk
of that big blue-black and white bird,
its gleam, its stare –
and I thought of Robert Lowell's skunk
that would not scare

but out in the gold of this October afternoon
caught in a sudden swirl of leaves
I think *Corryvreckan*,
but tell myself we're still very far
from winter's washing tub
and yes here I am
happed up warm and
out to buy whichever Hallowe'en cake in the
baker's window is putting the best face on it,
here I am
with a pomegranate in my pocket
like a bomb packed with garnets.

a pomegranate,
its scarred and shiny rind
both buff and blebbed with russet like
this air which rustles, crackles.

I think *late beauty is the best beauty as*
un-saluted
but with a hop skip and a jump in front
of me today's tally of magpies
flips from *one for sorrow to*

two for joy.

BEYOND IT

A Golden Shovel poem

In seas. In windsweep. They were black and loud.
                              – Gwendolyn Brooks

The bad weather is trying to get in,
so veils of rain become blatterings, seas
over-arch, they pound and rake our shores. In
they come – far, far beyond the high-tide mark with windsweep
and drag, splintering all they suck back in. They
make a nothing of all things that once were
our all-in-all, stood proud. The skies go black
with thick murk, this impenetrable cloud, and
more-than-weather stirs one boiling broth of chaos, irresistible
            and loud.

The Golden Shovel is a form invented to honour the work of the late great
black American poet, novelist and autobiographer, Gwendolyn Brooks. The
rules? First you have to quote, in full, a line, any line that somehow intrigues
you, from Brooks's work. And, acknowledging its provenance make sure
you use the all words of this line – in their original order – as the last words
of the lines in the new poem you are to compose. I was intrigued to be asked
to contribute to a new anthology of Golden Shovels, but not hopeful I'd get
anywhere. I found that if it feels initially like nothing more than a daft, fun
word game, you soon realise that, with luck, it just might take you to other
unexpected parts of your imagination.

HOW TO BE THE PERFECT ROMANTIC POET

Be born male.
Begin your career as a poet early.
Take advantage of your nursemaid's momentary distraction
by – not yet a twelvemonth –
crawling to the fire and snatching out a live coal, flamed
and glowing, learning
to brand Promethean sensation to your flesh and brain.
(This will also initiate you nicely into the twin satisfactions
of rousing the whole household with your shrieking
and getting a maid into trouble.)

Be orphaned ere you grow to double figures.
Ever after, idolise your father, disappoint your mother.
Have a sister (every Romantic poet worth his salt most certainly
has a sister). She'll be the one to hearken when you sing
Then come my Sister! come, I pray,
With speed put on your woodland dress;
And bring no book: for this one day
We'll give to idleness.

Even if you are not Lord Byron
be mad and bad and dangerous to know.

Be faithful to your Muse and marry the wrong woman.
Your Muse will most fulsomely reward you.

When in London, lodge at the Salutation and Cat,
that hotbed of sedition. Thrill to that.

Leave your long black hair unpowdered,
wear your blue topcoat with a white swansdown waistcoat,
your muddied stockings most spectacularly bespattered – but
most vehemently refuse to change them just to please your wife.

Dream, but
ere you're older (if you want to get much older)
attempt
to wean yourself off your predilection
for laudanum, opium, brandy,
drop the Kendal Black Drop for the more sedative stimulants
of egg-nog and Orinoko tobacco.
Soar,
escape the real world of gruel, sulphur-ointment, haberdashery,
pig-iron, cotton manufactories and silk mills;
worship all winged creatures – Angels, Harpies,
the starling, sea-mew, ostrich, owl, canary, vulture,
the nightingale, sparrow, thrush, bustard, tom-tit, dove, duck,
    linnet, lark
and, ah,
the albatross . . .

Dread, above all, becalming, stasis.
Love the wild wave,
the humble bird-limed thornbush; let nature be your teacher
but be a *library cormorant*, dive deep.
When it thunders
run bareheaded, harebrained, out into the rain.
Miss all deadlines – write all night,
tempt and court the Nightmare and the Succubus
in pursuit of the green radiance,
in pursuit of the fugitive colours of the day.

III. EKPHRASIS, ETCETERA

PHOTOGRAPH, ART STUDENT, FEMALE, WORKING CLASS, 1966

Her hair is cut into that perfect slant –
an innovation circa '64 by Vidal Sassoon.
She's wearing C&A's best effort at Quant
ending just below the knicker-line, daisy-strewn.
Keeping herself in tights could blow her grant
entirely, so each precious pair is soon
spattered with nail varnish dots that stop each run.
She's a girl, eighteen – just wants to have fun.

She's not 'a chick'. Not yet. Besides, by then
she'll find the term 'offensive'. 'Dollybird' to quote
her favourite mags, is what she aspires to when
her head's still full of *Honey* and *Petticoat*.
It's almost the last year that, quite this blithely, men
up ladders or on building sites wolf-whistle to note
the approval they're sure she will appreciate.
Why not? She did it for *their* benefit, looks great.

Nor does she object. Wouldn't think she has the right.
Though when that lech of a lecturer comments on her tits
to a male classmate, openly, she might
feel – quick as a run in nylon – that it's
not what ought to happen, is . . . not polite,
she'll burn, but smile, have no word that fits
the insult, can't subject it to language's prism.
In sixty-six there's plenty sex, but not 'sexism'.

Soon: *The Female Eunuch* and enough
will be enough. Thanks to newfound feminism and Greer
women'll have the words for all this stuff,
what already rankles, but confuses her, will seem clear
and she'll (consciously) be no one's 'bit of fluff'
or 'skirt' or 'crumpet'. She'll know the rule is 'gay' not 'queer',
'Ms' not 'Miss' or 'Mrs' – she'll happily obey it
and, sure as the Pill in her pocket, that's how she'll say it.

This photo's saying nothing, is black and white, opaque.
a frozen moment, not a memory.
The boyfriend with the Pentax took it for the sake
of taking it, a shot among many others, randomly,
to see how it would develop. Didn't imagine it'd make
an image so typical it'd capture time so perfectly.
How does she feel? Hey, girl, did it feel strange
to be waiting for the a-changing times to change?

SOME OLD PHOTOGRAPHS

Weather evocative as old-fashioned scent

the romance of dark stormclouds
in big skies over the low wide river,
                   of long shadows and longer shafts of light

of smoke,
          fabulous film-noir stills of Central Station,
of freezing fog silvering the chilled, stilled parks
          of the glamorous past
          where drops on a rainmate are sequins
          under the streetlight, in the black and white

your young, still-lovely mother laughs, the
hem of her sundress whipped up
by a wind on a beach
somewhere doon the watter
before you were even born

all the dads in hats
are making for Central at five past five
in the snow, in the rain, in the sudden *what-a-scorcher*,
in the smog, their
belted dark overcoats white-spattered by the starlings

starlings swarming
in that perfect and permanent cloud
above what was
never really this photograph
but always all the passing now
and noise and stink and smoky breath of George Square

wee boays, a duchess, bunting, there's a
big launch on the Clyde
and that boat is yet to sail

'THE SCULLERY MAID' & 'THE CELLAR BOY'

by Jean-Baptiste-Siméon Chardin

1. THE SCULLERY MAID SPEAKS:

He liked me fine, the Master,
called me 'pretty as a picture'
the day he stopped me at my scouring.

I was more than a mere scullery maid to him he said –
or rather as something to pay attention to today
than a bonny scullery maid like me
he could think of nothing better.

He never called me by my name – I think he never knew it,
or needed to – nor so much as touched my rough-work apron
that he said had a coarseness he liked the look of
as so he did my good clean house-frock's unbleached
nothing-sort-of-colour that set off nicely
the peach-ness of my skin.
That got me blushing, but I needn't have bothered.
Looking back, I can see his glad eye
was as greedy for copper, earthenware, old cooperage,
the glimmer in the long-handled pan I worked at.
He made every bit as much of that daft cellar boy
who is the bane of my life always with his crude remarks
and grabbing hands given the half-a-chance I aye
have to make sure he never gets. The Master
made him look human, almost handsome, yes,
he certainly stands out
there in his kitchen-whites
against the cellar's dimness beside the old tub
among his jugs and flask and funnel.
To him we were a pair.

'Hold still!' he said and that was the only time
he ever spoke to me with any hint of sharpness.
And I might have said, 'Never mind, M'sieur Chardin,
that I've work to be done the mistress won't be letting me off with
and these pots won't wash themselves!' – except it wasn't
my place to, was it?
Besides, squinting at me through those spectacles,
dabbing at his canvas, tutting,
I could see that he was hard at work
and I liked that.

It gave me pause.

2. THE CELLAR BOY SPEAKS:

He's no wi the toun at aw, the Maister.
He's in a warld o his ain, plooterin
Wi paint on cloth stretched roon wid frames, footerin
Wi crayons, burnt twigs o charcoal, broken chalks, in a slaister
Amang the thick oil-stink o linseed, the sherp sting
O turpentine, gum arabic, white spirit. Pride o place
Aye to the palette an the easel staunin tall aboon the mess
That the maid got a richt flea-in-her-ear for tidying.

First day he drew me? Whit maist I mind
Is thon rat the cook's terrier stertit-up from oot the coarner stour.
Chased fur its life, it leapt richt ower the Maister's fit
But he peyed nae tent to it. Never even seen it – blind
Tae awthin but the task in haun, he never heard the poor
Rat's last heich, sair squeal, nor the snarlin o the dug eftir it.

Somethin o thon stubborn terrier in him!
Noo his dander was up the hunt was on
And he had nae choice but to get me doon.
He had me in his sights, his thumb

Oot at airm's length like he was pressin in a tack
Nailing me to nuthin. He lukked at me. I lukked back.
He's never liked me. That day he couldnae get enough
Till his tea was cauld and the Mistress in the huff.

Specs on his neb's end, een screwed up, squintin, he
Was eftir somethin – whit I dinna ken – in me.

THE ART OF WILLIE RODGER

is essential essentially

it's   made by hand   created from the heart
from the heart of this most creative family

with perfect and perfected   economy
with nothing but
the eye   the cut
the dab hand
the knife   the lino, ink and roller
the perfect paper (the black and
not *quite*
white?)
with maybe the black on softest red?   the black on buff?
with the never too much   the always enough
the dab hand the either/or
the both, the and

with   essentially
the block and the roller   the paper
the ink
its light, deep funny, sad per-
jink

who else but he
in a print   can make a Scottish *haiku*?
Willie *sees*
and what he sees *shows* face to face

it's full of grace.

A MAN NEARLY FALLING IN LOVE

After the linocut by Willie Rodger

no one is more dangerous
no one
than the man nearly falling in love
his eye gone from glad-eye to gaga
his mouth open in an *oh no!*

get him
plucking out
that arrow which
almost
pierced him in the heart and
where it hurts.

he's floored   temporarily
he's fallen
for someone   almost
fallen for her but
not
in love no
not exactly.

lethal.

someone   he'll make sure of it
someone
will have to suffer for this.

IN ALAN DAVIE'S PAINTINGS

An ee
an open ee
whit seems but an ashet o
bools and penny-cookies mak an arabesque
an arra-heid edder frae ablow it
gaes serpent-slinkan
yont the picture frame.
a jazz o bird-heids, herts, peeries, playin cairts
the crescent mune –
a the shapes and symbols frae
ankh to ziggurat, corbie-steppit.
whiles a rattle-stane blatter
whiles a hurly-gush o colour – wow
this lovely lowe o cramasie, soy-saft,
noo the reid, reid, reid o thunnercups,
a braid and tappietourie swag o
emerant
yallochie
blae.

THREE STANZAS FOR CHARLES RENNIE MACKINTOSH

On the centenary of the opening of the great architect's building for the Glasgow School of Art, 15 December 2009

I.

It is but a plain building that is required.
North light, set dimensions for studios, that budget inspired,
in no way constrained, you. Dear Ghost, Dear Genius,
a plain wonder of a building's what you gave to us.
Volume, light, line, astonishing rhythms of space,
guts, harmony, surprises, seemliness, a great place
to work in, learn in, live in, take for granted.
Much more than they ever knew they wanted
was what you gave Fra Newbery, the Governors, the World, the
        Future –
changing for ever the possibilities of architecture.
A prime modernist squarely in the Scotch Baronial tradition
and proud of it! Definitively beyond definition.
Your details delight us endlessly with their endless variation.
Always decorated construction, never constructed decoration.

II.

Art is the flower, you said, *Life is the green leaf*.
Time is the judge. Time is the thief.

III.

Die Hoffnung ist – graphic, 1901.
Wee motif: the blaeberry of the Mackintosh clan.
The other? Abstracted, a sprig of heather for your Margaret.
There is hope lettered in your own alphabet –
blaeberry and heather twinned in that symbolism you devised.
So what if that motto you made your own was plagiarised?
There is hope – yes – in honest error, none
in the mere stylist's icy perfection.

LABYRINTH

for the students of the Glasgow School of Art

first you have to know the rules to break them
not so   the artist says:
first you have to know there are no
rules not to break is
first
to know no rules
except

the unbreakable rules of the
call it your
'art'   or 'truth'   or 'muse'   or 'process'
the goddess accident
as she   very deliberately
shows you what you want to do

and exactly the rules you must first invent then
slavishly obey

this time   and this time only

it's as if Ariadne handed you the
tentative end of a ball of twine and now you know
the creature   and all creation
is   it really is
down there for you to get
for you can smell it

smoke or musk or dung   a reek of danger
most definitely danger

one good student testifies:
my art was once all about my dreams but my
dreams made no sense to anyone but me so

I started to explore caves
real caves with real paint
the exact spaces between
the walls and the
rule was it had to be real exactly as-was
and the intervals precise and the

more real I got the more people told me
my art was like their dreams

EMAIL TO ALASTAIR COOK

Thanks for sharing those images
from the Imperial War Museum website –
nine or ten photographs of
Greenock women in the Great War
working in the sugar sheds.

When their men were in the trenches
they were welcomed in the workplace
for the duration
to work their fingers to the bone
then, after that shift's overtime was over,
keep the home-fires burning too.
Hard labour
but these photos show they sort of liked it?
See them, what are they like, eh? –
skirts kilted thigh-high as they lug those sacks
of raw molasses to or from the hook and hoist
or paddle barefoot, shouldering heavy shovels,
up to their knees in those
great mounds and drifts of sugar,
white bings, shifting the stuff in jigtime to
the bagging room.
Strong women,
solid, archetypal as Millet's gleaners
or Degas's laundresses,
Queens of the Sweet Heaps,
singing their white-woman's blues.

And their voices were not refined.

They'd breenge brass-necked and raucous
through the toun streets at lowsin time,
pay-packets in their pockets, sure that
once this War was over

they'd no be sent hame and telt they'd better
learn to mak a guid pot o soup.

On another day – a black yin –
when Mairn and Mysie baith get their telegrams, they'll
greet wi them, greet sair, then rally roon
and bear them up, but today
they're no feart!
They're laughing as they brag out loud
about the legendary bandy-leggit Betty
who could smuggle oot three pokes in each leg o her bloomers
above the extra-strong elastic.
Nane o whose neighbours would ever
go short o a spoonfu to sweeten their tea.

Alastair, tomorrow
I'll meet you at Central, eh? And we'll go down together
to where the river widens and goes silver and I'll see
what you and Alec and Annie and the other artists
have made of this a century later,
have made of those spaces rendered lovely,
rendered elegiac, with disuse.

To enter one of your photographs
is to be in the presence of absence,
to be humbled,
to be where even the light is granulated
and the layered shadows seem to retain traces
of that burnt sugar smell.
And it's as if your open lens
wasn't only looking but was
listening for the traces –
Alastair, your glad eye for
the spaces and those places
make those absent voices

sing.

THE BALLAD OF ELSIE INGLIS

1.

1864. Elsie Maud Inglis, in India
was born, seventh child, favourite daughter
of a most enlightened father –
despite his being a servant of the Empire,
of the Raj and Queen Victoria.

Wee Elsie wanted to cure the whole wide world.
Blotches big and red as poppies
were the pockmarks and the mock-measles
that she painted on her dollies.

Daily she washed off the paint
from the dollies' faces,
daily she disinfected the dollies
in all the dollies wounded places.
Daily she tended to her dollies,
daily the dollies got better.
Elsie's (gentle) mother and Elsie's (just) father
had nothing but kisses and yeses
when Elsie told them, 'I am going to be a doctor.'

1886. Grown-up, back in Scotland,
soon as her medical training began
Elsie knew she had it in her to be a surgeon
as good as any man.
And many a suffering woman
would most certainly prefer
(if it came to baring her all beneath the surgeon's knife)
said knife be wielded by her.
They had to thole tyrannical husbands –
his property, in law – that was a wife.
He'd the right to refuse her an operation –
even one to save her life.

Surely everyone saw what Elsie saw?
'twould be only common decency
to have female specialists in obstetrics,
paediatrics and gynaecology?

1894. Doctor Elsie Inglis founded in Edinburgh
a Women's Hospital for the Poor.
1914. Somebody shot somebody in Sarajevo
and the whole bloody world was at war.

1914. *Britain Needs You!* and
young, green, lads were queueing up to enlist.
Elsie Inglis saw the necessity
for the doctor she was, for the suffragist –

for patriotic Elsie knew she could muster
all-female medical teams who would want
just as if they were fighting soldiers,
to be risking their lives at the front.

Then the injustice of further denying women the vote
would be more than crystal clear.
So off to the Castle, to the RAMC,
went Elsie to volunteer.

The man from the War Office smiled at Elsie
My good lady, go home and sit still.
Did this make Elsie Inglis angry?
If it did, it was grist to her mill

for Elsie smiled back at the man, said nothing.
She really did not want to be rude.
Thought: If my Government doesn't want Women's Field Hospitals
surely some other government would?

2.

Her father's daughter –
she'd never minded this, just taken it for the compliment
she knew whoever had come out with it
certainly meant it to be.
But, Edinburgh Castle, the War Office,
1914, that buffoon in charge of the RAMC . . . !
Elsie was not *his*, nor what he would call
either a *lady* or *good*.
That she'd have to get round this damnable obstacle
Elsie well understood.

3.

My good lady, go home and sit still.
But she did not, would not, could not, could she,
take no for an answer?
She was almost fifty years old already, already ill
(though she kept this close to her chest) with the cancer
she, and only in her last days, swearing her to secrecy,
confided to Mary, that long-serving hospital-cook she trusted,
she had a . . . *certain malignancy*
she was sure she'd survive and not be bested
by. Oh, the pain it was truly chronic,
it really gave her what for,
and none of her nice nieces would ever get to ask her
aunt Elsie, what did you do in the war?

But all this was 1917
and after three long years of that terrible War
throughout which Elsie'd always known
exactly what she was fighting
and what she was fighting for.

Written for the John Bellany and the Scottish Women's
Hospitals Exhibition in the Scottish Parliament, 2016.

GALLIMAUFRY

for the re-opening of Glasgow's Kelvingrove Art Gallery in July 2006

1.
thon big gink
that skinnymalink giraffe
– the round-shouldered knock-kneed giraffe
with its half-daft embarrassed bug-eyed face-of-an-alien
and its *square spots* for godsake! – oh
ho you
better duck   giraffe   because watch!
a Spitfire's coming over

and has, just as good as new,
swooped through
(very nearly scraping the balconies on either side and
taking the whole place down with it)
hangs fire in mid air
more brazen than the ten pendent electroliers
and almost as brilliantly
engineered as the seagull that flies beneath it

here's a hero for us
Spitfire
your matt drab dark green khaki-emblazoned LA198
each badged wing making an
OK-I-double-dare-you mockery of a target
with those insignia roundels of red and blue
we could almost touch your wingtips
can't but
contemplate how very skinny the snakehips of the
young men in the myth   in the history
who had to lift the lid and shimmy into your fateful cockpit
we can't but marvel
at the precision of the six guns of your cannon
and the five blades of your propeller

2.

the smogs of the fifties   the emanations of old raincoats
a century of Capstan and cigars the
fusts and filth of the air factories bad
breath blitz and bombast that
tarry earl o hell absolute black-mockitness
made up of such a mixtermaxter as would make you dizzy
all that's
been just pure stripped from
this pale clean stone
in one miraculous
latex peel

so now I want to go there
take my nephew
say Davie you were only seven
the last time we could lift you up to
look into the glazed eye of Sir Roger the Elephant
and now you're ten and
it's three more years since the morning
his keeper gave breakfast
to that wrinkled and cynical as a general old veteran
of the Scottish Zoo and Variety Circus –
then handed him over
his beloved elephant Sir Roger
to several soldiers and a man with an elephant gun

Davie, I want to show you
the bones of the Baron of Buchlyvie
and his two horse shoes   Benin bronzes
the biggest spider and the smallest pygmy shrew
teach you all the names of the birds you can see in your garden
goggle with you at the fabulous skeleton of the giant Irish deer
at the ceratosaur the chiffchaff the willow warbler
the ebonised writing desk by Mackintosh that holds open its doors
like a Japanese lady holding out her arms akimbo in a kimono

show you amulets scarabs and talismans
the eye of Horus
and the hand of Fatima
show you the clouded leopard,
the dogsteeth necklace
the head of the Endrick Pike
fossils as lucid as the blueprint photograms of Anna Atkins
the mandrill
the masks of Menander
the La Faruk Madonna
the eyewitness watercolours of Auschwitz by Marianne Grant
the orrery and the beaded and birchbank souvenirs for tourists
made by the Metis and the Cree
show you
the King Billy banner from the Orange Lodge
the Statue of St Patrick
say *sectarianism is history*
show you
that Cézanne
say *how do you like them apples*
show you
the bright and savage
Joan Eardley weans in the picture queue
and Stanley Spencer's
tummelling their fatbum wulkies eternally around the railings
of *The Glen Port Glasgow*
I want you to keek back at that tousle-headed man
keeking out at you
at the snow
from *Windows in the West*
I want you to hear the orchestrion giving it laldy
and gawp at the Goliath birdeater that eats birds
I want us to wonder together
at the ptarmigan and the polecat and the Great Auk
and wonder why there are turnips engraved on the splendid

armour of the Earl of Pembroke,

I want to measure your height
against the long legbone of the giraffe,
say *hey*
Davie the last time you were up to here and
here!
now you're up to there

3.
look at that gorgeous girl that
real Glasgow stoater done up to the nines
who is a perfect specimen of the present
if only we could preserve her

and she's gawping at that
very swanky perra black satin platforms
she says
haw lookit, lookit that toty wee perra peerie heels in see-thru plastic
made by Jean Rimbaud Paris in
nineteen fifty something,
jist gorgeous eh no?

come and I'll show you
the pretty tiny embroidered bootee
to cover the stump left by the work of the footbinder in China
the flamboyant neckties of Emilio Coia
in Italian silk
I'll show you the branks and the jougs and the nursing corset
the ladies' silk safari suit
and (tho she wore it to the opening a hundred years ago
it's still fresh as a daisy)
I'll show you the bonny pink frock of the Duchess of Fife

4.
one man gave his wife
that peacock brooch in enamel on silver another a bunch of fives

and pit her to the branks
stitched her up and banged her in that scold's bridle

what is the taste of iron on the tongue?
whit like is it?
and what are we like?

we are here
and there
and even that is neither here nor there because

this one is suddenly back in a Saturday in the sixties
walking with her dad and
hearing the sound of the skelp of her brand-new sandals
on the marble floor

that one remembers
sitting right there next to Alasdair Gray at Miss Jean Irwin's
Saturday morning children's classes in the nineteen fifties and how
he just had it, even then

the lonely divorcee
looks at the beaded deerskin moccasins
the Native American hunting coat of sealskin reads
the designs a woman painted on her husband's coat
are guided by his dreams

there's a new widower in Egyptology
with a heavy heart –
an Orpheus among the faience and elegance
and he's studying the Book of the Dead
wishes he could *bathe in gazelle's milk*
the eye of Horus
wishes he could bring her back

look at
these lovers, these Sunday-afternoon lovers
beneath their flung-on clothes still naked
from their Saturday night and long Sunday morning
blink and stare at the suit of armour amazed
what could anyone want with armour?

well, ask the Temminck's pangolin, the
nine-banded armadillo, ask
the man in the seventeenth century who wore this
thick buff coat of elk hide with the
real blood and the bullet mark

Mammy, Mammy I want to go back to the diaroma
see the hare change its coat
winter to summer and back to white-and-magic winter again
I want to overhear somebody else's granddad explain
to that wee boy who isny even interested
the name of the device that makes it work is *Pepper's Ghost*

5.
there should be a cliché that goes
as greedy as Glasgow
glad-eyed Glasgow
that's aye grabbed its chances goodstyle, gone
loot from Lucknow?
oh aye, sees it
the emperor of China's cloak, seized from the Summer Palace?
aye, sees that
sees yon ghost dance shirt
they sent us from Lakota, Dakota
(OK it's a replacement) and
sees our jade
our gesso panels

our Man in Armour
our Orange Blind
sees our Noel Paton
sees our Avril Paton
our Salvador Dalí

Glasgow flourish?
Oh aye no hauf oh
whit a
gallus gallimaufry!

let us haste to Kelvingrove . . .

WAY BACK IN THE PALEOLITHIC

Long long ago
what do you know
even back then
in them caves of Lascaux
more than thirty thousand years ago
way back in pre-history
this was already the essential mystery:

Art, art, what is it for?
To bring into being what never existed before.

It's that elemental
artistic vibe
that binds us together as part of the tribe –
every father, mother, every sister, every brother
every man and every woman
needed them animals on the cave walls
to define themselves as human.

Art, art, what is it for?
To bring into being what never existed before.

Way, way back and long ago
in the caves of
Chauvet, Altamira, Lascaux
those first folk –
those first about-to-be artists – had to face
that blank wall only Nature so far had had a go at
somehow put it in its place.

So they bravely turned their hand to it,
stencilling in its outline with the spatter and the spark
of the spat and blown pigment
that drew so clearly where their hands both were and weren't

and they made their mark – with Art!

Art, art, what was it for?
To bring into being what never existed before.

In the Cueva de las Manos,
in Chauvet, Altamira and Lascaux
already this fundamental inclination
that drives pro creation
forced those folk to fashion
something beyond religion or ritual – Art!

Art, art, what was it for?
To bring into being what never existed before.

Fetishes of priapic phalluses,
amulets of big-bellied round-hipped split-vulva-ed Venuses,
objects of clay, bone, antler, stone
for they knew man could not, should not
live by meat alone.

No they were
not just hunters tasked with bringing home the bacon
but artists
with a mammoth undertaking!

Images of aurochs, bulls and bison,
ochres, oxides, charcoal, mineral pigments,
fierce felines, fleet equines, bear and deer –
made from the life
and from imagination's figments.

Because their truest impulse was
to *capture something*
soon running wild on the walls were

hordes of realer than real creatures
the torches in the firelight
flickered into the first motion pictures.

Did they dance?
They danced themselves to trance.
How do we know?
Bone flutes we found, stone drumsticks tell us so.
In the firelight, in the cave, beyond
all the other ordinary passing glories,
beyond the fugitive music and the stories –
on the walls
their Immortal Art!

IV. KIDSPOEMS AND BAIRNSANGS

HOW I'LL DECORATE MY TREE

Written as a banner – with lines from London school children – for the
Norwegian Christmas tree in Trafalgar Square, 2014

It was still very far from Christmas
when my mamma said to me:
tell me, Precious, what *you* going to hang
on *our* Christmas tree?

I said: the fairy-lights that Dad just fixed
and . . . jewel-coloured jelly-beans from the pick'n'mix –
oh, and from it I'll dangle tinsel in tangles,
sparkles, sequins and spangles,
a round golden coin (chocolate money),
that cracker joke that was *actually funny*,
my rosary beads – and a plastic rose
as red as Rudolph Reindeer's nose,
the gnome that grows the tangerines,
the picture of me with my tambourine,
and (this is Mum's favourite, she says)
the photo of all of us in our PJ's!
The Ladybird book that Lola lent me,
the blue butterfly bracelet that Brittany sent me,
the ear-ring I lost,
a pop-up Jack Frost,
a space-hopper, an everlasting gobstopper,
a pink-eyed sugar mouse,
the keys to my grandfather's house,
a tiny pair of trainers with silver laces,
and – now my smile is straight – gonna hang up my braces!
A marble, an angel-scrap, a star,

the very last sweetie out my advent calendar,
a kiss under the mistletoe,
a mitten still cracked with a crunch and a creak of snow,
that glitter scarf I finally got sick of,
a spoon with cake-mix still to lick off,
the Dove of Peace that our Darren made,
some green thoughts in our tree's green shade –
I'll hang up every evergreen memory
of moments as melted and gone
as that candle that was *supposed* to smell
of cinnamon –
memories big as a house and as small's
the baubles I used to call *ball-balls*.

With pleasure I'll treasure them
then, on *proper* Christmas Day, I'll show them all to you
between the Queen's Speech and *Doctor Who*.

GLASGOW NONSENSE RHYME,
NURSERY RHYME, FOR MOLLY

*– who, fetched by her new parents, Graham and Julie, from distant Jiangxi
province in China just in time for her first birthday, came home here to Glasgow*

Molly Pin Li McLaren,
come home and look
at the pictures in your brand-new book –
a tree, a bird, a fish, a bell,
a bell, a fish, a tree, a bird.
Point, wee Molly, and say the word!

Oh Molly, I wish
you the moon as white and round as a dish
and a bell, a tree, a bird and a fish.

Touch! Taste! Look! Smell!
(tree, fish, bird, bell)
and listen, wee Molly, listen well
to the wind,
to the wind in the tree go swish
(bird, bell, tree, fish)
to the shrill of the bird and the plop of the fish
and the clang of the bell
and the stories they tell
the stories they tell,
Molly, the tree, the bird, the fish and the bell.

*Glasgow's coat of arms has motifs of a tree, a bird, a fish and a bell, hence the
traditional – this is the tree that never grew / this is the bird that never flew
/ this is the fish that never swam / this is the bell that never rang.*

NINA'S SONG

Nina, come to Scotland
Nina come soon
We'll show you the wee-est field mouse
And the biggest, roundest moon.

The million-zillion stars'll *amaze* you –
So bright and so far . . .
Pick one and we'll sing you
Twinkle, twinkle little star.

Come soon, Nina,
Come and never wonder why
There can be three perfect rainbows
In just one wide sky.

Just enjoy the bonny colours
Nina, never mind their names –
Although it's true
We will very much enjoy teaching you
Your *red, orange, yellow, green and blue*
Your *violet and indigo*,
And every colour that we know
Wee Nina, all the same.

And everything will be glad to see you,
All the singing birds will go,
Nice to meet you, new wee Nina,
Hey, Nina – hello!

IN GAIA'S POETRY

Gaia does not care to rhyme.

She's right of course.
To start to put down words that end the same –
soundwise – is to get on a horse
that's going to take you where you might not really want to go,
make you say what you – maybe – didn't want to say?
Not be true to what you're writing
so
(as truth's the thing) *that*'d be no good, no way!

And Gaia's got a point – *except*
there's the fun of what you don't expect –
the *half*-rhymes, echoes, chimes,
the *internal* (inside a line) and unstressed rhymes
where the sense doesn't end on the rhyme-word with a clunk.
There's the fun too of the thought you never would've thunk
were it not for the rhyme that took you there.
There's the *couplet* (a new rhyme after every pair
of lines – AABB), there's the interlaced *quatrain*
that goes ABAB, or (complicated) the sestet, the sonnet –
none of which beats getting it down plain
because you're thinking about what you're writing about
and are *on it*.

This is Gaia's gift.

I'm thinking of the diary that you, Gaia, let me read
which gave me such a lift.
Each day recorded was a joy indeed.

THE FRUIT OF THE WORD

Apple says 'a' – it was true.
Ah, but the 'a' said 'apple' too.

I'd like to hold again that wee stub of pencil,
let it make again the mark my mind could never cancel
after the first down-stroke of that slant stem, attached –
ah! – to the sound of it
in the shape of the fat globe of the round of it,
the first fruit-of-the-word,
the apple.
How it matched
the sound, was the shape
of that sound, the 'a'
to the apple, the apple to the 'a'
the apple to the 'A'.

Boys and girls: what does the apple say?

V. MAKAR SONGS, OCCASIONAL AND

PERFORMANCE PIECES MAINLY

POETS NEED NOT

Poets need not be garlanded;
the poet's head
should be innocent of the leaves of the sweet bay tree,
twisted. All honour goes to poetry.

And poets need no laurels. Why be lauded
for the love of trying to nail the disembodied
image with that one plain word to make it palpable,
for listening in to silence for the rhythm capable
of carrying the thought that's not thought yet?
The pursuit's its own reward. So you have to let
the poem come to voice by footering
late in the dark at home, by muttering
syllables of scribbled lines – or what might
be lines, eventually, if you can get it right.

And this, perhaps, in public? The daytime train,
the biro, the back of an envelope, and again
the fun of the wild goose chase
that goes beyond all this fuss.

Inspiration? Bell rings, penny drops,
the light-bulb goes on and tops
the not-good-enough idea that went before?
No, that's not how it goes. You write, you score
it out, you write it in again the same
but somehow with a different stress. This is a game

you very seldom win
and most of your efforts end up in the bin.

There's one hunched and gloomy
heron haunts that nearby stretch of River Kelvin
and it wouldn't if there were no fish.
If it never in all that greyness passing caught a flash,
a gleam of something, made that quick stab.
That's how a poem is after a long nothingness, you grab
at that anything and this is food to you.
It comes through, as leaves do.

All praise to poetry, the way it has
of attaching itself to a familiar phrase
in a new way, insisting it be heard and seen.
Poets need no laurels, surely?
Their poems, when they can make them happen – even rarely –
crown them with green.

CONNECTING CULTURES

for Commonwealth Day in Westminster Abbey, 2012

I am talking in our lingua franca.
Tell me, do you drive on the left or right?
Is your football team the *Botswana Zebras*
or *Indomitable Lions of Cameroon?*
Can you take me to *Junkanoo*
and is there a mangrove forest?
Is it true that a lightweight business suit
is the appropriate city garb and shaking hands
the usual form of greeting?
Are there frigate birds? Diamonds? Uranium?
What is the climate? Is there a typical hurricane season
or a *wind of change?*
How many miles of coastline in your country?
Is the currency the Kenyan shilling or the
Brunei dollar – or is it also the word for *rain* or *a blessing?*
Do you speak the lingua franca?

Communication can mean *correspondence,*
or *a connecting passage or channel,* can mean
a means of imparting and receiving information such as
speech, social media, the press and cinema.
Communications can mean *means of transporting,*
especially troops or supplies.

Commonwealth means
a free association of independent member nations bound by
friendship, loyalty, the desire for
democracy, equality, freedom and peace.
Remembering how hard fellow feeling is to summon
when Wealth is what we do not have in Common,
may every individual
and all the peoples in each nation
work and hope and

strive for true communication –
only by a shift and sharing is there any chance
for the welfare of all our people and good governance.

Such words can sound like flagged-up slogans, true.
What we merely say says nothing –
all that matters is what we do.

RANDOM

*for Robyn Marsack on the occasion of the re-opening of the Scottish Poetry
Library, 28 October 2015*

Go take a book down from the shelf and open it.
Listen, this isn't 'book' but box,
box full of sound you lift the lid on, opening.

Yes, open any item in this place and you'll release
some specific human noise and voice and
song that doesn't need a tune to all-the-truer sing.
Pick one. Pick anything.
Slim volume or expansive, all-inclusive, fat anthology –
neither's a dumb tome of texts to tease mere 'meaning' from.
The song's the thing.

And the beauty is, it does away with time and makes it meaningless.
When – this is random, but, say, you flick a page,
here's . . . oh, Ben Jonson
and one man's singular, centuries-old, grief. *On my First Son –
here doth lie*, said he,
his best piece of poetrie –
so chimes and rhymes
with that here-and-now sorrow of your very own
that, hurt by his and stung to tears,
you're somehow almost comforted
because he had the guts to tell it terrible and true.

Love and the other stuff? Well, poets do this too.
Listen, this library-silence thrums
with lyric, epic, L=A=N=G=U=A=G=E, Lallans,
loud hip-hop or rap, maybe the Metaphysicals,
the Silver, Black Mountain, the Beats
and all the big-stuff always – Shakespeare's sonnets,
oor ain bard Burns (*Chiefly in the Scottish Dialect*), Gaelic's òran mór.
Here's the murmur of the Modernists,

the auld breath-and-beat of the balladeer –
oh, and – a word in your ear –
they've got a lot of her, thank God, so – *hypocrite lecteur*,
ton semblable, ta soeur et ton frère –
dae mind *Anon*.
She's aye been baith *the real McCoy*
and your perfect contemporary.
All that. And yet it's not cacophony.

Go in. Pick up a book. Enjoy.

OPEN

On the occasion of the opening of the fourth session of the Scottish Parliament, 2011

Open the doors wrote the Poet Morgan
eight years ago
on the occasion of the opening of this building,
singing out about 'our dearest deepest wish' –
that the work of this, Our Scottish Parliament, begin
and the 'light of the mind' shine out
as the light of that new day shone in.

Now 'Justice' is a fine and bonny word
to engrave upon a mace
as are: 'Integrity', 'Compassion' and 'Wisdom' –
grand Concepts, qualities to grace
every last thinking person of our Parliament –
but above all: Open-ness.

How else to turn an abstract noun, a name,
into a concrete verb – *a doing word*?
Open your ears, listen, let the people petition and be heard.
Justice, Wisdom, Compassion, Integrity?
Open your eyes – and *see*.

Integrity, Compassion, Justice, Wisdom?
Wisdom, Integrity, Justice, Compassion?
Open your hearts – and hope.
Open your minds – to change.
Open the future – because it's not yet written –
it's as Open as that it's coming yet is true!
But close the gap between what we say and what we do.

SPRING 2010, AND AT HIS DESK BY THE WINDOW IS EDDIE IN A RED SHIRT

He likes a red shirt, does Eddie – you should've
       seen him last year on his 89th birthday when he
       came over to Edinburgh to the Poetry Library for
       the opening of his Archive in a scarlet-trimmed
       mock-Warhol T-shirt embossed with a metallic
       gold, silver and red-striped applique of an iconic
       Tunnock's Caramel Wafer with, instead of the
       brand-name, *Glasgow*.

He's wearing a red shirt in the photograph
       on that page from March, 2005
       in the *Herald* that turned up the other day during the
       long-overdue big redding-out of my study.
       I smile.
       Article's about his newly-published
       Tales from Baron Munchausen. Here
       Morgan comes out, again.
       This time about his folklorist son Mahmoud he
       had to 'the enchanting Leila I met in Cairo
       during the Second World War'.
       From whose whispering lips, apparently, the
       pillow-talk was of the
       One Thousand and One Nights – initiating
       him to this long storytelling life of a poet . . .

But, see, I was wanting to talk of that day back in
       the autumn of 2004.
       I've come down to see him with the
       embargoed email version of his poem
       for the opening of the
       new Scottish Parliament Building.
       From the photographs he's seen, and celebrated,
       Eddie loves it.

Petals . . . curves and caverns, nooks and niches . . .
syncopations and surprises.
Leave symmetry to the cemetery.
But he's too shaky on his pins these days
and, next week, I've to read it
out loud and clear for him on the big day.
Terrifying honour! Four minutes of tongue-twisters.
What do the people want of the place? . . .
A nest of fearties is what they do not want.
A symposium of procrastinators is what they do not want.
A phalanx of forelock-tuggers is what they do not want . . .
Well, we'll rehearse it and mibbe I'll get it right.
He's a good director.
'Liz, *not wholly the power, not yet wholly the power, but . . .*
you're not getting enough out of the
not yet . . . '

Try again.
I'm standing in the open door of the bathroom, declaiming.
There's
       amazing Eddie, mild at his neat desk
       in this nursing home on the Crow Road.
There's
       the dialogue between the cancer cell and the
       healthy cell, here're Cyrano, Cathures, Saturn,
       Glasgow Green, Cinquevalli, Jesus and Gilgamesh,
       randy apples and red shirts and starlings
       and strawberries.

WHEN THE POEM WENT TO PRISON

After a visit to HM Prison Barlinnie

Apprehensive, the poem goes to prison.
Is photographed, has its bag searched, a form to fill
checks in money, mobile, rheumatism pills,
has to declare itself and state its reason.
Brute clang of steel door, bars, barbed wire, fear
of what they did or didn't do – and that's none
of the poem's business. Time that must be *done*,
not lived, *tholed*. Scratched off on walls. A love poem? Here?

We could just stey in oor cells, mind, this is oor choice.
Among the din of D Hall, eight men in jail-uniform able
to sit down and face the poem, the whole poem,
    and nothing-but-the-poem around this table.
Gey tremulous to start, it soon will find its voice
and in all innocence, all ears, these men will bless
this grateful love poem with their open-ness.

LISTEN

Written for the Children's Panel, to encourage new voluntary members, 2012

Trouble is not my middle name.
It is not what I am.
I was not born for this.
Trouble is not a place
though I am in it deeper than the deepest wood
and I'd get out of it (who wouldn't?) if I could.

Hope is what I do not have in hell –
not without good help, now. Could you
listen, listen hard and well
to what I cannot say except by what I do?

And when you say I do it for badness
this much is true.
I do it for badness done to me before
any badness that I do to you.

Hard to unfankle this.
But you can help me.
Maybe.
Loosen
all these knots and really listen.
I cannot plainly tell you this, but, if you care,
then – beyond all harm and hurt –
real hope is there.

THE SILK ROAD

for Jane as she leaves for her new job in Singapore, 2006

The Silk Road
was the trademark on the motto in the fortune-cookie
I got on China Day when we all
came round the corner from the Art School and
every one of us was
gluttonous on five-spice chicken
in the sunshine
in the Garnethill Garden for the Elderly
and it read:

He who dies with the most toys is nonetheless dead.

Jane, we've never needed fortune-cookie philosophy
to tell us this.
The getting and spending's
never been the thing for either of us and now
we *women of a certain age* know one thing
for certain sure is that there are no certainties
except
one day (and may
it be many brand-new nows from now)
one day, as your father said to you,
our old bones will make very good soup.

So be it. *The intrinsic optimism of curiosity*
this was, someone said,
the key quality of a poet friend of mine.
You own that too.
One thing I know:
for a School of the Creative Arts, anywhere, anywhere,
than you there could be none better.
Already I see you journeying, yes

in the silks of your deconstructed tartan jacket,
in your jet-black beads of felt,
yes, felt and silver –
(for one thing we women of a certain age have learned
is that things are very seldom made of what they seem . . .)

And the currents of air beneath the wings
are silk banners flying
yes, are the silks of the sky
the clouds beneath you are buoyant as all the
love and the luck that speeds you
from all here who will miss you.

This is China Day and they are
teaching us new ceremonies – so yes
I'll write that wish-label, take it from the pile in the little pavilion
of the Garden for the Elderly
and I'll fling it high,
high in some Scottish tree on this the day of
your festival,
your farewell picnic, and all it'll say

is, 'fly, Jane, fly'.

IN PRAISE OF MONSIEUR SAX

On his 200th Birthday, 6 November 2014

Monsieur Sax, Monsieur Sax, the great Adolphe
who invented the howl of the urban wolf.
He made the saxotromba, the saxtuba, the saxhorn
then finally came up with that magical instrument that pure
caught on!
Yeah, he tinkered with all that brassy trash and then – tout 'suite –
struck gold with the Daddy of them all who could sure
toot sweet.

Though – as the cliché says –
he came from that place
famous for nobody but Jacques Brel, the
bloke that thought up Tintin, and René Magritte –
Adolphe Sax, it was you
it was you,
it was you
made that thing
that makes that sound
that snarls from midnight Manhattan windows or curls
like the steam from the grilles in the street,
the sound that howls its blue, blue loneliness then
coos real low, cool and sweet.

All praise to Monsieur Sax, the blessed Adolphe
who invented the authentic howl
of the urban wolf.

GRACE

Written for the Royal Incorporation of Architects in Scotland on the occasion of the Annual Fellows Dinner, 2012

Once in Moab
before *the land of milk and honey*
it was written in Deuteronomy
that before breaking bread together, friends, we should
take pause, and then say grace.
Which was to say we were to bless
what blessed us with everything that was good.
God – or the
land of the wheat and the barley, the
source of all our food,
the land of the vine and the fig and the pomegranate,
the land of the oil-olive and the syrup-date.

But this is Scotland, this
our one small country in this great wide world, which is
our one, wondrous, spinning, dear green place.
What shall we build of it, together
in this our one small time and space?

We are far from Deuteronomy,
far from long forgotten
Moab, far from any *land of milk and honey* –
we are *where nothing is written*

Yet tonight
together
for good food and even better fellowship,
whether we have a God or not
our gratitude cannot be denied.

And we shall eat, and we shall be satisfied.

LINES FOR THE CENTENARY OF THE SCOTCH WHISKY ASSOCIATION

Freedom an whisky gang thegither – Robert Burns

1.

When we sit wined and finely dined,
dressed up in oor best, braw and fancy,
oh, it's a far cry tonight, in this company bright,
from the rude and hoorin howff o Poosie Nancy.

Friends, we hae a history:
rough stuff. 'Rascally Kilbagie'
mair fiery by faur than 'lost Ferintosh' and fit,
fit for but 'the most rascally part',
fit for the bard's Jolly Beggars,
fit only for 'rectifying' into Hollands gin
– in the back lanes of London,
Mother's Ruin.

Sing, drunk for a penny,
blin fou for tuppence, quaff
an ye shall hae straw for free
when you maun sleep it aff.

2.

Two hundred and fifty years . . .
How many thousand bottlings
to the honeyed finish,
aromas of lavender, sherry-cask or gorse;
essences and esters of salt, pine, nutmeg, smoke;
tinctures of topaz, amber, mahogany;
palest straw, purest gold, liquid?
Liquors, elixirs, infused with – is that a
hint of anise, even liquorice?

Toddies tea-coloured, smooth and soothing –
can you taste tobacco, heather-nectar, rain or moorland,
smell the sea?
How many thousand bottlings, angel's shares,
new market leaders in the field,
till today's best blends and the triple-distilled?

3.
Ask MacDiarmid, ask Ettrick Hogg –
wha took his whisky 'by the joug' –
ask Rab himsel, an he will tell you whether –
language made essence, thought distilled –
inspiration's whit a dram might yield?
If poetry an whisky gang thegither?

Consider.
Answer. Aye, right well thegither.
(Though – taken by the jug-fu – either yin's reduced to blether.)

4.
And friendship an whisky surely gang thegither?
It's the *aqua vitae* we imbibe wi yin another.
A hip-flask in the cauld, uncorked, a shared swig,
a deal sealed wi a word and a dram,
och, see us a splash of water from thon china jug,
gie us a drappie in my coffee mug,
there's aye a drouth for true companionship, until at last
the luggit cup o the quaich is passed.
Sweetness sipped from a chinked glass, cheers!
Savour friendship.
Its flavour will mature for years.

5.
And – if freedom an whisky gang thegither –
how do you like your freedom? Swallowed neat?
Distillations of history, language, weather
in an usqueba o barley, burn water, peat.

FROM A MOUSE

The present author being, from her mother's milk, a lover of the poetic effusions of Mr Robert Burns and all creatures therein (whether mouse, louse, yowe, dug or grey mare Meg), was nonetheless appalled to find, in her slattern's kitchen, sitting up washing its face in her wok, the following phenomenon.

It's me. The eponymous wee moose
The *To a Mouse* that, were I in your hoose,
A bit o dust ablow the bed, thon dodd o oose
That, quick, turns tail,
Is – eek! – a living creature on the loose,
Wad gar you wail.

Aye, I've heard you fairly scraich, you seem
Gey phobic 'boot mice in real life yet dream
Aboot man-mouse amity? Ye'll rhyme a ream!
Yet, wi skirt wrapt roon,
I've seen ye staun up oan a chair an scream
Like Daphne Broon.

But I'm *adored* – on paper! – ever since
First ye got me at the schule, at yince
Enchantit – wha'd aye thocht poetry was mince
Till ye met Rabbie,
My poor, earth-born companion, an the Prince
O *Standard Habbie*.

For yon is what they cry the form he wrote in
An you recite. Gey easy, as you ken, to quote in
Because it sticks. I will allow it's stoatin,
This nifty stanza
He could go to sicc lengths wi, say sicc a lot in –
Largs to Lochranza,

Plockton to Peebles, Dumfries to Dundee,
If a wean kens ony poem aff by hert, it's *me!*
Will greet ower ma plough-torn nest, no see
The bit o' a gap
Atween the fause warld o Poetry
An baited trap.

Get Rentokil! Get real! Wha you love
'S the ploughman in the poem, keen to prove –
Saut tears, sigh, sympathy – he's sensitive.
Wee sermon:
Mice, men, schemes agley, Himsel above
Cryin me vermin.

Ploughman? That will be right! Heaven-taught?
He drank deep o The Bard, and Gray, and Pope – the lot.
I, faur frae the spontaneous outburst you thought,
Am an artifact.
For Man's dominion he was truly sorry? Not!
'Twas all an act.

Burns, baith man and poet, liked to dominate.
His reputation wi the lassies wasna great.
They still dinna ken whether they love to hate,
Or hate to love.
He was *an awfy man!* He left them tae their fate,
Push came to shove.

Couldnae keep it in his breeks? Hell's bells, damnation,
I wad be the vera last to gie a peroration
On the daft obsession o this prurient nation,
His amatory antics.
He was – beating them tae it by a generation –
First o th' Romantics.

Arguably, I am a poem wha, prescient, did presage
Your Twenty-First-Century Global Distress Age.
I'm a female mouse though, he didna gie a sausage
For ma sparklin een!
As for Mother Nature? Whether yez get the message
Remains to be seen.

THE THEATRE MAKER'S CREDO

for David McVicar, Ralph Riach, Siobhan Redmond, Ann Scott Jones and
D.C. Jackson, who are all quoted here

Tell the story
make it make sense –
whether you've got a budget of three hundred grand
or fifty pence
just tell the story – in the present tense.

Tell it in prose
tell it in rhyme
tell it in words of one syllable
tell it in mime
give it the old softshoe
with the once-upon-a-time . . .

Tell it with a soaring operatic aria
or a wee folk song.
Tell it with a pure heart and an open mind
and you won't go far wrong.

Tell it to the world and his wife –
and their illiterate friend
who doesn't even know Hamlet
dies in the end.

Tell it complete with undeleted expletives.
Tell it short and sweet.
Show it so I'll know it
With a silence, a look, or a beat.
Tell it in extravagant verbal flights of fancy –
oh audibly – gie us a chance! –
even (over my dead body)
tell it in dance –

but just tell the story.
Not necessarily loud, but clear.
Don't show me where we're going,
take me there

By telling me the story –
let me in.
Are we sitting comfortably?
Then let us begin.

Doesn't have to be a new story –
the old ones are, whiles, the best.
Just: is it a good story?
That's the acid test.

Tell it like it is, but!
Don't forget
the isle being full of many noises, plenty brand-new voices
ain't never been heard from yet!

Spare us the protagonist's monologue
just show what he or she does
and, as old Shakespeare himself says, we'll see
what Hecuba is to us.

If you're determined to be tragic,
well . . . gie's the odd laugh, please,
even if you're up to your oxters in blood
(think Euripides).

On the other hand Molière
was right on the money
with his cast of gloomy obsessives
who were just so fucking funny.

So take a long look at life, tell the truth,
play it as it lays –
oh, plus K.I.S.S. (Keep it Simple, Stupid)
as the Man Mamet says.

Part one of the Process:
go back to square one
and just tell the story all over again.
Don't forget to have fun –

let's not get arty, nor earnest
(God, earnest is the worst).
Fuck them if they can't take a joke –
but don't tell the punchline first.

Yeah, tell it in the right order
and you'll really put us through it.
Through hoops, loops, one fell swoops
and *Ohmigod! I knew it!*

To hell with telling folk what they should think –
that's just not polite.
Don't try and change people's minds –
mibbe just try change their night?

For the message is: There is No Message –
heaven forbid! –
Let the audience *think on* bout what happened,
but be damn sure what did!

Though it *is* Show Business Not Tell Business
nevertheless – have I said this before, eh? –
the business of the whole show
is to Just Tell the Story

and though non-narrative theatre
seems to be all the rage
with the funders – if not the punters –
let us put on the stage

the one-and-only, ever-loving, rootin-tootin Story
Which will out, in the end.
Long live the Story
although it depends –

Whether it's a living nightmare
or a Midsummer Night's Dream
yup, depends on each and every member
of the Creative Team

not fucking up the story
(however hard to stage)
and them all telling the Same Story,
being on the Same Page

telling it with style and pace
(one to ninety, back to zero).
Do 'get right inside your character'
Monster, Everyman or Hero –

but it's not *your* story,
no, it's not about you,
it's not about the Bad Divorce
the leading actor's going through

it's about the people in the play
And what happens next.
Just tell the blooming story,
stick to the text.

IN NUMBER ONE DRESSING ROOM, A PORTRAIT OF THE LEADING ACTRESS

In celebration of the 2015 re-opening of Glasgow's Theatre Royal

Backstage
in Number One dressing room
on this, the last night of the run,
before *Beginners* and after her *Five-minute Call*
just time for one last time
to centre herself, apply one last scoosh
of that antique cologne she wears to
get in character with just this character,
bin the dregs of it, kiss
her lucky rabbit's-foot mascot that
got her grandad through the war, drop it
in the maw of her packed carpet bag.
She's counted the champagne corks
before chucking them,
unpeeled from their blu-tack all the good-luck cards,
stacked them to save and take on top of those
drawings from her children that
sent
their *lots and lots of love Mummy!*
but gave her guilt.

The over-the-top flamboyant flowers
her agent sent are drooped and dying,
ditto the bonny bouquets from friends,
even the single rose from her secret lover.
She smears the lipsticked messages and kisses
on the merciless mirror, risks
a final check in it, bares her teeth.
God, but she's glad of that nap under her wrap
before the half –
one last night to get every last thing right!
There's a plane ticket in her handbag.

Beginners, and out she goes along breezeblock corridors
to the wings, the wings

which give her flight.

NICK DOWP, FEELING MISCAST IN A VERY ENGLISH PRODUCTION, REHEARSES BOTTOM'S DREAM

Tie up my lover's tongue? Yon's censorship!
Hae anither English apricock and button your lip.
Neither dewberry nor honey bag from humble bee'll keep
Me silent, I hate it!
Fish oot o watter in this green wid, I hope
To funn mysel translatit.

Proud Titania – yon's who yon posh quine is –
She hus a faur, faur better pert than mine is!
Her 'R.P.' Shakespeare-spiel, oh as befits a lady fine, is
In couplet verse.
Whauras I get *mere prose* o which the bottom line is
That I'm an erse!

Shakespeare's (excuse me for being cynical)
Attitude to Scotch verse is that it's kinna like McGonagall's
And only guid enough for thae Rude-Mechanicals
An Loss-the-Plots
To tumpty-tum their numpty lyricals
In accents Scots

Ach, but here goes! In ma ain wurds!
I have had a maist rare and unco and byornar Vision. I have
hud a dream . . . telling ye, I'm daunerin aroon in a dwamm
like a hauf shut knife tryin to shake mysel free o it, but och, it's
beyond Man's kennin to say whitlike a dream it wis.
I'm dumfounert, fair dumfounert.
I'm naethin but a cuddy if I ettle to expound upon it at ony
length. See, whit I thocht – naw, naw I'm saying nuthin! But,
aye, naw, aye, I thocht I *wis* . . . an I thocht I *hud* . . . an that a the
lang nicht lang, we actually . . .

But you'll get hee-haw oot o me on sicc maitters, Nick Dowp here is ower much o a gentleman. An I tell ye this: Man's een havena heard, man's lugs havena seen, his fummlin,fouterin hauns havena the gumption to taste, nor his tongue to mak heid nor tail o. Nor yet his yammerin hert to let dab whitlike thon dream o mine was.

I'll mibbe get somebody to write it doon for me to elocute? 'In the Doric', do they no cry it? Them that canna thole 'keelie-talk', nor 'kailyerd', nor the 'deservedly much despisit and debasit accents o the urban poor'? Sicc snobs! Love-o-goad almighty, could somebody no mibbe dae somethin hauf-wey guid in the Glesca-patois to gie us a laugh and let me an the Mechanicals sook in with the Duke an his Leddy at the finish-up o oor play?

For oor cast has a wheen o erses to kiss
Us workin-joes, we hae to hae a hit, we canny miss!
And still we areny really oot the wids wi this
Heedrum-hodrum humdrum --
For thon Shakespeare-felly thocht it funny to take the piss
Oot o am-dram!

So his jyner, tailor, wabster are no very smart
But guid-herted cheils -- gey willin to learn their part.
Only when it gets richt spooky dae they get feart
An run awa in alarm.
While I dream! Mindin it will aye wind aroon my heart
Like a hairy worm!

EPISTLE TO DAVID

for David MacLennan (1948–2014), a fellow theatre-maker

The heart aye's the part aye – Robert Burns: Epistle to Davie, A Brother Poet

Dear David, I scribble this because today
We did the read-through of your three-hundredth play –
We open in two short weeks (eek!) on Monday 20th May –
Imagine! Three hundred plays which did not exist before
They *premiered at one p.m.* at Òran Mór.

OK, flashback. Best part of a decade ago,
So the story goes and as far as I know,
Once upon a time in the West – Byres Road t'be exact –
You, David McL, bumped into one Colin Beattie, who was, matter
    of fact,
Up to his oxters in turning a derelict church into a dream he had.
He (you-don't-have-to-be-crazy-etc.-but-it-helps) was mad
To make it much more than a super-pub and mega wedding
    destination,
Was dying to show you the story-so-far of his new creation,

So he jams a hard-hat on your heid and . . . in you baith go.
David, you could not believe your eyes (at least you told me so)
Th'whole place, the space, the colour, the light,
Stained-glass, half-restored splendour, and – at a great height –
Alasdair Gray on his back on scaffolding, a latterday Michelangelo
Painting Sistine-esque intricacies on the ceiling – and, D, what
    d'you know,
Colin goes: What would *you* like to do in this venue?
You don't blink, don't even think, just open your mouth and then
    you
Come out with your *own* mad idea, and, as a result, you
Are a legend in your own lunchtime – which is not to insult you,
In fact, D, it prompts this fond epistle – I just thought: ach, might
    as well,

In praise of you, old pal, Producer Extraordinaire, produce a line or
  twa o doggerel?

Because, thon fateful day, this was your reply:
I've got a good idea. Hey Colin, why
Don't we do Lunchtime Theatre here?
Say it's: *A Play, A Pie and A Pint?* Let's try . . .
They pay us tenner, they get a play, they get a pint, they get a pie.
C'mon, Colin, say aye!

And from that first season –
September 2004, the first of twelve plays
To the annual thirty-eight productions and forty-two weeks of
  nowadays.

Whit Taggart was it you were in? Actors used to get asked this all the
  time, before.
Now it's: *Haw, when did you last dae an Òran Mór?*

Could be a monologue, a musical, a comedy, a tragedy, a panto,
  a rom-com
Just check it out on www.playpiepint.com
All hail PPP – a veritable and a venerable fixture
With a welcome-to-all-comers open-to-all-ideas repertoire that's a
  total mixture.

Say you're a brand-new writer or one new at least to writing plays
Òran Mór's audience'll fairly teach you how to play it as it lays.
It is hard to get a start, but, David, you're out to change that.
As for us old hands – you're aye careful to arrange that
We don't feel left behind either, don't feel left out,
That we drop our jaded attitudes, are . . . still in with a shout?
David I confess today it made me very proud
To hear my wee three-hander – your three-hundredth play – if not
  yet up on its feet, at least out loud.

But, though the play's the thing,
You do like to tell it like it is, David
(I'm remembering *Dear Glasgow*, those *Letters From the Arab Spring*)
Oh, it's a big wide world and –
We want to tell you a story
We want to make it to make sense
We know what the gig is –
To tell the story in the present tense.

And by telling them the story, David, letting them in,
We'll go, *Are we sitting comfortably?*
Then let us begin . . .

PORTRAIT OF A GENTLEMAN AT SIXTY

for Ralph Riach, on his birthday

In fair Rose Terrace there lives a man
Of grace, of style, *d'un certain* age and pure élan.
He is always elegant, it matters not a toss
Whether 'tis kilt, socks and sandshoes, or Hugo Boss.
He likes a good joke wi sweerin, he is, let's say no prude,
But it must be rhythmical, inventive, funny and no jist crude.

And he knows the Rare Occasion when 'twill not quite do
To tell the tale of the Broon Coo and the White Coo.
When fans accost him, how graciously he bends to answer
Their *who urr you again? Settle a bet! Were you in Chancer?*
Naw! It's thingwy ooty whidjie, whit is it you're on?
Were you the baddie in – Naw! It's TV John!

May his every *Taggart* get re-repeated!
May his every *Guardian* crossword get completed!
May Redmond phone him up and go *Hey, tell us*
What is fifteen down? . . . And then get pure jealous!

May he get his country cottage, the sort eh?
Where he may freely play his piano, forte!
May he (and all the other *Hamish MacBeth* individuals)
Get yet another series at double fees plus residuals.

He is never O.T.T. We may always expect
Minimum effort, maximum effect.
His timing's nice, he is often praised
As master of the demi-beat, the eyebrow not quite raised.
We appreciate his talent, but each appreciator
Knows his talent for friendship is even greater.
No better pal than he, ach,
Many Happy Returns to you, Ralph Riach.

ADDRESS TO A SEPTUAGENARIAN
GENTLEMAN AT HOME
for Ralph Riach, on his birthday

Gardener's Cottage. Des Res is not the word!
Out of the poky wee sow's ear that was Bon Accord
You made such a silken purse. Oh, the trouble
You took to coax this floribundant garden from the rubble
A green-fingered glory; to furnish this home-from-home
With a welcome warm enough to make all comers come
From aw the Airts and Pairts for R&R
For music, food and friendship, for Just You to be the Way You Are
Our dear Ralph, a genial generous host to either pop in on
Else stay (and stay) till any other bugger'd say, Begone!
Och, gie any of us an inch and we'll take a mile!
But, Christ, you even nag our arses off with style.

Seventy summers. Three score and ten
Could be considered a good age! In lesser men
Well, fuck it, let's face it, *tempus fugit*
And we're all knocking on a bit – but you don't look it.
To say 'You wear it well' is to state the obvious
And you're the most likely of all of us
To – thirty years hence – have Prince William
(Once he's the King) send you *That* Telegram.

Meanwhile, may you have sunshine in the garden a.m. till p.m.,
Many, many Methven Arms lunches, new piano pieces, *carpe diem!*
Oh and *carpe per diems* as well,
For I wish you more parts in films than tongue can tell,
That many lucrative wee tellies
As to make all your many thespian friends pure jealous.

May there be acres of that bonny needlepoint cross-stitchin
To blossom at your fingertips in Mrs Jolly's Kitchen.
May your every cross word be in the *Guardian*

May you be daily forced to phone a friend and say, 'A hard yin,
Right enough, it was today, but me, I got it done –
Even that hoor-o-a-clue eight down! – by early afternoon.
See, I'm aye on *Araucaria's* wavelength, that wee twist
I enjoy much more than *Bunthorne* or *Enigmatist*!'

May we watch *Bullets Over Broadway* till we know it off by heart.
All the lines, not just Chazz Palminteri's part.
May we bring in many a New Year together, would be good, eh?
And you could show us Elaine Stritch, Ethel M. and Judy.
Long may we have to swither 'ere we can decide
Whether to have smoked salmon on our scrambled eggs
        or on the side.

Dearest Ralph, I wish you all you wish yourself, but selfishly,
I wish you many hours to spend with *me!*

FOR MYRA MCFADDEN ON HER SIXTIETH BIRTHDAY

Surely some mistake! Better get it fixed eh?
Nah,
A little bird told me
That Myra's sixty!
Sixty?
Sixty?
Surely no!
Jeepers, creepers
Who's that girl in them tartan brothel creepers?
Aye it's Myra,
Myra
Oor Myra.

You can keep your Little Eva, you can keep your
Brenda Lee,
Though her voice *penetrates* like their's do
(And though she's *wee*)
You can keep your Little Eva
You can keep your Brenda Lee
Cos Myra, she's the girl for me.

Myra, she sing rock'n'roll
She sing loco
She sing local
She sing like a lintie in a leafy tree
Because Myra she's the zinging singing girl for me.

If I was Ian Dury, if I could sing . . .
Except my singing scores a lot less than zero
But if I could
I surely would
Do for Myra what Mister Dury did
For Sweet Gene Vincent, his hero.

Myra's friends – and, oh my God,
Oor Myra's friends are myriad –
We're all to record a memory of some bit of fun with Myra
That we've had
(And *digitally?*
Ohmigod, give-me-a-break I'm a Luddite, that willnae be me
But I'm supposed to . . . *document* this memory?)
Been wracking my brains for the right anecdote –
Well I've got plenty – but not one
She'd want me to quote.

Cos –
She's a wonderful friend to be on-the-same-page with
She's a very dangerous woman to be on the same stage with
(Ask Siobhan,
Ask Siobhan,
Ask anyone!)
Give her one line, give her . . . a look
And no one else will get a look-in,
heigh-ho
Just give her one note
And who's the star of the show?

She's The One that everybody remembers
In musicals, comedies and dramas
Because she's both the dogs bollox and the cat's pyjamas.

You all will have got the picture:
I simply Think She's Great
But *Sixty?* . . .
(Well, suppose she must be since I am sixty-eight . . .)
Well you can bet your ass
I'm dying to see what that that girl's gonna do
with her Freedom Pass.

Myra – what's she like, eh?
Myra, Myra –
Tho we all love her to bits –
She's *oor Myra your Myra a'body's Myra* –
And tho – like every other bugger –
I am her greatest admirer
I just canny put it intae words, she's
Just Myra!

Myra, ach, impossible to describe her.
You just have to get in her company and
Positively imbibe her!

SONG FOR A DIRTY DIVA

Why are my friends all friends of Dorothy?
Now, I'm cool and glib about gay lib
But suddenly it's got to me
That all of my friends are friends of Dorothy.

Now, I get on great in gay bars and the boys adore me –
We even fancy the same film stars and the crack is frank and free.
They'll do my clothes, my hair, my decor
But they won't do me.

Yet I can go some from here to kingdom come.
Hey, man, you must be barmy
If you think you could exhaust me, yeah, you and
Whose army?
I could ball a rugby team and cream them all to orgasm.
Take a caveman, and his club, to fill ma yawnin chasm.

All those guys who're really nice, but not interested,
All those nancies who don't fancy the tried and tested,
Who turn the other cheek and spurn
What can't be bested,
Oh they huff and they puff and they get real vexed
About my mainstream addiction to
Hetero-sex.

My thoroughly modern girlfriends all say to me
You aint tried it don't knock it you should suck it and see.
I say thanks a lot but no thanks
It's not for me.

I want a real man with a rock-hard dose of the horn
Who these days is as rare as
A unicorn.
Oh I wish he'd pure skewer ma penetralia

And spatter ma sheets with a map of Australia

But 'cause all my pals who are gals
Are strictly Sapphic
They seem to deem it disgustin and pornographic.
But my sex life's at a standstill –
There is no through traffic
So – at the risk of sounding . . . politically incorrect
I need a crash-course collision
With something erect.

Yet all of my friends are friends of Dorothy,
Yeah, friends of Dorothy.
Now, I'm cool and glib about gay lib
But suddenly it's got to me
That all of my friends are friends of Dorothy.
And why oh why do they get that vexed
About my mainstream addiction to
Hetero-sex?

ANOTHER, LATER, SONG FOR THAT
SAME DIRTY DIVA

'Just visiting, honey? Dream on . . .
This, ma darlin, is the ladies' john
Of the Seniors Association of Greater Edmonton
And Ah'm here to tell you, girl, one fine day
You're going to find yourself permanently here
In the Sunshine Café
Fitting in perfectly among us old-timers
With the arther-itis and the arteriosclerosis and the
Alz-heimers.
– Which is *not* my problem, baby –
No, cruel thing is I can remember way back when still
Ah'd some ooze in ma cooze
And he'd a leettle lead in his pencil.
OK, these days it's not the same
But give it a little elbow grease and I'm still game.
Though when you are more
Than three-score-
And-ten
It's very fucking unlikely to be raining men.
Soon you, too, will be grubbing round for the *last* of the
Last-of-the-red-hot-lovers
'Mong the 'lasticated leisure-suits and the
Comb overs . . .

Ah, it was a very good year – yeah, back in
Nineteen-fifty sumthin when ma sex life was just begun
And the fact you shouldn't was . . . just part of the fun.
(Oh boy, the joy
Of being underage, oversexed and in the back
Of someone's daddy's Cadillac . . .)
Soon the swinging sixties
And ooh baby I swung,

Got all the action that was going –
And plenty in ma twenties when I was young
The permissive society? Remember?
A great club. I was happy to be a member.
Fantastic! Fuck-all forbidden
And everybody perked up at the prospect
Of bein
Bed-ridden.
Yes, in sixty-nine it was a very good year, damn fine
For moon-landings and . . . sixty-nine.
And in the seventies did I slow up a tad?
Not a whit, not a bit of it. Are you mad?
For there was always sex-and-drugs and having a laugh –
When 'a selfie' was certainly not a
Photograph.

Ah, once there was
Powder in the powder room –
You could get it on, no bother
And every which way,
When two-in-a-cubicle used to mean something other
Than what it means today
Here in the Sunshine Café
Remember, before?
When two paira shoes, under one locked door
Signalled sex, illicit and acrobatic?
Now it's likely to be 'a carer' and 'a client', geriatric.

Once there were
Pills, poppers,
Downers, uppers,
All on offer – and no lack o
More than a whiff of more than a spliff of that wacky tobacco.
Now ma handbag still harbours drugs of every description
But these days, darlin,

They are all . . .
pre-scription.'

And she snapped her lipstick back in her purse,
Gave me a wink that said: 'Could be worse'.
Yes, she said all this with a single look.
It was eloquent (oh, I could read her like a book).
It said,
'Forget the nips and tucks, they are not the answers.'
And off she hobbled to join her team
Of geriatric line-dancers.

Yes, off she went leaving me alone
Before the mirror in the ladies' John.
It felt a little flat without her . . .
She left a kinda . . . absence in her wake.
I sighed and looked around me and then, fuck-sake,
Saw something I'd never seen the like of, never since
They started dishing out the complimentary condoms
In the Eighties, remember? Yes. Like . . . after-dinner mints?

Well, what can I say?
That day
In the female comfort-station of the Sunshine Café,
There, then, in the ladies' john
Of the Seniors Association of Greater Edmonton,
Bold as brass, gratis and for free,
Openly out there on the counter between the soap dispenser
and the pot-pourri
Right before my very eyes
Lo and behold, very much to my surprise –
Free incontinence supplies!

IN PRAISE OF OLD VINYL

In the beginning was the chord
The perfect combo of the melody and the word
Played at thirty-three and a third

Four in the morning, crapped out, yawning
Still crazy after all these years.

    Old vinyl . . . old vinyl
    Nostalgia's everything it used to be
    When you're half-pissed and playing that old LP

You make me feel . . . You make me feel . . . You make me feel
It's not-so-easy listening without protection
When you open Pandora's Record Collection –
May you never lay your head down
Without a hand to hold
Lord knows when the cold wind blows it'll turn your head around
Little things I should have said and done
I just never took the time
But I always thought I'd see you a –
No more I love yous
Language is –
Hey that's no way to say
Go way from my window
Leave at your own chosen speed
I'm not the one you want babe
I'm not the one you need
I keep singing them sad, sad songs, y'all
Sad songs is all I know.

Talking 'bout the box you've never even opened since your last flit
Full of all you could rescue from that Bad Split –
The albums, seminal and antique,
You saved up pocket-money for, week after week –

The ones that took your teenage soul apart,
The ones that broke your thirty-something heart,
The ones you stole from old lovers,
With muesli in the grooves, coffee-stains on the covers
And printed lyrics that that were pure
Lonely bedsitter literature –
I learned the truth at seventeen . . .

Oh Dusty and Joni and Nico and Emmylou,
Dylan, Van-the-Man and Rhymin' Simon too . . .
Songs to flood you with all that came to pass
Between 'Piece of My Heart' and 'Heart of Glass'
Once had a love and it was a gas . . .

      Old vinyl . . . old vinyl
      Nostalgia's everything it used to be
      When you're half-pissed and playing that old LP

Annie and K.D. and Eddi and Ella for when you're home alone
Inventing a lover on the . . . Saxophone!
When he's gone and you and those lonesome blues collide
A certain Canyon Lady knows just how you feel inside . . .
The bed's too big, the frying pan's too wide

Furry sings the blues? Well, if anybody can,
Sincerely L. Cohen – you're my man.
And (oh my sweet lord and he's so fine)
Gravel-voiced Tom Waits with his Blue Valentine –
An' Otis 'n Elvis 'n some-kinda-Wonderful Stevie were the men
When you picked yourself up 'n tried to love again –
But . . . Baby I know – the first cut is the deepest . . .

      Old vinyl . . . old vinyl
      Nostalgia's everything it used to be
      When you're half-pissed and playing an old LP . . .

I want to walk in the open wind
I want to talk like lovers do
I want to dive into your ocean
Is it raining with you?

Come on, c'mon, c'mon, don't kid on
You don't remember when
Yesterday was young and it was raining men?
Believe me . . . believe me . . .
Though it's an achey-breaky this-old-heart of yours – it's murder –
Old Stereo's still in working order!
Needle gets in the groove and proves as it plays
That all tomorrow's parties are now yesterday's.
From Sinatra to Suzi Quatro to Suzanne
It takes a lot of pain, it takes a lot of pain
Love hurts, love scars, love wounds and mars,
Ooh ooh love hurts . . .

But – oh sex and drugs and rock and roll! –
Buddy Holly, Billie Holiday and Billy Fury,
Janis Joplin, Janis Ian and Ian Dury
Have little in common, as a matter of fact,
Except – one hook, and they fair take you back!
I'm sorry that I made you cry . . .
Apple, Island, Rough Trade, HMV and Stiff
Label me, turntable me, and let me riff!
Do me wrong, do me right, tell me lies but hold me tight . . .
Oh and you'll be back in love again, back at school,
Back in the USS – back where your memories will unspool
Like that audio-cassette your midnight-caller compiled
With 'Easy Like Sunday Morning' and 'Born to Be Wild'
He comes for conversation . . .

Old vinyl . . . old vinyl
Nostalgia's everything it used to be
When you're half-pissed and playing that old LP . . .

May you nev – nev – nev – nev – nev . . .

Oh hear those nice, bright colours,
Hear the greens of summers,
You'll be wearing rags and feathers from Salvation Army counters,
You'll be Marcie in a coat of flowers –
Mama, please don't take my Parlophone away.

Old vinyl . . . old vinyl . . .

INDEX OF TITLES